RURAL POLITICS IN NASSER'S EGYPT

A Quest for Legitimacy

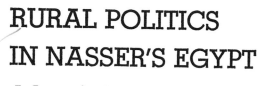

RURAL POLITICS
IN NASSER'S EGYPT

A Quest for Legitimacy

JAMES B. MAYFIELD

Foreword by George Lenczowski

UNIVERSITY OF TEXAS PRESS
AUSTIN AND LONDON

International Standard Book Number 0-292-70136-5
Library of Congress Catalog Card Number 70-165910
© 1971 by James B. Mayfield
All rights reserved
Type set by G&S Typesetters, Austin
Printed by Capital Printing Company, Austin
Bound by Universal Bookbindery, Inc., San Antonio

To Merlene J. Mayfield

CONTENTS

MAPS

FOREWORD

Poverty, disease, and ignorance are the triple evils of the under-developed societies of Afro-Asia. Moreover, they tend to be self-perpetuating and to reinforce each other. The result is physical debility, low productivity, apathy, and the reduction of vast masses of humanity to a subsistence level. The aim of modernization is to break this vicious circle and, by infusion of new ideas, organization, and techniques, to launch a society upon the path of development in which literacy and knowledge will replace ignorance and supersti-tion, health will dislodge debility, and production of goods will meet the material needs of civilized citizenry. Among the countries of Afro-Asia undergoing various experiments in modernization, Egypt is one of the most strategic. An ancient country, whose people have produced in the remote past a splendid civilization and which, in due course, became a leading center of Islam, Egypt has assumed in the mid-twentieth century a new role as the fountainhead of Arab nationalism and social revolution. Its experience with the process of modernization should have a profound effect not only on the Arab world but also on the broader Afro-Asian community of nations.

A vast distance separates the urban from the rural sector in Egypt. The urban environment provides the compactness, com-munication facilities, and concentration of motivations and skills that render the task of modernization more feasible and hopeful. By contrast, the rural areas with their tradition-bound peasantry present tremendous obstacles to innovation. No matter how success-

ful in the cities, Egyptian modernizers will face ultimate defeat if
they fail to extend their reforms to rural Egypt as well.

In concentrating his study on the modernization in rural areas,
Dr. Mayfield has undertaken an ambitious and pioneering task in a
field that thus far has received rather scant attention from Western
scholars. Most Western studies on the politics and economics of
Egypt have tended to focus on broad problems of governmental
policies, either in terms of institutions or practices. Egyptian village life has traditionally been the preserve of cultural anthropolo-
gists and of observers with no ascertainable professional skills. Thus
it is refreshing to see a young and vigorous American political
scientist address himself to the "micro" world of politics in the
Egyptian village.

In his well-researched study, Dr. Mayfield describes and analyzes
the functioning of the Egyptian village as a political community
embracing three interlocking organizations: the local branch of the
Arab Socialist Union (ASU), the centrally appointed administrative officials, and the village council. The purpose of the ASU is to
act as the chief psychological agency of change and modernization.
More specifically, its purpose is to mobilize, indoctrinate, watch
loyalty, check on the performance of bureaucrats, generate enthusiasm for improvements and reforms, and serve as a two-way channel
of communication with the political leadership of the country. The
task of the centrally appointed officials—headmasters, health officers, veterinarians, agronomists, and social workers—is to implement government-designed policies. And finally, the purpose of the
village council, a mixed body of elected, selected, and ex-officio
members, is to serve as a deliberative and executive agency that attends to local interests within the framework of policy guidelines
handed down from above.

In analyzing this institutional structure and its performance, Dr.
Mayfield leaves no aspect of the political process untouched. His
account is enlivened by personal observations of behavior of the
officials and villagers; and he judiciously puts his study within a
broader context of the cultural and religious heritage of rural Egypt.

For Western researchers who describe and interpret general and

local politics of the Middle East, the greatest challenge is to overcome the linguistic barrier and cultural gap that separate them
from the subjects of their study and thus to gain an intimate knowledge and understanding of the local conditions while, at the same
time, preserving both a scholarly detachment and a perspective
based on a systematic mastery of the concepts and methods of
political science. Few foreign observers have been able to fulfill
these specifications. It should be a source of pride for the American
political science community to see one of their members succeed so
eminently in this difficult task. By undertaking and executing his
mission of research with enthusiasm and distinction, Dr. Mayfield
has not only enriched our understanding of the vital sector of
Egypt's political process but has also written a lively story of
absorbing human interest.

GEORGE LENCZOWSKI

University of California, Berkeley

PREFACE

On September 29, 1970, President Gamal Abdel Nasser died of a heart attack. World leaders were stunned, while men, women, and children from Morocco to Iraq careened through the streets, weeping and tearing off their clothes. In Egypt, all theaters, athletic events, and places of amusement were closed for a forty-day period of mourning. Radio and television carried funeral chants and readings from the Koran. From throughout the countryside thousands of Egyptians streamed into Cairo. They came by all methods of conveyance—trains, buses, cars, donkeys, or on foot. The almost hysterical outpouring of grief at the state funeral dramatized the depth to which the loss of this charismatic leader has shaken the Arab world. Few men have achieved the love, prestige, and adulation that Nasser experienced from the Arab masses. Yet, in reality, Nasser's life was a tragic story.

Forced to choose between domestic needs and international challenges, Nasser's attention too often drifted beyond the borders of Egypt. His visions of renewed Arab greatness, his dreams of Arab unity, and his concerns for Arab justice and development often distorted his perception of his own country—Egypt. And while nobody who had personally conversed with Nasser doubted his sincerity in wishing a better life for the peasants of the Nile Valley, many have noted the tendency of Nasser to allocate resources more on the basis of dreams and less on the realities of Egypt's own domestic problems. This book seeks a careful analysis of Nasser's belated attempts to modernize the rural areas of Egypt. Granted permission to move freely through Egypt's twenty-five provinces prior to the post-1967 travel restrictions, I gained the unique opportunity of personally observing Nasser's dramatic attempts to bring progress and development to his people. This study attempts to portray graphically the political, economic, and social factors that made Nasser's dream for his people unattainable in his lifetime. The bitter reality of Egypt's slow progress toward modernity and prosperity is not due to Nasser's lack of leadership or determination, but rather to the frustrating awareness that the gap between the industrialized nations and the newly emerging states is widening—not diminishing—and that no leader, whether enlightened and dedicated or ruthless and demanding, can quickly eradicate the centuries-old social and cultural imperatives that block progress, hinder development, and destroy the hopes of those who would seek a better life for their people.

Most of the research for this study was concluded prior to the death of President Nasser and thus focuses on Nasser's rural reforms as an ongoing set of policies. Although Nasser's untimely death now makes this study history, it must be recognized that Nasser's impact on Egypt has been profound, that his ideals and aspirations will live long beyond his death, and that events in Egypt far in the future will be colored and shaped by the two decades of Nasser's rule.

Few will deny that Nasser was one of the truly great Arab leaders of this century. I have accepted the challenge to analyze Nasser's policies in rural Egypt both as a friend and as a scholar. As a friend, I have been deeply moved by Nasser's great hope to establish dignity and prosperity for the Egyptian people. I left Egypt gladdened by the friendship, the hospitality, and the warmth extended to me by Egyptians in all walks of life and in all parts of the Nile Valley. As a scholar, I must critically evaluate what I have observed—not for the purpose of belittling or destroying, but for the purpose of clarifying and delineating both the achievements and the mistakes of Nasser's programs. Thus, hopefully, the achievements will be recognized and the mistakes will be rectified.

J. B. MAYFIELD
Middle East Center
University of Utah

ACKNOWLEDGMENTS

My first debt of gratitude is owed to my wife and family. It has been my wife's constant encouragement, her willingness to sacrifice, and her desire to see this project through to its completion that has urged me on. Her wholehearted support has immeasurably eased the burden of my task.

I would also like to express my debt and my gratitude to the many colleagues and friends who have helped me, directly and indirectly, in discussions, correspondence, and many other ways. They include, in particular, Dr. William S. Livingston, Dr. H. Malcolm Macdonald, Dr. James R. Roach, Dr. Wilfred D. Webb, Dr. Orion F. White, Dr. Robert Fernea, Dr. Paul English, Professor William Zartman, and Dr. Tareq T. Ismael.

Dr. Sami Hanna, of the University of Utah Middle East Center, graciously consented to carefully read my manuscript for accuracy and consistency both in subject material and Arabic transliteration. His frank and persistent criticism helped me to tighten up my analysis and corrected some of my interpretation of rural Egypt.

I am also indebted to several graduate students in the University of Utah. Safwat Souryal and Judy Jarrow, as research assistants, carefully proofread the manuscript and offered many valuable suggestions. D. Sherman Ross and Bud D. Pate, graduate students in the Geography Department, were especially helpful in the preparation of the maps and charts used in this book.

Although many people must remain anonymous, I still wish to publicly thank my many Egyptian friends who freely gave of their time and counsel. A word of thanks is necessary to the Egyptian government officials in the Ministry of Local Administration, the Ministry of Agriculture, and the Ministry of Social Affairs who made the extra effort to meet with me and to provide me with the data and information used in this book.

Mention also must be made of the assistance provided by a Fulbright-Hayes research grant, which financed my research field trip to Egypt in 1966–1967 and a research grant provided by the Middle East Center of the University of Utah to finance the final updating research during 1969 and 1970.

As a final acknowledgment, I must mention three individuals. First, I am particularly grateful to Carl Leiden of The University of Texas at Austin for assisting me in the planning of this research, for giving valuable criticism during the compilation of data, and for reviewing the manuscript to assure good style and the accurate presentation of material. During the past few years, Dr. Leiden has not only proven to be a close friend and confidant, but has also stimulated a critical approach to political science that has proved to be invaluable. Second, I must thank Dr. Loren C. Tesdell, formerly of the American University in Cairo, for his cooperative assistance and warm friendship. His encouragement and support played a key role in ensuring the completion of this project. Finally, I must thank Dr. George Lenczowski for his friendship and guidance, his willingness to write the foreword for this book, but above all for his example as a scholar and gentleman.

Whatever merit there is in this work must be shared by those who made its completion possible; for the errors and failings, I alone am responsible.

RURAL POLITICS IN NASSER'S EGYPT

A Quest for Legitimacy

1 ▣ Introduction

THE RURAL AREAS of the United Arab Republic are experiencing revolutionary changes. The vast majority of these changes are unplanned and spontaneous reactions to the world-wide cultural diffusion inherent in the transportation and communication revolution penetrating the emerging nations of Asia and Africa. After the Revolution of 1952, Nasser's regime voiced a strong commitment to reform and development. Nasser sought to introduce new processes and institutions through which this reform and development might be encouraged and advanced. This study will seek to analyze the interaction of these revolutionary changes and the new structures founded by the Nasser regime.

This research is based on the assumption that the political, economic, and social structures presently functioning in rural Egypt can be understood only through a detailed account of the political culture within which these structures must operate. Political culture is portrayed in terms of certain fundamental historical, social, and psychological factors that have determined the general beliefs, attitudes, and sentiments that give order and meaning to the Egyptian political process. This suggests that the perceptions and images held by the peasants and rural administrators must be considered

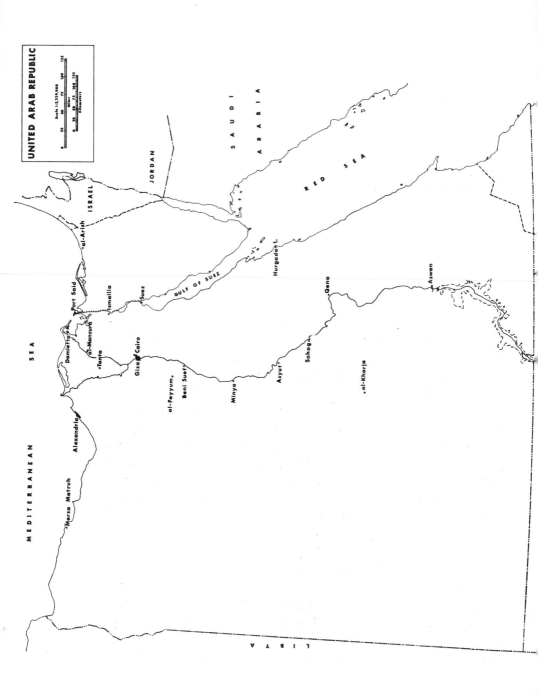

UNITED ARAB REPUBLIC

Scale 1:5,250,000

Miles

Kilometers

MEDITERRANEAN   SEA

ISRAEL

JORDAN

al-Arish

SAUDI   ARABIA

RED   SEA

Port Said

Ismailia

Damietta

al-Mansura

Tanta

Giza Cairo

Alexandria

Mersa Matruh

al-Fayyum

Beni Suef

Minya

Asyut

Sohag

Suez

GULF OF SUEZ

Hurghada I.

Qena

Aswan

el-Kharja

LIBYA

if one is to understand the effectiveness and functioning of the structures and institutions presently operating in rural Egypt.

One central theme of this study is the concept of political legitimization, the process of inculcating and deepening the belief among members of a society that the present political institutions, procedures, and ideals "are right, are good, and are appropriate." More explicitly, one might define the process of legitimization as the gradual development, among members of a political system, of a deep and unambiguous sense of identity with the national government—its leaders, policies, institutions, and procedures. The problem of legitimacy is especially crucial for the newly emerging nations that are caught between the demands of traditionalism and modernism. All traditional societies must face the revolutionary impact of modernization. The violent overthrow of established values and institutions creates a crisis of legitimacy in which neither the old nor the new is completely acceptable.

The concept of political legitimization is particularly applicable to the dramatic changes now taking place in the rural areas of the United Arab Republic. Modern Egypt is a complex mixture of the old and the new, and this "gap" in the society must be recognized if one is to understand present-day Egypt.

With Syria's secession from the United Arab Republic in 1961, Nasser began to realize, as never before, the significance of this cultural gap separating the intellectual and governmental elites from the rest of his people. Strange as it may seem, the problem of the Egyptian elites is accentuated by the fact that they are, in certain basic respects, strangers to the values, attitudes, and motivations of the fellahin. To be sure, many of the intellectuals are well versed in the Muslim cultural heritage as it developed and flourished in previous times. But when it comes to linking this heritage with the culture of the masses as it exists today, and to interpreting it in terms of their current attitudes, cherished values, and social organizations, the leaders continually find themselves faced with this gap.

Starting in 1961 Nasser embarked upon a determined policy to weaken the traditional political structure of the rural provinces

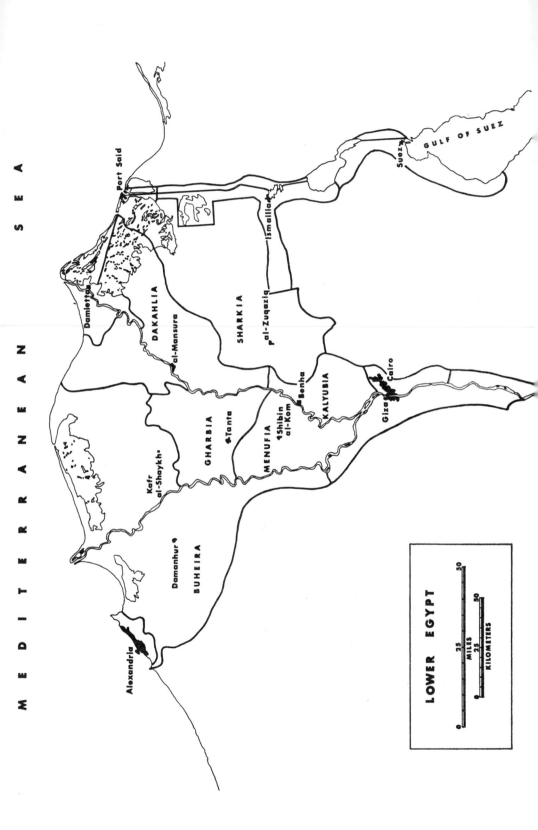

MEDITERRANEAN SEA

SEA

GULF OF SUEZ

Port Said

Suez

Damietta

Ismailia

DAKAHLIA

al-Mansura

SHARKIA

al-Zuqaziq

Benha

KALYUBIA

Kafr
al-Shaykh

GHARBIA

Tanta

Shibin
al-Kom

MENUFIA

Giza Cairo

Damanhur

BUHEIRA

Alexandria

LOWER EGYPT

MILES
0   25   50

KILOMETERS
0   25   50

in Upper and Lower Egypt. This policy was an attempt to create new political and social relationships in the villages, which would then be more conducive to the changes necessary for modernization. Thousands of university-trained civil servants (doctors, agronomists, social workers, and schoolteachers) were sent to the villages; the Arab Socialist Union (Nasser's single political party) established Institutes of Socialist Studies in many of the provincial capitals for the purpose of training the active elements in each village; community development projects were springing up everywhere, and nearly a fourth of the villages were given their own local council.

These various programs and institutions were generally interpreted as a rational extension of Egypt's present nationalist ideology. The many programs of the central ministries, the political party activities, and the local government institutions now developing in the rural provinces of Egypt were heralded as positive proof of Nasser's concern for the fellahin. The actual impact of these central government activities, now that Nasser is gone, will depend upon the extent to which Nasser's rural campaign reflected the real needs and desires of the fellahin.

The modernization process in Egypt requires that appropriate plans, programs, and technical innovations be implemented to alleviate the major problems of Egyptian society, such as an exploding population, a limited agricultural system, illiteracy and poverty, and a lack of capital formation. In addition, an effective relationship between the government and the peasantry requires that some kind of mutual trust and reinforcing harmony be established by which both levels come to understand and appreciate the other's problems, interests, and aspirations. This process of developing trust, confidence, and a meaningful two-way system of communication in its broadest sense is the process of legitimization.

The policy-making and policy-implementing process in a society is a gigantic system of communication and learning. The urge for development and the willingness to change are not equally present in all peoples. In the Egyptian peasant there are motivations that encourage change, but there are also far more conflicting feelings

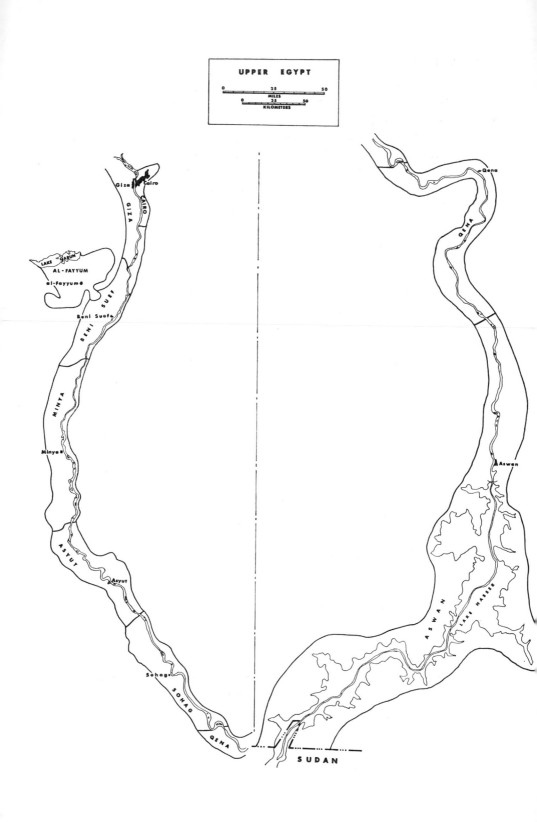

UPPER EGYPT

0   25   50
MILES
0   25   50
KILOMETERS

GIZA

CAIRO

Giza   Cairo

LAKE QARUN

AL-FAYYUM

al-Fayyum

BENI SUEF

Beni Suef

MINYA

Minya

ASYUT

Asyut

SOHAG

Sohag

QENA

QENA

Qena

QENA

ASWAN

LAKE NASSER

Aswan

SUDAN

of resistance to change. The factors that determine these motivations and resistances are cultural, social, and psychological. Associated with every technical and material change there is a corresponding change in the attitudes, thoughts, values, beliefs, and behavior of the people—all of which are learned and communicated within a common cultural milieu. Men's attitudes, and consequently their behavior toward their government's effort to neutralize the barriers to change, will depend primarily upon their orientation and perspective toward the political process, which is a function of their political culture.

Leaders in Egypt seldom have difficulty in creating enthusiasm, zeal, and optimism for new programs and projects. Great hopes and dreams rest on the High Dam, Egypt's ownership of the Suez Canal, and the oil discoveries in the Western Desert—yet these "headline makers" do not generate the kind of commitment needed to ensure an effective legitimization process.

How does a political process stimulate the kind of commitments and attitudes needed to persuade a local clerk in an agricultural cooperative not to demand bakshish for his services; to induce the landowner to charge a reasonable rent to his tenant farmers; to encourage a woman to use the "loop"; to persuade the village doctor to remain in his village more than three or four hours a day; to induce the fellah to drink from the tap instead of the canal; to encourage the local social worker to treat the villagers as equals and not inferiors? Legitimization, conceived in terms of these kinds of problems, is best conceptualized as a function of the political socialization process that determines appropriate behavior patterns and role expectations within the political system of rural Egypt.

Thus legitimacy is extremely crucial. The future of the new post-Nasser regime may well rest upon its ability to substantially meet the needs and aspirations of the masses of Egypt. Yet these needs and aspirations will be achieved only to the extent that individual Egyptians feel motivated by and committed to such programs and projects. The gap that exists between the elite and peasant masses is a reality that Nasser's successors cannot afford to ignore. Communication, understanding, and cooperation are urgently needed.

Three secondary political socialization structures of importance in rural Egypt are the traditional village leadership system (the village *'umdah*), the single political party system (the Arab Socialist Union), and the local administrative system (village councils). These structures must be described in terms of their organization and their functions. The traditional, charismatic, and legal-rational aspects of legitimacy are considered within the context of these rural structures.

Utilizing this Weberian analysis, one might easily conclude that the obedience extended by the fellahin to their rulers rested primarily upon tradition and custom, habit and convention. However, tradition is not enough to explain the political history of Egypt. Such charismatic men as Ramses II, Muhammad the Prophet, Salah al-Din, Urabi, Zaghlul, and Nasser have driven the passive, fatalistic fellahin to sporadic gestures of fervor and ecstacy. Yet few have left a lasting mark upon the fellahin. In the past, tradition meant status quo while charisma meant change and revolution. Profound change required more than a mere coup d'état because real change demands significant alterations in the social, economic, and cultural matrix of the community. The success of Islam in Egypt was no doubt due to the charisma of Muhammad and his close associates. Yet the impact was lasting only because values, norms (goals and procedures), attitudes, and perceptions of reality were transformed and internalized.

The great task facing Egypt's new leadership is to transform Nasser's coup d'état into a genuine social revolution. Nasser's charisma is not to be doubted. But if this transitory phenomenon is to take on the character of a permanent relationship between Egyptian leaders and citizens, it is necessary that Nasser's charismatic authority be "routinized," be institutionalized into structures, organizations, and procedures that are considered legitimate.

Egypt's leaders today must face the same problem Nasser faced, the problem of creating a new society—a society that traditionally has been forced to accept the rules and demands of its government, but a society that today requires the active support of its citizens if the government is to introduce change and modernization. Nasser's ideological commitments to social justice—the eradication of poverty and misery and the establishment of a "true democracy"— required that his regime gain the active, enthusiastic support of its citizens. Nasser's ideology (Arab Socialism) postulated a certain kind of political process and organization; the legitimacy of this process and organization was not based on past tradition or the rational norms of a bureaucratic state. To the contrary, Nasser's new political system was considered legitimate only to the extent that it was perceived as the express will of President Nasser himself. But his charismatic appeal, while explaining short-term acceptance, cannot guarantee long-term legitimization.

There are two approaches to the study of rural politics in Egypt: the descriptive and the interpretative. The descriptive facts are usually found in legal or official documents and administrative pronouncements on policy and procedure. The main approach here is interpretative. This involves an analysis of the subjective attitudes, opinions, ideas, and assumptions that members of the Egyptian society have about their political institutions. The major deficiency in most descriptions of the local administrative organizations of Egypt is their failure to consider the subjective attitudes of individuals and the role these attitudes play in determining how citizens respond to their political institutions, what value and support they will give to them, and, consequently, the eventual effectiveness of these institutions. Since legitimacy presupposes subjective evaluations of the political process, I have collected data on four types of governmental representatives: the traditional village mayor ('umdah), the village party leader, the village council chairman, and either the village doctor, the village schoolmaster, or the village bank director. This analysis thus focuses on the subjective attitudes of these government employees in terms of: (1) how they described and perceived their own duties and responsibilities in the village; (2) how their superiors perceived and described their position in the village; (3) how they evaluated each other; (4) how the villagers evaluated their functions and effectiveness in the village.

This study analyzes the rural politics of Egypt from these points of view. First, I will deal with the historical, cultural, and psychological factors that impinge upon the political culture in Egypt. Many of the attitudes and value judgments expressed by individuals interviewed about their government and its local representatives can only be understood as a function of their history and cultural milieu.

Second, I will outline past, present, and proposed structures and organizations, including the theoretical foundations and legal functions of these governmental institutions. I will trace the relationships of these structures both among themselves and to the central government in Cairo. These political structures include the traditional *'umdah* system, the various community development structures, the local village political party organization, and the newer village councils and proposed popular councils.

Third, I will analyze the effectiveness of these various structures and organizations in socializing the Egyptian peasant into the new political culture envisioned in Nasser's Arab Socialism. Changes in rural Egypt were largely due to President Nasser's charismatic leadership. Many villagers identified with Nasser and thus accepted many of his regime's innovations. Whether Nasser's charisma eventually will be "routinized" depends on whether the villagers consider the new regime's party workers and government officials competent and dedicated to the solution of rural problems.

The political system in the rural communities of the U.A.R. is composed of three groups of leaders: the local traditional leaders, the new emerging party leaders, and the ever-present administrative functionaries. These three groups are not mutually exclusive but are indicative of the conflicting values, cultural norms, and behavioral patterns that provide rural Egypt with such a "mixed" political process. All three must be invited to play an important role in legitimization, and all three are presently seeking ascendance in the political life of rural Egypt.

In 1960 a presidential decree (Law 124) announced the establishment of a new system of local administration—a system committed to "decentralization, local autonomy, and popular democracy." This system was to be institutionalized at the village level in the form of village councils. These councils were to be composed of elected, selected, and ex-officio members. (These three types of members should not be equated with the three types of leaders mentioned above.) This pluralistic approach to membership recognizes the diffuse nature of the political process in the Egyptian village and seeks to integrate different, if not conflicting, bases for political power.

What are the sources of legitimization? What role can an ideology, an organization, or even an individual play in generating legitimacy, and what are the implications for change and development when these different sources are used separately or together? What institutions, roles, and procedures in Egypt seem to be acquiring legitimacy, and what is the process by which some structures and individuals gain legitimacy and others lose it? Given these sources and objects of legitimacy, what conclusions for policy, procedures, and institutional organization are warranted for a society committed to rapid modernization? With these questions as guidelines, let us proceed to an analysis of the Egyptian political culture.

Nasser's death provides a break in Egypt's ongoing drive for modernity and allows us a brief pause for reflection. The new rulers of Egypt must now look hard at what Nasser has accomplished and, perhaps more important, what he did not accomplish. His accomplishments were great, yet his unfulfilled dreams were even greater. This, then, is the challenge awaiting Egypt's present leadership.

2 ▣ Political History
of the Egyptian Fellahin

EGYPT, since the days of Muhammad Ali, has been sub-jected to the political, economic, and social influence of Western civilization—probably one of the first non-West-ern nations to be so invaded. Despite this early exposure, Egyptian society in its basic structure has seen little change. Most barriers to change are primarily cultural: the basic values of the group, its concepts of right and wrong, and the nature of its attitudes, be-havioral norms, and traditions. The way a man acts depends largely upon his perspective, which is one's ordered view of the world—what is taken for granted about the attributes of various objects, events, and human nature. It is an order of things remembered and expected, as well as things actually perceived, an organized conception of what is plausible and what is possible; and it con-stitutes the matrix through which one perceives his environment. Culture, then, in its broadest sense refers to a perspective shared by a particular group, one that motivates common reactions. This emphasis on a cultural perspective or orientation is extremely val-uable in analyzing the political, social, and psychological barriers that face a developing nation such as Egypt.

Yet this study does not purport to include a complete study of the complex and extremely diffuse Egyptian culture. Rather, I will focus on the narrower problem of Egypt's political culture, which Verba defines as "the empirical beliefs, expressive symbols, and values which define the situation in which political action takes place."[1] Specifically, political culture consists of the fundamental beliefs that the members of a given society hold concerning the nature of their political system and the role they should play in it.

The primary aim here is to describe in broad terms certain major historical trends, social structures, and psychological parameters applicable to an understanding of the present political culture in Egypt. Political systems are never "ideal types,"—either purely traditional or modern. Modernity and tradition are never fully distinct in reality, hence the political culture of even the most "modern" countries is, in fact, a blend of the traditional and modern.

One is often impressed by the neatness with which historians segment the flow of Egyptian history. It is customary to distinguish the Pharaonic, the Greco-Roman, the Byzantine, the Arab, and the Ottoman periods, while modern Egyptian history usually starts with the rule of Muhammad Ali in 1805. To understand the attitudes of the Egyptian peasant toward his government, one must first trace the evolution of the political organization in the Nile Valley, including the factors that have shaped his concept of authority. During the ancient Pharaonic period, the ruler was God; his word was obeyed without question. The many officials of his court ruled by the stick and the whip. The all-too-vivid pictorial records in the tombs of the kings leave no doubt that flogging and beatings were the common forms of discipline. In describing the Pharaonic era one writer notes: "The excesses of autocratic and bureaucratic terror are an extreme manifestation of human behavior under total power. Institutionally, however, they are probably less important than the innumerable acts of terror that were perpetrated as a matter of routine and within the flexible frame

[1] Lucian W. Pye and Sidney Verba, eds., *Political Culture and Political Development*, p. 593.

of despotic law. It is this routine terror in managerial, fiscal, and
judicial procedures that caused certain observers to designate the
government of hydraulic despotism as 'government by flogging.' "²

The lives and conditions of these early peasants of ancient Egypt
were indeed arduous. Digging, sowing, working the *shadūf* (a
primitive irrigation device) from morning to night for weeks,
straddled with consistently high taxes, and subject to long periods
of forced labor (corvée), the existence of these peasants (fellahin)
was generally unchanging. The ties between ancient Pharaonic
Egypt and the modern Egyptian are admittedly tenuous—yet Cromer's description of the late nineteenth-century Egyptian scene
with its corvée, its bastinado, and its use of corporal punishment,
closely parallels what we know of life in ancient Egypt.³ Although
it is impossible to measure the impact of this Pharaonic tradition
upon modern Egypt, the absolute and capricious governmental
practices so prevalent in the rural areas during the nineteenth and
early twentieth century certainly are not unique in Egyptian
history.

In describing the historical factors that have impinged upon
Egyptian political culture, no tradition is more all-encompassing
than that of the Arab Muslim invasion of the seventh century. The
Arabs of pre-Islamic days had not developed a system of government superseding the tribal system. The political structure was
rudimentary and presents a tradition of government that modern
Egyptian leaders may well seek to emphasize as they prod the
fellahin into an active and purposeful participation in the governmental process. This earlier tribal society was generally patriarchal,
for descent was counted only through males, and the head of the
tribe was the *shaykh*, who was perhaps regarded as the wisest man
of the tribe.⁴ Succession to this high office was not necessarily
hereditary and the *shaykh*'s son, or close relative, became chief
only if acceptable to the leading clans of the tribe. The *shaykh* "held
his office thanks to his personal prestige, which, though in part was

² Karl A. Wittfogel, *Oriental Despotism*, p. 143.
³ Lord Cromer, *Modern Egypt*, II, 402–405.
⁴ Bernard Lewis, *The Arabs in History*, p. 29.

due to his noble lineage, sprang mostly from his qualities as a leader, his generosity, and his ability to deal with people."[5]

The *shaykh*'s authority, though it was a private prerogative of the person or persons involved, was, in fact, preeminently an authority on behalf of the group as a whole. It had to be exercised in the interests of the members and thus was not freely appropriated by the incumbent. One major characteristic of this early desert *shaykh* was his lack of a strong administrative staff: "He is hence still to a large extent dependent on the willingness of the group members to respect his authority, since he has no machinery to enforce it. . . . Obedience is owed to the person of the chief, not to any established rule. But it is owed to the chief only by virtue of his traditional status. He is thus on his part strictly bound by tradition."[6]

The *shaykh*'s powers were not absolute or even primary. The advice of the tribal council (*majlis*), consisting of heads of families and representatives of different clans, was sought on all matters pertaining to the entire tribe. Therefore, his powers were centered in the functions of arbitration rather than command. He was able to influence people only by example, by advice, or by other non-compulsory means. He was rarely more than a first among equals. The life of the tribe was regulated by the Sunna (practice of the ancestors), which owed such authority as it had to the general veneration for precedent and found its only sanction in public opinion. Legitimacy rested not upon religion, but upon tradition and the sanctions of custom and mores. The tribal *majlis* was the institutionalized symbol of the tribe, its mouthpiece and sole instrument. Consequently the tribal chief followed rather than led tribal opinion. "The *sayyid* (chief) had no powers to enforce his bidding. Sometimes he became guilty of arrogancy, but as a rule his prerogatives did not infringe on the essential equality of all members of the tribe. He was freely accessible. No ceremonial protected him and his position."[7] Decision-making was primarily by consensus,

---

[5] G. E. von Grunebaum, *Medieval Islam*, p. 155.
[6] Max Weber, *The Theory of Social and Economic Organization*, p. 346.
[7] G. E. von Grunebaum, *Medieval Islam*, p. 155.

forged by blood ties and the hardships of desert life. The Bedouins saw tribal organization merely as a necessity in time of war.[8]

Many customs, institutions, and attitudes toward family and authority of the Arab tribal community are present in the modern Egyptian village. For example, the village council is traditionally the agency charged with the maintenance of law and order; even its composition reflects the traditional authoritarian concept. "Prestige derived from age, experience, and sobriety combined with power attached to landowners and heads of large families who are well known for their hospitality, are the main qualifications for selection in these councils."[9] The Arab tribal belief that blood relationships alone determine one's role, duty, and position in society is still prevalent in Egyptian village society. The old Arab practice of blood revenge, in which each clan and family must pursue a private justice against a thief or murderer of one's kinsman, is still a serious problem in Upper Egypt.

The most significant and pervasive source of modern Egyptian political culture is the Islamic period. The Islamic community was based upon a brotherhood of believers who were all equal before Allah. According to Islamic doctrine, the condition of freedom and equality of all Muslims before God is a juridical right.[10] Under traditional Islam the converted followers were united in a theocracy, a commonwealth in which political power was held by God, who delegated its administration to the Prophet Muhammad. Legitimate political power was conveyed to Muhammad through his divine mission. There was no distinction between temporal and spiritual authority. While the West distinguishes among civic, political, social, religious, and moral obligations, these in Islam are all viewed as moral obligations derived from a revealed source of values and ideals, perceived as both objective and transcendental. Through the Prophet Muhammad the religious tenets of Islam, including all civil legislation, were communicated from the divine

[8] W. R. Smith, *Kinship and Marriage in Early Arabia*, p. 9.

[9] Hamed Ammar, *Growing Up in an Egyptian Village*, p. 60.

[10] W. M. Watt, *Islam and the Integration of Society*. Watt presents a most interesting analysis of Islamic political institutions during Muhammad's lifetime and their similarities to traditional tribal structures and concepts.

authority to the people. Man must obey them, and law and obedience to law had from the beginning the character of a religious obligation. This system of rules comprising every part of a Muslim's life, from the humblest details up to the principles of his moral and social existence, is termed *sharī'ah* (the Islamic Law).[11] The *sharī'ah* encompassed both obligatory and prohibited activities. It was a system of laws as well as a system of morality. Theoretically, the *sharī'ah* derives essentially from the Koran and the Hadith, or tradition of the Prophet's deeds and sayings. Its purpose is not to determine the relations between men, but to define the standards of right and wrong on the basis of one transcendental standard.

Both leadership and authority were needed to implement this legal system, to defend the Islamic community (*'ummah*) from its enemies, and to spread the word of God to other nations. Thus, the Islamic community demanded some political organization. Obedience to a political structure sanctioned by God was a natural outgrowth of this new process of legitimization, one based on direct revelation. Few will question the obviously normative aspects implicit in the obedience and acceptance extended to the Prophet Muhammad in this early Islamic state. The Koranic formula, "obey Allah and obey the messenger and those of you who are in authority," sums up this approach to obedience.[12]

Gradually, during the first three centuries of Islam, various aspects of the general field of jurisprudence were denied the *sharī'ah* courts. First, the administration of criminal justice, and later, an ever-increasing share of the law of contracts and obligations, had to be relinquished to practice and custom.

As more and more of the functions of the polity were freed from the demands of the *sharī'ah*, the growing discrepancy between Muslim theory of state and the actual administration of political power became a concern of jurists and scholars. Most thinkers of

---

[11] Most of this discussion makes use of material and views found in the following works: J. Schacht, *Origins of Muhammedan Jurisprudence*; T. W. Arnold, *The Caliphate*; R. Levy, *An Introduction to the Sociology of Islam*, 2 vols.; E. Tyan, "Le Califat," in *Institutions de droit public musulman*; and M. Gaudefroy-Demombynes, *Les Institutions musulmanes*.

[12] *The Koran*, Chapter IV, Verse 59.

the earlier periods insisted that the caliph be obeyed—but only so long as he did not order something which was contrary to the *shari'ah*. During the later Abbasid dynasty, obedience tended to become an absolute duty, and even an unjust ruler was regarded as better than none at all. Only a small minority of political writers ever suggested that rebellion could be legitimate.

The paradox of the historical unity of religion and politics . . . is related to two circumstances, the first of which is historical and the second rather more theological. The historical circumstances which gave rise to ideological concern over the relationship between religion and politics is [that] the *ulama* held ever more strongly that the sphere of politics was to be dominated by the sphere of religion—even while, in fact, the sphere of politics came ever more strongly to dominate the sphere of religion. At the very least, this enormous generalization is true as regards the institutions of the caliphate and the sultanate. The theological circumstance is . . . that Islamic theology cannot accept the idea of tension between religion and politics.[13]

By the eleventh century, the ruthless realities. the tremendous gap between the normative dreams and the actual conduct of state had become so marked that Islamic theologians had to make a choice. The choice was summarized by al-Ghazzālī, who tried to legitimize power by submitting it symbolically to religious authority at the same time that he sought to confirm authority by linking it to political power.

The concessions that we make are involuntary, but necessity makes permissible that which was prohibited. . . . Who is there . . . who would argue for the avoidance of the *imāmah* in our days because of the lack of the requisite qualifications? . . . Which is better, that we should declare . . . that all appointments are invalid . . . that all executive actions in all parts of the earth are null and void . . . or to recognize that the *imāmah* is held by a valid contract, and that all acts and jurisdictions are valid given the circumstances of the times.[14]

Thus, "circumstances," not God's transcendental order, must be used to justify the existing political ruler. Whoever had the power,

---

[13] Leonard Binder, *The Ideological Revolution in the Middle East*, p. 51.
[14] Abu Ḥāmid al-Ghazzālī, *al-Iqtiṣād fī al-i'tiqād* (Cairo, A.H. 1320.) quoted in Nadav Safran, *Egypt in Search of Political Community*, p. 22.

be it de jure or merely de facto, a tyrant or a corruptionist, must be considered legitimate. After all, anything was better than anarchy. Fearing political instability more than bad government, the religious authorities urged political quietism. The logical consequence of this approach tended to legitimize any ruler as long as he was Muslim. Yet, if the consequences or the situations can hold final authority in political legitimacy, then authority has no moral foundation. Al-Ghazzālī's thought tended to justify a situation that already existed. Many Muslim rulers and their regimes were no longer based upon *sharī'ah* principles of justice, honesty, and morality in interpersonal relations, and thus the moral basis of obedience was significantly weakened. Dishonesty, bribery, and corruption gradually became a common legacy to the Muslim's political system. With a disillusionment bordering on cynicism, the common man viewed the ruling elite with feelings of utter hopelessness and resignation.[15]

Although Egypt's Islamic heritage can be traced back to the Arab invasions of the seventh century A.D., it was not until 1517 that Egypt became a province of the Ottoman Empire, whose sultan, as caliph, proclaimed the traditional authority of the earlier Islamic empires. Weber defines this type of government as "sultanism":

The members are now treated as subjects. An authority of the chief which was previously treated principally as exercised on behalf of the members, now becomes his personal authority [which] he is entitled to exploit, in principle like any economic advantage—to sell it, to pledge it as security, or to divide it by inheritance. The primary external support of patrimonial authority is a staff of slaves, coloni, or conscripted subjects. . . . Where authority is primarily oriented to tradition but in its exercise makes the claim of full personal powers it will be called "patrimonial" authority. Where patrimonial authority lays primary stress on the sphere of arbitrary will free of traditional limitations, it will be called "sultanism."[16]

In Egypt, as elsewhere in the Ottoman Empire, the people were divided into two great classes: the ruling class of Ottomans and the vast majority of subjects whose main function in life was to produce

[15] G. E. von Grunebaum, *Medieval Islam*, pp. 167–168.
[16] Max Weber, *The Theory of Social and Economic Organization*, p. 347.

wealth by trade, industry, and agriculture for the benefit of the sultan and his ruling class. Egypt was established as the granary of the Ottoman Empire just as it had been for the empires which previously ruled in the eastern Mediterranean. The land of Egypt itself was a great tax farm that the governor purchased from the sultan, usually on a two-year contract. The governor, in turn, sub-leased the land to tax farmers (*multazims*), whose function was to make sure that the lands were cultivated and that the taxes were collected and delivered to the treasury. By the end of the eighteenth century, this tax-farm system (*'iltizām*) was the predominant fiscal system in Egypt.[17] The *multazim*, in return for his services, was allowed to keep a portion of his collections (*mīrī*) as profit for himself. The entire system was structured to exploit the land and produce wealth—first for the *multazim*, then for the governor, and, finally, for the sultan.

Usually, the lands of a village were held under several *'iltizāms*, and each *multazim* (tax farmer) appointed one of the village notables as his responsible chief or *shaykh*. The *shaykh* representing the *multazim* with the greatest amount of land in the village was usually designated chief *shaykh* or *shaykh al-balad*. He was the main intermediary between the Ottoman hierarchy and the village, and was in charge of coordinating and directing the activities of the other chiefs and village officials. As the chief executive officer, he presided over the village council of elders when it met, acted as magistrate and arbitrator in village conflicts, and supervised all tax collections. Though he was often harsh and tyrannical, his position was respected, and the fellahin often turned to him for assistance, advice, and support. Each village in effect was an isolated, yet self-contained unit, where life had changed little since the days of the pharaohs and was largely regulated by a body of tradition and custom. As its relations with the Ottoman government were

[17] The following works are especially valuable for understanding the political and administrative history of Ottoman Egypt: Sir Hamilton Gibb and Harold Bowen, *Islamic Society and the West* 2 vols.; S. J. Shaw, *The Financial and Administrative Organization and Development of Ottoman Egypt*; E. Comb, *L'Egypte ottomane*; and Helen Rivlin, *The Agricultural Policy of Muhammad Ali in Egypt*.

limited almost exclusively to the payment of taxes, it would not be inaccurate to describe these villages as largely self-governing.

The immense gap between the sultan and the peasants in one of his provinces probably precluded any significant commitment or sense of loyalty to the sultan or his representative tax collectors. In fact, the peasants tried to deceive the government agents whenever possible. "All the fellaheen," says Edward Lane, "are proud of the stripes they receive for withholding their contributions, and are often heard to boast of the number of blows which were inflicted upon them before they would give up their money."[18]

The life of the fellahin had been unchanging for centuries. Their political and economic organization was strictly based on the kinship system. However, in terms of political control and economic exploitation, the village, not the family, was the unit of measure. Individual peasant ownership of land was completely unknown prior to the nineteenth century, since "village lands were held in common and periodically redistributed among the peasants."[19] Although some fellah families did gain certain "traditional rights" to certain pieces of land, which were transmitted to their children, still they did not own this land, nor could they sell it or even lease it without permission of the *multazim*. In addition, the village was considered the unit of administration in fiscal matters—the village as a whole being responsible for the payment of taxes to their *multazim*. Thirdly, it was a village responsibility to provide all corvée labor, which was called periodically to maintain irrigation canals, build roads, and even work on the lands of the *multazim*. These three pressures made the villagers a closely knit group, highly integrated and fully aware of their mutual interdependence. The peasant's world was divided into his own villagers and the "foreigners." The outsider was distrusted, feared, and avoided. Lane describes the wealth of the governor and the poverty of the peasant with these words:

[18] Edward W. Lane, *Manners and Customs of the Modern Egyptians*, pp. 132–133.

[19] Gabriel Baer, "The Dissolution of the Egyptian Village Community," *Die Welt des Islam* 6 (1961): 56.

The revenue of the Báshà of Egypt is generally said to amount to about three millions of pounds of sterling. Nearly half arises from the direct taxes on land and from indirect exactions from the felláheen. . . . The felláh, to supply the bare necessaries of life, is often obliged to steal and convey secretly to his hut as much as he can of the produce of his land . . . Most of the governors of provinces and districts carry their oppression far beyond the limits to which they are authorized . . . and even the sheykh of a village, in executing the commands of his superiors, abuses his lawful power: bribes, and the ties of relationship and marriage, influence him and them, and by lessening the oppression of some who are more able to bear it, greatly increases that of others.[20]

Government authority on the local level was inclined to be arbitrary, and life uncertain. It is probable that the village functionaries tended also to come from the wealthier families of the community and were often related, except for the financial managers, who were generally Copts (Egyptian Christians).

Nineteenth-Century Egypt

In many ways Egypt's modern history began with Napoleon's invasion. Napoleon's forces landed in Egypt in 1798 and won their decisive victory near Cairo at the Battle of the Pyramids. The Mameluke-Turkish army, composed of a large number of fellahin conscripted for the emergency, were quickly scattered, some of them fleeing with Murad Bey, the Mameluke leader, to Upper Egypt.[21]

Napoleon's efforts to win over the ulema (local religious leaders) by professing a profound respect for Islam and by assuring them of his desire to liberate them from Turkish oppression were received with distrust and suspicion. French forces shelled a religious institution (al-Azhar) in quelling a popular revolt in Cairo three months after the Battle of the Pyramids. Further evidence of Napoleon's apparent duplicity was found in the behavior of the French troops, who completely disregarded the tenets of Islam and thereby deeply offended the ulema. The fellahin also were alienated, since

[20] Edward W. Lane, *Manners and Customs of the Modern Egyptians*, pp. 132–134.
[21] J. Christopher Herold, *Bonaparte in Egypt*, pp. 225–262.

their tax burdens were increased. French provincial inspectors employed Copts, who were extremely efficient, to collect taxes. This was a further insult, since never before in Islamic Egypt had Coptic Christians been on equal terms with Muslims, nor had they collected taxes for a conquering infidel army. "The mere sight of the French infidels ruling the land patronized by the House of the Prophet shocked the religious sentiments of the people and aroused their corporate Moslem feelings to the pitch of a *jehad*."[22]

In 1801, Napoleon's forces, defeated by the Turks and the British, evacuated Egypt. The sultan's power and influence were then gradually reestablished. By 1805, an ambitious young Albanian officer in the Ottoman army, Muhammad Ali, had gained control of the whole country. The ulema, who found it expedient to recognize Muhammad Ali's authority, provided leadership for the rebellious fellahin whose economic status was almost unbearable under the rule of the local Turkish governor.[23] Led by the ulema, forty thousand fellahin converged upon the Cairo courts in 1805 to demand the deposition of the governor, basing their case on the religious tradition that permitted the people to depose an unjust caliph. So impressed was the Turkish judge by this mass display of power that he declared their cause to be just.[24] The governor was dismissed, and Muhammad Ali became the new ruler of Egypt.

Although the extent of the spontaneity of fellahin participation in the deposition is questionable, it is certainly true that the fellahin had suffered severe economic hardship since before the French invasion, and that their situation had worsened thereafter. Forced out of their circumscribed village life by conscription into the Mame-

[22] M. Rifaat Bey, *The Awakening of Modern Egypt*, p. 12.

[23] Jamal Mohammed Ahmed, *The Intellectual Origins of Egyptian Nationalism*, p. 3.

[24] Rifaat quotes al-Jabarti, a contemporary of this period: "*The Turkish Delegate*: How can you depose the man whom the Sultan has nominated to be your governor? Have you forgotten the divine commandment to obey God almighty, His Prophets and those in authority over you? *The Egyptian Leader*: Those in authority referred to in the Sacred Book are the noble *sheikhs*, the lawgivers and the just Sultan. But this is an unjust man; and it is customary from the earliest times for the people to depose their governors and even kings or Khalifas if they misgovern or persecute the nation" (Rifaat Bey, *The Awakening of Modern Egypt*, p. 19).

luke army, they had been aroused from their apathy by the defeat
of their lords by the infidel and still further shocked by the French
occupation and the suddenly intensified collection of taxes. The
prestige of their rulers was considerably diminished; no longer were
they invincible. The infidel had roused the fellahin to united action,
making them forget, at least temporarily, their inimical attitudes
toward the inhabitants of other villages. Having banded together to
fight against the French, they were ready to rebel against their
former masters. To a large extent the revolt of 1805 seems to have
been spontaneous. "The fellahin of Egypt opened a new chapter in
the history of their country. Not only did they venture to depose the
Governor without referring the matter to the Porte, but they also
asserted their full right of self-determination in choosing their own
head of state."[25]

Muhammad Ali's power and influence was not merely a function
of popular support, however. He was a clever man who was aware
that his success in maintaining power depended upon the strength
he could draw from the potentially rich province of which he was
now the temporary master. He set himself, with boundless energy
and determination, to make Egypt a country richer and stronger
than its nominal master, Turkey. Out of his struggle and effort,
modern Egypt was born. Between 1805 and 1816 Muhammad Ali
dealt one by one with the English, the Turks, the Mamelukes,
and finally the Albanians, who had helped him to power. By 1816
he had successfully disposed of all serious challenges to his power
and had only to contend with the latent jealousy and hostility of
the sultan.

In this same period he reformed the tax system by abolishing
the *'iltizām* practice of farming out the land tax, readjusting the
tax base, and arranging for taxes to be paid directly to the government. By successive steps from 1808 to 1814, he swept away the
privileged classes of landowners that had developed under the
Mameluke regime and gathered into his own hands the nominal
ownership of all the land in the country. Yet he did not break all

25 Ibid., p. 20.

ties with Turkey. A historian of his day said of him: "He, however, [still] professes allegiance to the Sultán, and remits the tribute, according to former custom, to Constantinople: he is, moreover, under an obligation to respect the fundamental laws of the Kur-án and the Traditions; but he exercises a dominion otherwise unlimited. He may cause any one of his subjects to be put to death without the formality of a trial, or without assigning any cause; a simple horizontal motion of his hand is sufficient to imply the sentence of decapitation."[26]

In 1826 Muhammad Ali announced the creation of an Advisory Council (*majlis al-mashūra*) made up of 156 members: 33 high officials, 24 district or local officials, and 99 village notables. Its major function was to advise in matters of administration, education, and public works, to receive complaints, and to put forward suggestions. These limitations reflect the restricted concerns of the government, which were largely fiscal and judicial. He completely reorganized the provincial government, dividing the country into twelve *mudirīyāt*, each headed by a *mudīr*. Each *mudirīyah* was further subdivided into *marākiz*, each headed by a *ma'mur*. This attempt to superimpose the French administrative system upon rural Egypt proved largely ineffective. In actual practice these changes were superficial, and the whole system continued to be administered by the whip (*korbaj*), tempered with bribery.

The strong secular state that Muhammad Ali tried to set up was at variance with the traditionally weak Islamic state. Muhammad Ali's goal was to build an Egyptian empire ruled by his dynasty. He believed that such an empire would be possible only if it had complete control over the entire society. As he describes the situation: "I collected all power into my hands in order to ensure efficiency. The question is one concerned with production, and if I fail to act, who else would? Who is going to provide the necessary funds, suggest the plans to be followed and the crops to be planted? Who is going to force the people to acquire knowledge and sciences which made Europe progress? I was forced to lead this country

[26] Edward W. Lane, *Manners and Customs of the Modern Egyptians*, p. 113.

as children must be led because allowing it to function alone would only lead to chaos again."[27]

Muhammad Ali claimed all of the land to be his and granted large tracts, both cultivable and uncultivable, to members of his family and entourage, the remaining Turko-Circassians, including high-ranking civil servants, and other foreigners. The newly appointed government representatives in the villages, the *shaykhs al-balad*,[28] were also frequently recipients of grants of land. They were linked to Muhammad Ali through the provincial and district administrators.

Life within the village continued as before with very few changes. Each fellah was alloted three to five feddans (approximately 3.1 to 5.2 acres) and the necessary seeds and implements for their cultivation. These transactions were carried out by the *shaykh al-balad*, who was also responsible for the reapportioning of land and the collection of taxes, all of which was not very different from the Ottoman system. The *shaykh al-balad* had considerably more authority, however, than did his counterpart under the Ottoman rule. He was responsible for the assessment of taxes, the recruiting of fellahin for the corvée and for service in the newly instituted fellah division of the army, and for work in Muhammad Ali's factories. Corvée duty, which had never been salaried, now took the fellahin far from their villages to build roads, canals, and barrages on the Nile, and to increase the area of cultivable land. The corvée drained the manpower of the village, and the fellahin detested it.

Under this system thousands of persons were forcibly employed every year without pay, without any provision of food, without any proper tools, or any organization of labor, and often far from their homes, and this system, hard enough if it had been justly worked and the burden had been divided between the rich and the poor, has been so unjustly carried out that the rich have almost entirely escaped from any contribution either in money or labour, while the poor have borne it all. . . . Statistics as to the numbers called out yearly for the corvée up to 1878 are not forthcoming. In the years 1878, 1879 and 1880, it is esti-

[27] Muhammad Shafīq Ghurbāl, *Muhammad 'Alī al-kabīr*, p. 113.
[28] A village headman was known by the title *shayhk al-balad* during the early nineteenth century, but later his title was changed to *'umdah* (mayor).

mated that 188,000 men were summoned, and that of these, 112,000 on an average, were annually employed for the space of five or six months during low Nile.[29]

The army and factory conscripts were also away from their villages for extended periods and came into prolonged contact with a new world of city life for the first time. The labor shortage thus created in the village added immeasurably to the tax burden laid on the fellahin remaining at home.

In many ways Muhammad Ali, and his successors as well, pursued policies that should have led to an equitable distribution of land among the fellahin. In actual fact, there gradually developed a thin stratum of large landowners sharply differentiated from the mass of fellahin. Increased taxation, especially among the smaller landowners, became so burdensome that many peasants were forced either to sell their land or merely to abandon it. The general exodus of the fellahin during the 1840's and 1850's belies the commonly held notion that a fellah would never leave his land. In an effort to escape army conscription, corvée duty, or the heavy taxation, many fellahin even escaped as far as Syria and Turkey. Muhammad Ali's ostensible reason for declaring war on Syria in 1831 was over the issue of extradition of the fellahin who had sought refuge there.[30] In fact, requests for permission to abandon land apparently reached such proportions that it had to be forbidden by decree in 1865. Most of the abandoned land fell into the hands of the large landowners or village *shaykhs*, especially during and after Khedive Ismail's reign (1863–1879). When drawing up his cadastral survey, Muhammad Ali allocated five percent of all village lands, tax exempt, to each *shaykh al-balad*. In theory, income derived from them was designed to meet the expenses of hospitality that each *shaykh al-balad* was supposed to extend to visiting strangers and dignitaries.

From among the leaders of these large landowning families, the central government would appoint the *shaykh* with the strongest

[29] Sir E. Baring, *Report of the Conditions of the Agricultural Population in Egypt*, p. 6.
[30] Helen Rivlin, *The Agricultural Policy of Muhammad Ali in Egypt*, p. 204.

reputation in the area to be the chief *shaykh* or *shaykh al-balad*. "Although this was a subordinate position in the civil-service hierarchy, it was one of influence in determining landownership relations within the village. . . . In many villages the office of [*shaykh al-balad* or] *'umdah* remained in the same family for generations."[31]

Since the *'umdah* was the single government representative in the village, he controlled all matters concerning village lands, and the central authorities generally upheld his decisions. Prior to the 1850's the *'umdah* arbitrarily redivided all lands left to the state by the death of one of his villagers. Although new laws of inheritance that were passed during the second half of the nineteenth century somewhat curtailed the powers of these village leaders, still they had great influence in the village community. Baer notes that these *'umdahs* "had a large and sometimes decisive say in fixing tax assessments; they determined virtually alone the classification of land for purposes of taxation; and they decided which land should be classed as 'unproductive' and, therefore, exempt from taxation for a considerable period. It was on the strength of what the *'umda* told him that the *mudīr* decided which land should be expropriated for public use."[32]

The *'umdah* had still another powerful source of influence. Since the government generally accepted his recommendation as to which of his fellahin would be conscripted into the army or forced to work on corvée, few of the villagers would ever challenge his position or his decisions.

The problem of the corvée was aggravated by the gradual extension of private property to the fellahin through the government decrees of 1855 and 1871. Now that a peasant was individually responsible for his tax payments, corvée duty imposed during the planting or harvesting season meant the loss of his crops. As many of the landlords of the large estates were allowed by government to exempt their fellahin from corvée duty, this put an additional

31 Gabriel Baer, *A History of Landownership in Modern Egypt 1800–1950*, p. 51.
32 Ibid., p. 52.

strain on the remainder of the population, especially during the building of the Suez Canal. Furthermore, the corvée was misused by influential landowners who forced the fellahin to work on their estates for nothing. In 1878 the British consul observed in a letter to Lord Salisbury, "the result of the arbitrary and uncertain demands of the government, made at seasons which do not coincide with the harvest, is that the cultivator is often driven to borrow money at usurious rates of interest, ranging up to 7 percent per month, or even to sell his cattle and land, and not the least of the economic evils resulting from this deplorable absence of system is that the class of small proprietors tends to disappear."[33]

The transition to a money tax, instead of in-kind, was started under the Khedive Abbas (1849–1854), and by 1880 all taxes had to be paid in cash. Now, instead of having to abandon his land or starve, especially in the event of flooding or drought, the fellah who owned his land could be granted credit on its security. To make matters worse, Western concepts of land mortgaging (heretofore unknown in Islamic law) were adopted with the establishment of the Mixed Court System in 1875. To quote the Dufferin Report, "In the same way as the introduction into India of British codes invested the creditor with new powers, so in Egypt the International Tribunals have, on the one hand, stimulated the fellah's borrowing instincts by constituting his holding a legal security, and on the other, they have armed the mortgagee with far too ready and extensive power of selling up the encumbered owner."[34]

Fellah indebtedness started to become a problem at the beginning of Ismail's reign, in the early 1860's. The cotton boom, spurred on by the American Civil War, led many small landowners to increase their cropped area on the basis of loans, principally from Greek, Armenian, and Syrian merchants. The sudden end of the cotton boom and a coincidental rise in taxes caused widespread bankruptcy.

Loss of land through sequestration by the government for nonpayment of taxes was only surpassed by foreclosures of loans from

[33] Ibid., p. 36.
[34] Great Britain, *Correspondence 3554*, pp. 6–7.

the Greeks, Syrians, and other Levantine Christians. "Although shaikhs and notables also lent money to fellahs, it appears that most dispossessions were due to foreigners. Villiers Stuart tells of one village where 'the Greek had 200 acres, and no other inhabitant had more than a few acres left, even the sheikh had only twelve acres. The Greek's estate had been carved out of theirs.' "[35]

The foreign population of Egypt grew from only 3,000 in 1836 in Muhammad Ali's reign, to over 68,000 in 1875.[36] Many of these foreigners became large landowners. To facilitate their commercial and land transactions, the Khedive Ismail introduced large portions of the Napoleonic Code as well as the French court system. The purchase of many a fellah's land occurred in these courts, and the ignorant fellah, who even today regards the Cairene as a "foreigner," was totally unable to accrue any legal redress. Although he might have been aware of the existence of these courts, his cynicism in regard to their value is evident in the response of a peasant in Lower Egypt who was asked to describe how justice is administered.

It is all by bribery; a poor man has no choice. If he is wronged, if it is a small debt, or if he has been maltreated, or beaten or robbed . . . the constable of the village reports the case to the Mahmour [district representative of the Ministry of Interior], who, if he deems it sufficiently important, reports it to the Mudir. If it is a land dispute, e.g., about boundaries or successions, it goes to Tantah [provincial capital]; three or four years may elapse before it is settled. If he has a buffalo or a cow, he must sell it to make presents for Chief Clerks and their subordinates, and even higher officials. He is soon ruined. In other cases which are reported . . . to the Mudir, the man who can afford to bribe highest gets the most favorable reports.[37]

As taxes continued to rise, the discrepancy between the wealth of village notables and 'umdahs, some of whom had estates of eight hundred to a thousand feddans, and that of the rapidly growing group of indebted and landless peasants gradually increased.

[35] Gabriel Baer, *A History of Landownership in Modern Egypt 1800–1950*, p. 36.
[36] Charles Issawi, *Egypt in Revolution*, p. 29.
[37] Villiers Stuart, *Egypt after the War*, pp. 21–22.

The peasant may or may not have resented this: in any case, he did not revolt against the 'umdah; he merely left his land. The property law of 1871, which became mandatory in 1874, gave absolute property rights to the owner provided that he pay six years of taxes in advance, which was utterly beyond the ability of most peasants. A low Nile in 1878, coupled with the depression of the 1870's, was disastrous, and again whole villages were abandoned.

In order to maintain a firm hold on the rural areas and to impress the foreign powers with the extent of his liberal, modern ideas and with the extent of his popular support, Ismail set up a constitutional body, the Chamber of Deputies, in 1866. It was composed of rural notables and village 'umdahs, whose election to office was encouraged by the government. Its function was to listen to the khedive's demands for additional revenue and to acquiesce. While the deputies discussed agricultural problems and expressed concern over the growing number of migrants, they had little control over Ismail's financial policies since they had no control over the budget. The property law of 1874 was indicative of the extent of the khedive's indebtedness and his lack of success in meeting the demands of his European creditors. Ismail's bankruptcy in 1876, the establishment of the Anglo-French Debt Commission with control over Egyptian finances, and Ismail's deposition in 1879, seriously undermined the authority of the khedivate in the eyes of all Egyptians who understood the situation.

When the Anglo-French Commission, intent upon reducing government expenditures, sharply cut back the size of the army, it provoked a military demonstration that forced the government to pay up arrears in army pay. Then the Turko-Circassian minister of war, Osman Rifki, provoked the anger of a number of fellah army officers by reducing the number of years of compulsory reserve service, a policy that discriminated against the "peasant" officers as opposed to the Turko-Circassian officers (who had enjoyed a monopoly over the officer corps until the 1850's).[38]

[38] Mary Rowlett, *Founders of Modern Egypt*, p. 51.

Colonel Ahmad Urabi, an *'umdah*'s son, and several other army officers presented to the prime minister a petition registering their grievances and demanding Rifki's resignation. They were arrested for insubordination, but their troops staged a demonstration demanding their release, thus forcing the government not only to release Urabi, but also to dismiss Rifki. The summary dismissal of Rifki's successor, Sami el-Barudi, some months later by the khedive, in an attempt to reassert his own authority and that of the Turko-Circassian elite led to a demonstration by Urabi and his partisan troops. Urabi demanded reform and the calling together of a legislative assembly in the name of the people. This gave Urabi much popular support, and the khedive was forced to accede to his demands. Sherif Pasha, the leader of the constitutionalists, became prime minister, with Urabi as undersecretary of state for war. This cabinet represented a temporary coalition between the liberal constitutionalists and a certain number of the army officers. Their party, the National Society, advocated constitutionalism and opposition to foreign intervention.

In 1882 Urabi forced the khedive to legalize the constitution. Some Turko-Circassian officers allegedly plotted to take Urabi's life, while Urabi considered deposing the khedive. The utter stalemate that ensued between the cabinet and the khedive interfered with the business of government. An Anglo-French note demanded the prime minister's resignation and Urabi's exile. The cabinet resigned, and not long afterwards rioting broke out in Alexandria, resulting in the death of forty Europeans. Thereupon, the English decided to intervene actively, and defeated Urabi and his fellah army at Tel el-Kebir.[39]

Urabi's movement was aided by the weakened state of the khedivate and support from the fellah ranks of the army; he also had sympathizers from nearly every level of Egyptian society who opposed foreign intervention. The ulema in particular resented the

[39] For a comprehensive discussion of the Urabi Revolution as the forerunner of the Army Revolution of 1952, see Muḥammad Muṣṭafā ʻAṭā, *Miṣr baina thawratayn* [Egypt between Two Revolutions]. Also note Rifaat Bey, *The Awakening of Modern Egypt*; Wilfred S. Blunt, *Secret History of the English Occupation of Egypt*.

intrusion of secularization into Egypt, begun by Bonaparte and institutionalized by later rulers in the form of secular law courts and
a secular school system. The landowners were indignant because
the government had paid its debts to foreign creditors instead of
to them. In addition, those local notables and wealthy *'umdah*s
who had moved to Cairo must have resented the exclusive nature
of Turko-Circassian society and were inclined to sympathize with
Urabi's stand against the Turko-Circassian monopoly of the higher
echelons. Landlord, *'umdah*, and ulema had, therefore, various
reasons for encouraging popular support of the Urabi movement.
Friday sermons in the local village mosque were probably the most
effective way of awakening the people to active support, and the
subject of a jihad served to channel the enthusiasm aroused in this
traditional way.[40]

Urabi derived support from the fellahin because of his ancestry
and because many of them had served under him in the army.
They admired his defiant opposition of authority, and, furthermore, he promised to do away with their indebtedness to European
usurers. Even though their superiors did provide leadership, their
support of Urabi was probably fairly spontaneous.

The Urabi revolt is often called the first revolution of Egypt in
the modern period. It is argued that Urabi, being of fellahin origin,
attempted to rally the Egyptian peasants with the express aim of
driving out the foreigners and establishing an Egyptian republic.
Whether this was Urabi's aspiration is debatable. More crucial for
the analysis of the fellahin's political culture are their own views
concerning who the leader of Egypt should be. In comparing political attitudes of the fellahin in 1867 with those of 1967, one very
obvious difference is the present-day fellah's apparent awareness
and insistence that his leaders be Egyptian. Contrast this with a
nineteenth-century fellah's reply to the question concerning his
form of government: "We have a just and upright *Mudir*; he does
not accept presents [bribes]; he has been here about a year. All
the others before him were unjust and oppressive. . . . He's an

[40] Villiers Stuart, *Egypt after the War*, p. 155.

Osmanli [Turk]." "Would you prefer to have an Egyptian?"
"Well, if he governed uprightly; but in my experience, fellahs—
wealthy fellahs, in the time of Ismail, paid large sums to be made
Governors, and they oppressed the people more than all the
others.[41] This is hardly the voice of an Egyptian national.

The British Occupation

Urabi's trial and the exile inaugurated British rule. In many
ways this rule proved beneficial for the fellahin. The dual system
of administration that placed a British adviser at each level of
provincial government curbed the excesses of the *ma'murs* and the
mudīrs. *'Umdah* estates were split up and many new *'umdah*s
were appointed. Much of the authority of the *'umdah* was curtailed. His former responsibility for the assessment and collection
of taxes, the cruel use of the *korbaj*, the arbitrary selection of men
for the corvée, all were taken away from him.

The British were continually perplexed by the growth of crime
in Egypt during the 1880's and 1890's. The general opinion was
that this was due to deficiencies in the legal system. Part of the
problem lay in the internal difficulties and structures of the new
courts: the fellahin generally had neither the money nor the free
time for a court procedure that was both expensive and slow. Yet
the increase in crime is better understood in the framework of the
political culture in which conflicting values, attitudes, and behavioral norms toward authority were being forced upon the fellahin
at the time when traditional village unity was being disrupted by
far-reaching economic and social changes.

The local administrators—generally from the large and powerful
landowning families—were responsible, as we have noted, to the
central government for the establishment of standards of public
security sufficient for the collection of taxes and the maintenance
of the irrigation system. If this level of security were not kept up,
the local *shaykh al-balad* or *'umdah* was in danger of losing his
position. Consequently, he tended to be ruthless in his treatment of

[41] Ibid., p. 147.

the fellahin, arbitrary in his decisions, and susceptible to bribery. One fellah graphically described his *'umdah* in 1882: "In all things relating to the levying of taxes, of the conscription, or of forced labor [corvée] . . . the *Sheikh* is made responsible for it, and must wring it from the fellaheen as best he can. Like our country justices he gets no pay, but in Egypt great is *bachsheesh*. Power here means money, for it can spare one man at the expense of the others, and the *Sheikh* is influenced in the customary manner. He has despotic authority and he can be a most oppressive tyrant."[42]

It is not strange, then, that the peasantry built up a great fear and resentment against those in authority. One may easily surmise that the mutual and widespread distrust that prevails today in most villages of Egypt can and should be ascribed to the fellahin's fear of getting involved with an uncontrollable and unpredictable government. Sir Thomas Russell, the chief British police officer in the Ministry of Interior for many years, describes how village officials sought to escape involvement with superiors in the Egyptian bureaucracy. He was discussing the number of murdered bodies that were thrown into the Nile River and often floated down to other villages. Thus he notes: "Dead bodies from the south had a way of lodging up in these places and if pulled out went down in the district registers as murders of unknown origin; the police in order to keep their records clean kept a punt pole handy and pushed the corpses off into the stream again. *Hat al-midrah* ("bring the punt pole") had a very special meaning in those parts."[43] This attitude relegates the prudent fellah to the narrow and confining realm of his own personal affairs. This fear separates him effectively from other members of the wide community to which he also belongs.

No peasant would ever come forward to present evidence in a criminal case, not only because he dreaded entanglement with the central government, but also for fear of reprisals from the accused or his friends. The fellahin's unwillingness to avail themselves of

[42] Ibid., p. 23.
[43] Sir Thomas Russell Pasha, *Egyptian Service 1902–46*, p. 52.

the new courts enabled a few criminals to tyrannize the entire community. In the old days the village *shaykh* would simply have used his superior police powers to rid the community of these troublemakers. Under the new system, where such individuals had to be convicted in a court of law and were free to do as they liked as long as no one would testify against them, there was little the government could do.

Murder was notoriously prevalent and belied the seemingly peaceful, monotonous life of the typical Egyptian village.

The Egyptian fellah (peasant), as one meets him in one's ride through the fields and villages of Egypt, seems to be a peaceful law-abiding and hard working fellow with an excellent sense of humor, and the last thing that you would accuse him of would be criminality. A very few days, however, of residence in the districts brings one up against this murder complex. . . . Murder is so common that it barely excites comment, it is a private affair which hardly affects the community. Eighty out of every one-hundred of these murders are the result of private feuds [and blood revenge *(thār)*] which is a thing he cannot escape; he did not cause it, but his code of honour compels him to carry it on, and he is proud to do so. Vengeance or *'intiqām,* however, for other affronts or injuries, is of his own deciding and forms the shield and buckler of his manhood and his honour. Brought up from childhood to stories of violence, having listened from his cradle of the deeds of revenge of 'Antar and Abu Zeid, he almost welcomes an affront so as to demonstrate to the world his manliness in avenging it.[44]

The traditional Egyptian village communities still have their own set of rules for keeping public order. For the past hundred years this system of customary law has existed alongside the newly es-

---

[44] Ibid., pp. 30–32. Russell also shows the large difference in the number of crimes committed in the cities as opposed to the villages by noting: "The average number of crimes committed annually in the five years of 1940 to 1944 was 7,900, of which 1,800 in the four cities of Cairo, Alexandria, Port Said and Suez and 6,100 in the provinces. Out of this total of 7,900 crimes there was an average annual total of 2,957 murders and attempted murders, of which 212 were in the four cities and 2,745 in the provinces." Various types of village crimes and the importance of blood revenge are discussed by a man who spent much of his life among the fellahin as a government public health inspector. (Muhammed Fakhr al-Dīn al-Subkī, *Mudhakkirāt ṭabīb fī al-'aryāf* [*Memories of a Rural Doctor*]).

tablished law of the central government. When operating efficient-
ly, both maintain the security and tranquility of the country,
although in a rather brutal way. The new codes forbade resort to
violence, blood revenge, and other deeply ingrained techniques
and customs of village life. Yet these so permeate the community
that the central administration still has been unable to stamp them
out. An entire community might be torn by a blood revenge dispute, but no one in the community would give evidence to legal
or police authorities.[45] In this sense, then, the new codes were not
accepted because they clashed with the established and traditional
values so prevalent in the political culture of rural Egypt.

For many the rising crime rate has been attributed to peasant
animosity toward the British after the tragic "Dinshaway Incident" of June 13, 1906.

A small group of five British officers, while participating in a
pigeon hunt near the village of Dinshaway, accidentally shot a
peasant woman. In the struggle that ensued, harsh words led to
open hostilities in which four peasants were shot in their legs and
two British officers were beaten with sticks. One British officer,
Captain Bell, who had been hit over the head, ran to the British
base, some five miles away, to get help. That evening Captain Bell
died of an attack brought on by a sun stroke and not the blow to
his head—at least according to his attending physician. A tribunal
composed of three British officials and two Egyptians convened in
an atmosphere of near hysteria as the court condemned four of
the villagers to death. Two peasants were sentenced to life im-
prisonment, one for fifteen years, one for seven years, and three
to one year of hard labor, while six other peasants were sentenced
to fifty lashes to be given publicly before their fellow villagers.
The "Dinshaway Incident" proved to be a symbol of British

---

[45] Although criminal attacks have been greatly reduced in the rural areas
since the Revolution, in February 1967, I read in the newspaper *al-Akhbar* a
story entitled "Would you be willing to die for your family?" The story explained how in one village a family feud had been in existence since 1938 and
that 67 people had been murdered. Now there had to be another murder to
make it an even 68.

"brutality" that few Egyptian peasants were ever allowed to forget.[46]

Other factors, of course, must be considered in explaining Egypt's rising crime rate. Egypt's population almost doubled between 1881 and 1917 (from 6,800,000 to 12,750,000), which resulted in an increase in the criminal segment simply by numerical progression. On the other hand, perhaps the dissolution of village solidarity based on individual responsibility for land, tax payments, and labor as a substitute for the former collective manner of solving these problems, and on the changeover from basin irrigation (which was again a collective operation) to perennial irrigation, is responsible.[47] Certainly all these changes tended to weaken the village as the social unit of action. Villagers even today still tend to identify with a clan or extended family. Economic and social security rests generally on family and clan ties, not on village ties, as was the case prior to the 1850's.

Yet another factor which must be considered is the fragmentation and loss of land through inheritance as well as through debt. Islamic laws of inheritance entail a rather complicated formula for dividing the property of a deceased among his heirs. The Ottoman system of tenancy without ownership entirely bypassed this problem, which became more acute after the turn of the century when the property laws instituted by Ismail became accepted. The problem was exacerbated from 1900 onward when growing population pressure began to make itself felt, increasing the size of villages and contributing to the already existing fragmentation of land.[48] While peasants under the Ottoman administration had known changes of fortune, so that dispossession was not something entirely new to the peasant mind, nevertheless, the loss of land after one had actually owned it must have seemed like a particularly malicious turn of fate; especially since possession of land

[46] See G. A. Lloyd, *Egypt since Cromer*, pp. 46–49, and Christina P. Harris, *Nationalism and Revolution in Egypt*, pp. 74–75.
[47] Gabriel Baer, "The Dissolution of the Egyptian Community," *Die Welt des Islam*, 6 (1961): 66.
[48] Gabriel Baer, *A History of Landownership in Modern Egypt*, chapter III.

added to the social prestige of the individual.[49] The landless fellahin were and still are at the very bottom of the social ladder. Probably this latter group suffered most from the "dissolution" of village solidarity, for they were detached from the soil and gradually became a commodity to be bought and sold, which left them completely at the mercy of their landlords. Under the Ottoman system, they had been able to seek the support of the ulema against their landlords, but this no longer was effective—particularly if the landlord happened to be a European—and by 1901 foreigners owned 23 percent of all large landed estates (over fifty feddans in area) in Egypt.

Lord Cromer, who was in charge of British administration in Egypt until 1907, set up the Agricultural Bank of Egypt in 1902, ostensibly "to maintain and, if possible, to increase the peasant proprietary class, and thus create a conservative element in the country which would make for stability. It was hoped that the advances would enable the fellaheen to extricate themselves from the clutches of the village usurers, and would furnish them with capital for agricultural improvements and for extending their holdings."[50] A reasonably large number of peasants took out loans from the bank, but the economic crisis of 1907–1914 forced the bank to foreclose on peasant property so that many fellahin again became landless.[51] The Five Feddan Law of 1913 was an attempt to prevent the loss of land through debt, making it illegal to dispossess peasants owning five feddans or less; the Agricultural Bank could not, however, give credit under these terms, so that the peasant continued to rely on the moneylender.

All of these factors, operating in the circumscribed context of isolated, unchanging village life, help to explain the present fel-

[49] Saad Gadalla in his study of the consequences of the Agrarian Land Reform of 1952 noted that the acquisition of additional land resulted in the gain of added social status in the eyes of the other peasants (Saad M. Gadalla, *Land Reform in Relation to Social Development—Egypt*, p. 66).

[50] Quoted in Gabriel Baer, *A History of Landownership in Modern Egypt*, p. 87.

[51] Ibid., p. 88.

lahin's attitudes toward and opinions in regard to all outsiders, especially government officials.

The life of the cities remained totally separate and utterly remote from rural life, as indeed has always been the case. The rich landowning class was drawn more and more to the city where Western influence was predominant. The British during this period encouraged among these affluent city-dwellers an interest in constitutional government and set up a Legislative Council and a General Assembly which were, however, largely consultive in function.[52]

The growth of the press and of political parties in Cairo in the early twentieth century created an increasingly wide public interest in nationalism and constitutionalism in the large cities. The burgeoning nationalist feelings became stronger as the British occupation was more acutely felt. Certainly the presence of the British was more obvious in the cities than in the countryside. Actually, the urbanites on the whole had little interest in and much contempt for the rural areas. Issawi states that by 1913 the national government had still not penetrated into the rural areas with effective services, control, or administration.[53]

Egypt in Search of Independence

The outbreak of World War I in 1914 focused attention on the strategic importance of Egypt and the Suez Canal to British imperial interests throughout the world. When the Turks aligned with the Central Powers, Great Britain declared a protectorate over Egypt (1914–1922) and the nominal rule of the Ottoman Caliphate came to an end. Egyptian opponents of the British rule were temporarily silenced, but when the Allied victory appeared imminent, they again became vocal, demanding the immediate evacuation of British troops, complete independence, and constitutional government.

The dissolution of the Ottoman Empire, the convening of the Versailles Peace Conference, and the elaboration of President

[52] Jacob M. Landau, *Parliaments and Parties in Egypt*, p. 147.
[53] Charles P. Issawi, *Egypt at Mid-Century*, p. 47.

Wilson's Fourteen Points encouraged the politically conscious urban elite to hope that Egypt might gain her independence. Saad Zaghlul, judge and lawyer, a prewar parliamentary leader, and former minister of education and of justice, enlisted the support of several ministers of Egypt's General Assembly: together they requested permission to attend the Versailles Peace Conference. The newly installed Sultan Fuad, anxious to increase his authority and strengthen his own position, encouraged Zaghlul and his Delegation (Wafd) party in their determination to go to Paris even though the British refused to permit any of them to leave Egypt. A petition drawn up by the Wafd demanding that Zaghlul and his group be allowed to go to Europe to explain Egypt's demands was circulated throughout Egypt with the assistance of the palace and the ministry.[54] It was sent to the provincial councils as well as to local civil servants. *Mudirs, ma'murs,* and *'umdahs,* who had always resented the presence of the British advisers,[55] were only too eager to encourage the villagers to sign the petition.

Several influential factors contributed to the peasant support for Zaghlul. The economic grievances were all attributable to the administration, in the peasant mind. Added to this was fanatical religious hostility, fanned into open flame by the ulema who preached in the village mosques. They played up the term *himaya,* meaning the British Protectorate, which was insulting, as it implied the protection of Islam by non-Muslims and also was a reminder of the infidels' stupidity and lack of comprehension of the one true religion. If the ulema did not speak of jihad at this time, they were to do so later on. Stirred to the bottom of their religious souls, and perhaps flattered and threatened by their *'umdahs,* the fellahin rallied to the cause, even making financial contributions they could ill afford,[56] so that the Wafd could defy the British, go to the "infidels' land," and secure the freedom of the Muslim people. It is questionable that the fellahin understood

---

[54] Elie Kedourie, *Sa'ad Zaghlul and the British,* pp. 148–149.
[55] M. Rifaat Bey, *The Awakening of Modern Egypt,* p. 235.
[56] Jacob M. Landau, *Parliaments and Parties in Egypt,* p. 149.

that Egypt was a country apart from the rest of the former Ottoman Empire.

In March 1919, the British agreed to the Wafd's going to Paris but denied Zaghlul permission to accompany it. The other members of the Wafd refused to go without him, and Wafd members in the government cabinet resigned. The British in Cairo, convinced that Zaghlul meant to obstruct the formation of a new cabinet, therefore arrested him and three other leaders and exiled them to Malta.

The news of Zaghlul's arrest spread quickly throughout the Nile Valley from Alexandria to Aswan. Riots and demonstrations broke out in many of the provincial capitals. Peasants attacked railroad stations, telegraph lines were cut, and in the frenzy of their bitterness toward the foreigners, several Europeans were beaten to death and their property burned.[57]

By an unfortunate coincidence it was just at this time that London decided to allow Zaghlul to go to Paris with the Wafd. The new British high commissioner, General Allenby, hoped that his release would quiet the populace, but the Egyptians, convinced that their violent demonstrations had secured Zaghlul's release, continued to riot.[58] The Milner Commission, sent from London to investigate the situation, was impressed by the unanimous and intransigent opposition of the people to British rule. Since the cabinet refused to negotiate with the Milner Commission without Zaghlul, the Britishers were forced to depart ignominiously for Europe to seek out Zaghlul. This enormously strengthened his position as leader of the Egyptian people.

In his informal talks with Lord Milner, Zaghlul secured an unofficial agreement of partial independence for Egypt, which he

[57] Ibid. Most observers of this era argue that the peasant revolt of 1919 swept the entire Nile Valley and was universal in its impact on the rural areas. See A. M. al-'Aqqād, Sa'd Zaghlūl, sīrah wa-taḥīyah [Saad Zaghlul: A Biography and a Tribute]; 'Abd al-Raḥmān al-Rāfi'ī, Thawrat sanat 1919 [The Revolution of 1919]; Fī a'qab al-thawrah al-miṣrīyah [In the Wake of the Egyptian Revolution]; Earl of Cromer, Modern Egypt 2 Vols; Valentine Chirol, The Egyptian Problem; M. Sabry, La Révolution égyptienne.
[58] Elie Kedourie, "Sa'ad Zaghlul and the British," p. 151.

later repudiated as being too restrictive to be acceptable. When the details of the agreement were released to the press early in 1921, the British were forced to compromise. Then began a struggle between Zaghlul and Adli Yeghen, head of the Egyptian ministries.

To get on with these negotiations, "Adli formed a new ministry," but Zaghlul was now in Egypt and on the rampage. Though he was not in the government, he claimed the right to head the Egyptian delegation which was starting for London. Not unnaturally, Adli refused such a humiliating proposal, and Zaghlul started attacking him as a British agent and a traitor to his country. Riots and demonstration again inflamed the country; one particularly bloody affair took place in Alexandria on May 20 and 21 in which foreigners were murdered and their houses looted.[59]

In rural areas fellahin looted and destroyed property belonging to their landlords and to the government, as they also had done in March, 1919.

It is impossible to estimate to what extent these rebellions in the countryside were spontaneous and to what extent they were incited by the Zaghlul political machine. It is known that during the 1919 rebellion a number of provincial officials, Egyptian troops, and police were also involved in the rioting and looting.[60]

Sir Valentine Chirol argues that the major cause of the revolt stemmed from the hardships the fellahin underwent during World War I when thousands were forced into the labor corps.

Fear had crept into the minds of the labourers, and still more so into the minds of their relatives in the villages. The Corps had been under shell fire. Men had died whose deaths were not notified by the authorities to their relatives. Typhus had broken out and was making ravages. In the Egyptian villages the Labour Corps suddenly became synonymous with the bottomless pit. . . . In some places the fellaheen began to fly from their villages, and soldiers and police had to scour the country to bring the "volunteers" in under escort to the labour depots. The British military authorities needed the men and asked no questions. . . . It was in the villages themselves that the worst things

59 Ibid., p. 155.
60 Ibid., p. 149.

happened. The whole system of village governance in Egypt cries out
for inquiry and reform. . . . There are 3,600 of them ['umdahs] in
Egypt, and a considerable portion of them are petty tyrants who ter-
rorise their neighbors whilst maintaining themselves in office by pan-
dering in every way to their superiors. It can be imagined what a
chance the recruiting of the Labour Corps offered to their cupidity
and vindictiveness, and how greedily they availed themselves of it. . . .
But what the fellaheen as a whole felt and remembered were the
methods by which the Corps came to be ultimately recruited in their
villages. They quite wrongly ascribed them to the direct orders of the
British controlling powers, whereas they were just the old methods of
indigenous oppression revived by their own officials as soon as the
vigilance of the British controlling power was relaxed. But because it
was relaxed when it was most needed, we can not repudiate our
responsibility for what happened [thus] we had for the first time
profoundly estranged the agricultural masses that form the vast majority of the population.[61]

Chirol's account is an interesting description of the situation in
the villages during this period; nevertheless, the hardships he describes were hardly different from the tyranny and oppression
common during the Ottoman period, or in Muhammad Ali's day,
or even the suffering experienced during the depression of the
1930's, none of which precipitated a rebellion or general revolt.
Some have argued that the key to this rebellion was the personality
of Zaghlul—his charisma. Certainly Zaghlul's exile and his victory over the British shortly thereafter had appealed to the imagi-
nation of the people. His popularity was also assured by his opposition to men like Adli Yeghen, who was of Turkish origin and
therefore of the elite—an elite associated with the local notables,
foreigners, and tyrannical authority in general. In addition, Zaghlul, like Urabi, was of fellahin background and thus was considered
to be a true Egyptian.

One factor that many Western writers of this period failed to
include in their analyses of this peasant rebellion was religion.
The common ideology of all the Muslim fellahin centered in the
precepts of Islam. "For the villagers, the world is classified into

[61] Valentine Chirol, *The Egyptian Problem*, pp. 136–140.

believers and non-believers on the basis of the Moslem faith," and otherwise "they are hardly aware of concepts like race or class."[62]

It is interesting to note that in the course of many centuries of invasion, exploitation, and terror, the fellahin had broken out in widespread revolt only twice before 1919, and in both cases there was an "infidel" occupation or the impending threat of one.[63] The causes of the 1919 revolt were numerous and obviously complex. However, that the revolt stemmed from popular consensus in support of a Liberal Nationalist ideology is scarcely tenable. "What had happened was, rather, that a relatively small class of Western-educated Western-oriented Liberal Nationalists had managed to ride to a decisive political victory on the wave of two elemental and hitherto inchoate forces that moved the larger masses of the people: hatred of a religiously alien power, based on a Muslim view of the world, and excessive economic suffering."[64]

Zaghlul's determination to secure unlimited independence for Egypt was doomed by this last outbreak of violence. The landowners, anxious to prevent a widespread peasant revolution, collaborated with Allenby, who secured limited independence in 1922 while Zaghlul was again in exile. The revolution was officially over, ended because it had been almost too successful.

This was the last popular revolt in modern Egyptian history. Like the rebellion of the first decade of the nineteenth century and the Urabi revolt, it was directed essentially against the foreigner and was couched in the form of a jihad, at least as far as the peasantry was concerned. The peasants were acting in accordance with Islamic law in performing the duty of a jihad. The ulema led the fellahin against Napoleon and against the Turkish governor. Urabi was an army officer and not a member of the ulema, but he had

[62] Hamed Ammar, *Growing Up in an Egyptian Village*, pp. 72–73. Elie Kedourie also quotes Lord Cromer, indicating that, while some Egyptian leaders might wish to remove religion from politics, yet "[unless] they can convince the Moslem masses of their militant Islamism, they will fail to arrest [the fellahin's] attention or attract their sympathy" (Elie Kedourie, *Sa'ad Zaghlul and the British*, p. 156).

[63] The peasant revolt against Napoleon's forces in 1800 and the Urabi rebellion in 1882.

[64] Nadav Safran, *Egypt in Search of Political Community*, p. 107.

studied at al-Azhar and took his religious obligations very seriously, as did Zaghlul. Although the structure of society after Muhammad Ali's assumption to power precluded the ulema from
achieving a leading role in a widespread rebellion, their support
was utilized by both Urabi and Zaghlul.

The revolution of 1919 was unique in Egyptian history. The
nineteenth-century revolts occurred largely because the governing authority had already been weakened, while that of the twentieth century occurred when the British governing authority was
in a strong position. But in Islamic terms, the British constituted
an illegitimate government, and as this was not supported by the
king, there was no reason why it should not be defied. Zaghlul's
effective utilization of an incipient nationalism led to the eventual
weakening of the British position in Egypt. Like the earlier upris-
ings, this revolt against a foreign occupation also inspired a certain
amount of rebellion even against the local authority whose legitimacy ultimately rested on Islam.

Once "official" independence was recognized in 1922, the urban
politicians decided upon a constitutional system as the most suitable form of government. In practice this was still to mean the
rule of the rich landowning class, just as it had in the past parliamentary assemblies, with one difference: the fellahin were now
to have an opportunity to participate as electors in all national
elections. The power of the ballot proved to be a tragic myth for
the fellahin. As one analyzes the electoral system which this new
constitution set up and seeks to determine what factors played the
crucial role in deciding how the fellahin would vote, one sees that
the fellahin is caught within the landowner's economic pressure,
the local administrator's corruption, and the fellahin's own ignorance and simplicity. Tawfiq al-Hakim describes a village election
in the 1930's with this humorous, but unfortunately all too true
anecdote.

Please believe me. I am a *ma'mur* [district representative of the Ministry of Interior] with a sense of honour. I am not the usual sort of
ma'mur. I never interfere in elections and never say "Vote for this
man!" Nothing of the kind. My principle is—leave folk alone to vote

for whomever they want. . . . Well, that's my method with elections. Complete freedom. I let people vote as they like—right up to the end of the election. Then I simply take the ballot box and throw it into the river and calmly replace it with the box which we prepare ourselves.[65]

King Fuad was not very pleased with the plan for constitutional government and his opposition deterred its implementation for nearly a year. The king, however, took revenge by giving Zaghlul, who had had no share in organizing this new government, his support in the 1924 elections where Zaghlul, with the newly created Wafd party, won a resounding victory. From then on until the ending of the constitutional government in 1952, the Wafdist political machine was to dominate Egyptian political life, winning every free election in the interim.[66]

What was the source of its strength? Its platform was nebulous, stressing the need to achieve complete independence from Great Britain above all else, but lacking for the most part any social and economic plans for the amelioration of domestic conditions. Although Communists and leftists joined the Wafd in the early forties and demanded some reforms, the larger reactionary membership, the richer landowners, prevented the passing of much legislation aimed at improving rural conditions. These absentee owners left the management of their estates to stewards, often while they engaged in professional and business activities in the urban areas. This largely prevented the growth of any effective opposition party founded by distinct business or industrial interests, as opposed to landed interests. The Wafd was a little bit of everything, drawing its membership from the aristocracy, the bourgeoisie, and even leftists elements who defended the interests of the rural and urban workers. The basis of the Wafd power, however, rested upon the massive support of the fellah who had

[65] Tawfiq al-Hakim, *Maze of Justice*, p. 99.
[66] Elie Kedourie, *Sa'ad Zaghlul and the British*, p. 159. For more detailed information on the Wafd see Ernest Klingmüller, *Geschichte der Wafd-Partie im Rahmen der gesamtpolitischen Lage Aegyptens*; Jacob M. Landau, *Parliaments and Parties in Egypt*; and Nadav Safran, *Egypt in Search of Political Community*.

become accustomed to voting for his landlord when the latter wished to be elected to the local provincial council.

There were other reasons for fellah support. There was Zaghlul, the leader of the party until his death in 1927. He was a hero to the people and the leader of the original Wafd, to whom they had given their money in hopes that he would win his jihad against the foreigner. The Wafd party retained this Islamic appeal by its slogan stressing complete independence from the British. It reminded the peasants of the recent revolt against the British. This party's ideology became symbolic of the national determination for freedom and therefore appeared indistinguishable from the aspirations of the United Muslim community (*'ummah*). Consequently, those who disagreed with the Wafd's platform or its leaders were considered outside the pale, no longer a part of the nation, and traitors to the cause.

The Wafd sustained itself through a network of village committees extending throughout Upper and Lower Egypt.[67] Jacques Berque says that the influence of the Wafd grew steadily stronger in the village of Sirs al-Layyan during the period of 1919–1944. The Wafd was supported by one of the leading families of the village, the members of which were often elected to office. The Wafdist press also had a limited but growing influence on the inhabitants of Sirs al-Layyan.[68]

The king, first Fuad and later Faruk, resented the power of the Wafd and regarded it as a threat to monarchial authority. His only recourse against the Wafd was periodically to dissolve its government and to permit one of the other smaller parties to win by rigging the election. It was even necessary to prohibit Wafdist leaders like Nahas from campaigning in the countryside, as in 1930–31, for fear of rural demonstrations or additional support from the people.[69]

While constitutional government was bringing the people into

[67] Jacob M. Landau, *Parliaments and Parties in Egypt*, p. 147.
[68] Jacques Berque, *Histoire sociale d'un village égyptien au XXième siècle*, p. 14.
[69] J. Heyworth-Dunne, *Religions and Political Trends in Modern Egypt*, p. 44.

slightly closer contact with the urban political world, it was hardly educating them to appreciate the value of such government. The authorities were as arbitrary as they had been in the past. Irrigation officials from the government arbitrarily cut off water from the village lands, tax collectors threatened the fellahin with the loss of their harvest, while at the same time other officials forced the villagers to realize the extent of their dependence on the government.

The Wafd's role as the 'ummah of the people was severely damaged by the secession of a number of its prominent members in the 1930's. No longer could it claim to be the undivided community of the nation. But the outbreak of World War II and the fascist inclinations of the king and the Ali Maher government brought the Wafd to power through British support. From 1942 until the king dissolved the government in 1944, the Wafdists cooperated with the British, which in itself was a compromise with the party's earlier platform, at least insofar as the politically conscious public was concerned. The exposure of Wafdist corruption in 1943 further disillusioned many of the party's former supporters. The growth of the Muslim Brotherhood and the Communist and Socialist parties in the 1930's and 1940's was indicative of the failure of the Wafd, the king, and the constitution to give the country honest representative government.

The fellahin's standard of living grew progressively worse during the 1930's and 1940's. Fellah farmers suffered from the extremely low cotton prices of the 1930's and from the inflation and the food shortages of World War II. The class of landless fellahin grew even larger with the continued increase in population, which rose from 12,750,000 in 1917 to 19,022,000 twenty years later. Since only a few thousand feddans were added to the area of cultivable land during this period, the pressure of population began to make itself felt. Rents rose as a consequence and wages fell. A growing unemployment problem forced landless fellahin to leave their villages and migrate to the towns where they formed squalid *bidonvilles* on the outskirts. Others became seasonal migrants and moved between factories in the town and landed estates in the country seeking employment. Agricultural conditions became the concern of the press in the late 1940's and there were many discussions in parliament about land reform. Two concrete proposals for reform were turned down, although a law promulgated in 1946 distributed land amounting to three thousand feddans to landless peasants in the district of Gharbia between 1946 and 1949. Land put up for sale by the government in 1945, much of which was suitable for small farmers, remained largely unsold, as "the small peasant could not take advantage of the offer, mainly because of the very high immediate payment required."[70]

During World War II there was an outbreak of fellah crime and the fellahin remained unsettled and restless in the postwar years. In 1951, a general uprising of fellahin occurred on several large estates. The peasants attacked guards, set fire to offices, and squatted on the land, sometimes taking up arms and demanding that the government sell these lands to them.[71] The Egyptian press during this period is full of stories describing the general unrest in rural Egypt.

These local rebellions have been attributed to the severity of economic conditions and the social tension that had been building up since World War II.[72] Another contributory element was the virulent attacks of the Socialist party press on the king and royal family during the early 1950's.[73] Furthermore, the repeated government promises of land reform and perhaps the ex-

[70] Gabriel Baer, *A History of Landownership in Modern Egypt*, p. 86.

[71] Sir Thomas Russell Pasha notes the number of weapons finding their way into rural Egypt: "This vengeance-murder tradition is going to be a still more formidable problem in the future; so far from having improved in the last forty years, it has got worse owing to the jealousies now introduced into village life by political elections and by the infiltration of thousands of modern firearms into the hands of the fellahin. . . . Today it is the ambition of every young fellow of the village to own a modern military rifle . . . to show his toughness before the girls of the villages and to hold his own with the local brigands" (Thomas Russell, *Egyptian Service 1902–1946*, pp. 33–34).

[72] Gabriel Baer, "Egyptian Attitudes towards Land Reform," in *The Middle East in Transition*, ed. Walter Z. Laqueur, p. 97.

[73] Charles Issawi, *Egypt at Mid-Century*, p. 265.

ample set by distribution of land in Gharbiyah may well have incited the fellahin to action.

Although the Wafd party dominated the Egyptian party system during the interwar period, still other groups sought the support of the peasantry. There were Communist groups working in villages from 1944 onward, although competent observers report that the Communists were rather unsuccessful in the villages. The landless peasants, in particular, seem always to have been totally apolitical and apathetic. The Communists had better success in recruiting urban workers.[74] They apparently followed the tactics used in China and Southeast Asia of first consolidating their influence over lower and middle-class workers, as well as intellectuals, and then seeking to penetrate the countryside. In typical Communist style, "the whole operation was being carried out under the cover of social justice and resistance to imperialism."[75]

The Muslim Brotherhood was one group that gained the sympathy and support of the peasantry during the 1940's.[76] Their ideology was based on the Koran. They advocated a return to fundamentalist, Islamic principles symbolized by the solidarity of the 'ummah, and they encouraged an intransigent, anti-Western attitude. Like the Communists, they had a concrete program for agrarian reform and land distribution. They claimed to have established over 1,700 cells throughout Egypt and were concerned with improving the conditions of the fellahin.

They founded a society for raising the standard of living of Egyptian villages and the reform of the countryside. One of the Brethren set up a model farm on his land. In one village, four cemeteries for the poor and the impoverished were constructed. The Brethren of another village decided to feed 200 poor weekly for the three holy months. Branches competed in the feeding of the poor, the lighting of villages and the collection of alms during the month of Ramadan. . . . Some

[74] Gabriel Baer, "Egyptian Attitudes towards Land Reform," in *The Middle East in Transition*, ed. Walter Z. Laqueur, p. 94. See also Jean and Simonne Lacouture, *Egypt in Transition*, p. 256.

[75] Charles Issawi, *Egypt at Mid-Century*, p. 269.

[76] J. Heyworth-Dunne, *Religious and Political Trends in Modern Egypt*, p. 19.

also acted as arbitrators of disputes in the villages and one of the committees undertook to take statistics of the homeless children and poor families, in order to give children employment suitable to their ages and to aid the disabled who had no means of support.[77]

The Brethren were often teachers who had studied at al-Azhar and their profession gave them entrée into village life. They used the mosque sermons to explain their views and to express their sympathy for the people. Many fellahin who had formerly supported the Wafd were won over to them and even some of the ulema were attracted to their ideology.[78]

The activities of the Muslim Brotherhood undoubtedly had some part in the development of fellahin discontent at the end of the 1940's. Certainly, Nasser and Neguib, after the army officers' coup in 1952, had to take rural sympathy for the Brethren into account, especially during the trials of various Brethren in 1954. The Islamic Congress, set up in 1954, was intended to offset the popularity of the Brethren. The support that the Brethren enjoyed certainly must have influenced the army officers to copy their technique of delivering Friday sermons in the mosques, which proved so advantageous to Nasser during the Suez Canal crisis of 1956. By this means he was able to pose as the religious leader of jihad against the infidel Anglo-French invading forces.[79]

The Wafd party gave the new revolutionary regime far less trouble than the Moslem Brotherhood. Although both groups had an extensive network of committees scattered throughout the rural areas of Egypt, it appears that the Brethren were much more effective—not only in providing financial help, medicine,

[77] Ishak Musa al-Husayni, *The Moslem Brethren*, pp. 52–53. For additional information on the Muslim Brotherhood, see Christina P. Harris, *Nationalism and Revolution in Egypt*; Muḥammad Ḥasan Aḥmad, *al-'ikhwān al-muslimūn fī al-mizān* [The Muslim Brotherhood in the Balance]; Ḥasan al-Bannā, *Bayna al-'ams wa-al-yawm* [Between Yesterday and Today]; Franz Rosenthal, "The Muslim Brethren in Egypt," *The Moslem World* 37 (October 1947).

[78] Gabriel Baer, "Egyptian Attitudes towards Land Reform," in *The Middle East in Transition*, ed. Walter Z. Laqueur, p. 264.

[79] Keith Wheelock, *Nasser's New Egypt*, pp. 19–47; P. J. Vatikiotis, *The Egyptian Army in Politics*, p. 196.

and schooling for the villagers, but also in presenting a program legitimized through its commitment to traditional Islam. The strength of the Muslim Brotherhood is impossible to determine because it has been officially banned since 1954. Underground units are obviously still functioning. Over four hundred Muslim Brethren were charged with conspiring to overthrow the Nasser regime in early 1966. Most Egyptians questioned in Cairo by this writer are convinced that the Muslim Brotherhood, as an effective organization, no longer exists in Egypt. However, several village doctors, agronomists, and social workers have suggested the Brethren's ideology still has great appeal in both urban and rural areas. While the organization may have been destroyed and many of its adherents may have been "forced to flee to Syria," still the idea of a reformed Islamic state has great emotional attraction to people who are unwilling to bridge the cultural gap between traditional Islam and modern secularism. Unfortunately, some Egyptians are convinced that this dichotomy offers their only choice.

This brief sketch of the fellahin's role in Egyptian politics prior to the Revolution of 1952 clearly demonstrates some of the basic causes for the Egyptian peasant's inherent suspicion, distrust, and apprehension toward those in authority. Yet, interestingly enough, few Egyptian nationalist leaders have chosen to ignore the presence of these factors, or discount the role they play in a revolutionary situation.

While the fellahin remain generally apathetic, suspicious, and uncooperative, still every major political leader and movement of the nineteenth and twentieth centuries has sought their support. What is important to note is the fact that the fellahin can be induced to act, to revolt, and to destroy when their struggle is equated with a jihad (holy war).[80] Motivation still seems to be dressed in religious garb and active participation appears to require a foreign infidel (non-Muslim) enemy. We can conclude

[80] One merely had to read the Egyptian press during May 1967 to note how President Nasser relied on this traditional symbol to generate support and enthusiasm among the illiterate masses for his struggle with Israel.

that peasant energy has usually been channeled into destructive ends, has been colored with xenophobia, and has always been legitimized by traditional Islam.[81] As we now turn to the actual attitudes, opinions, and assumptions many fellahin seem to hold about their government and their relationship to that government, we shall see what a tremendous imprint this past history has made on the fellahin.

[81] Chapter 7 will describe in much greater detail efforts of Nasser's government to integrate the fellahin into a national consciousness and the role of the ideology and organizational structure of the Arab Socialist Union in its endeavor to create an atmosphere for the functioning of the process of legitimization.

3 ▣ Personality and Culture
of the Egyptian Fellah

To FULLY UNDERSTAND the complex relationship between the new political and social institutions being created in the rural areas of Egypt and the individuals who function within these structures, greater emphasis must be given to the individual—the peasant, administrator, and new party worker.

A complete investigation of an Egyptian personality would have to include an investigation of the type and adequacy of his home life, the nature and pattern of his schooling, an analysis of his psychological needs and drives, a careful description of his cultural environment, his interaction with social institutions, his work, religion, government, and the types of values, goals, and philosophy of life that motivate him. Unless these components are integrated, we have only a partial view of his personality and never really understand its nature. The data necessary for this kind of integrated analysis of the Egyptian peasant's personality are not available, but significant work by competent Egyptian and Western scholars has prepared the foundation upon which at least tentative generalizations can be made.[1]

[1] This portion relies heavily upon the works of Egyptian and American

For every generalization one might make about the "Egyptian personality," there are of course many exceptions. A synthesis of a whole set of factors described and elucidated by scholars, writers, and students of Egyptian life will be presented in order to place the fellah into some perspective. The composite personality here described probably will not be found in any one Egyptian peasant, yet the character traits discussed must be understood before the new structures and institutions of rural Egypt can be effective in stimulating the kinds of changes necessary for modernization. The Egyptian personality "has many sources: the nomadic bedouin values that permeated Arab society and Islam, the claims of the religious system itself, the long history of subordination, crushing poverty, and patterns of child rearing which stem in part from these sources and reinforce them in generation after generation."[2]

The personality traits discussed in this chapter have been formulated, described, and analyzed by scholars in many fields, and I owe a great deal to their ideas in my own analysis. However, the conclusions offered here are the result of personal observations, and the validity or inaccuracy of these observations must remain my own responsibility. Much of this chapter describes a traditional way of life and personality types that are in transition. This traditional life style is now being challenged, weakened, and gradually modified.

Village life in rural Egypt is traditional in that values, norms

---

psychologists and sociologists who have pioneered the first studies in cross-cultural psychology and especially the interrelationship between culture and personality. Especially helpful were several interviews held with Dr. Louis Kamel Meleika (professor of psychology, 'Ain Shams University, Cairo) and Dr. Hamed Ammar, Salah Faik, and Dr. Ali Mahgoub, all members of the staff at the Arab States Training Center for Education for Community Development in Sirs al-Layyan, U.A.R. Note also Ralph Linton, *The Cultural Background of Personality*; G. H. Mead, *Mind, Self, and Society*; Ruth Benedict, *Patterns of Culture*; Marvin K. Opler, *Culture, Psychiatry and Human Values*; J. J. Honigman, *Culture and Personality*; F. L. K. Hsu, *Aspects of Culture and Personality*; C. Kluckhohn and H. A. Murray, eds., *Personality in Nature, Society, and Culture*.

[2] Morroe Berger, *The Arab World Today*, p. 136.

of behavior, technology, and social structure tend to continue with little change from generation to generation. The social structure is hierarchical, with men above women, elders above youth, educated above illiterate, and wealthy above the poor. The individual's position in the Egyptian village is normally inherited rather than achieved. While the Egyptian peasant may work in his field from sunrise to sunset, still his productivity is low and his standard of living even lower.

Robert Redfield, in his analysis of the essential nature of peasants, has sought to delineate the fundamental characteristics of a peasant society.[3] His analysis in some ways is applicable to the fellahin in Egypt, although in many details, the Egyptian rural community is quite unique. As in all peasant societies, land is the prime value and ownership of land is the supreme goal of every peasant.

As one looks for key factors in the Egyptian rural environment that might help explain both patterns of social relations and the personality of the peasant, one is struck by the fellah's apparent willingness to accept his existence. Some years the Nile River provides an adequate amount of water and his crops flourish; other years there is either flood or drought and his crops are destroyed. While his *gamoosa* (buffalo), which he values almost as much as his wife and children, is healthy and strong, he may prosper; yet it may die, bringing disaster. Above all, his wife and children live or die for reasons he cannot clearly understand (though of course he invents a score of supernatural explanations for all of these things). Government representatives have traditionally cheated, robbed, beaten, and exploited his family and village. He has a keen suspicion for all outsiders and usually considers all individuals from outside his province as foreigners or *khawāga*.

In the face of all these events he is helpless and thus has invented a most complex and intricate system of folklore through which he gains a sense of comprehension. Although he is fatalistic, one

[3] Robert Redfield, *Peasant Society and Culture.*

must not assume he feels impotent, for that would imply that he believes that his position is not as it should be. To the contrary, he generally takes for granted that the phenomena of the world around him are arbitrary and not amenable to his efforts. The laws of nature are uncontrollable in his mind unless the spiritual powers that determine them can be persuaded to favor him. Thus the incomprehensible aspects of his life are built into a pattern of myths and folk charms.

The young fellah's induction into the political culture of Egypt is a psychological process, the end product being his set of attitudes and impressions about the political process and authority. In traditional cultures it is essentially an unplanned and implicit process, yet in those areas where modernization has penetrated, socialization continues beyond this into a whole sequence of experiences through the primary and secondary structures of society. As a consequence, the attitudes of every Egyptian toward the polity is a product of his whole life experience. Early socialization, learned ideas about politics, exposure to the political process, and his own reactions to all these events, both past and present, combine to give each person a particular image of the society and his role in it.

Life in an Egyptian village is hard—death comes easily. Many doctors interviewed estimated that in some villages, especially among the extremely poor fellahin, one-fourth of all children will die before they are twelve months old. In such a world, the extended family of several generations, in which all feel responsibility for all, is the very foundation of the village community and plays a decisive role in the material and cultural life of the rural aggregate and in molding the psychological characteristics of the rural individual. This family organization provides the first socializing mechanism for creating the attitudes and assumptions inherent in the fellah's political culture.

In Egypt the extended family also stems from the ownership and inheritance of land. As Ammar points out, young men—even though married—are discouraged from owning land while their father is still alive, and thus they remain a part of their father's household until he dies. Whether two married brothers with their families form one extended family "depends on whether they work cooperately on the land after their father's death or whether they divide it."[4]

One must note that the psychological roots of the fellahin's attitude toward authority lie in the family organization. The father is endowed with considerable powers and is entitled to utmost respect and obedience. His jurisdiction includes the area of physical punishment, which he may apply to wife as well as children. Obedience is the prime objective in the socialization of Egyptian children. They are taught to be inconspicuous and respectful and to respond readily to any parental command. "The children readily accept the authority of their seniors, whether in work or play, and they endeavor to avoid their anger. This ready acceptance of the authority of those older than the child is epitomized in the axiom: 'He who is one day older than you, is in fact wiser by one year.' "[5] Although any sign of rebellion or aggression toward an adult is forbidden and subject to grave punishment, expression of hostility among children, while not openly encouraged, is still very common.

The main objective of child training is to cultivate a docile and yielding disposition, yet the severity of the punishment leads the child to deception and trickery to evade punishment. Ammar states:

Very little chance is given to the child to justify his misdemeanour, and hardly any effort is made to persuade him to avoid falling into the same error. Moreover, in administering punishment, there is no consistency or regularity; for the same offense the child might be beaten harshly, or his offense allowed to pass unnoticed. . . . It does not require any emphasis here to point out that the effects of these techniques of fear as forcing children to resort to lies and deception are reflected later in the prevailing atmosphere of adult life which is charged with suspicion, secrecy and apprehension.[6]

[4] Hamed Ammar, *Growing Up in an Egyptian Village*, pp. 42–43.
[5] Ibid., p. 127.
[6] Ibid., pp. 138–139.

Children, through this kind of a socialization process, acquire a disposition to respect and obey authority which is generalized to all other spheres of their lives.

The Egyptian family, urban and rural, is fundamentally authoritarian in character.[7] It is organized around the central idea that children must accord unquestioning obedience to and respect for parents and grandparents.[8] Family authority is hierarchically structured, descending from the male parent to the oldest male sibling and so on down through the entire family membership. Decisions are rarely made on a democratic basis; children are not expected to participate in decisions concerning themselves, nor are they often permitted even to complain about actions they consider basically unfair. When a complaint does occur, it is likely to be in the form of an emotional protest, or even in the form of violent behavior. With rare exception there is little training in the kind of pragmatic give-and-take that a democratic polity requires.[9]

In such a hierarchical system, independent thinking is discouraged not only by the norms of society, but also by feelings of uneasiness or anxiety that may develop in a person making a decision outside the accepted framework. Such an action challenges the very authority he cherishes. By accepting the traditions of the village and the authoritative decisions of one's superior, this anxiety can be avoided.

The fellah, by tradition and culture, has tended to assume that his desires and judgments must be subjected to the demands of his superiors. A natural corollary of this assumption is the concomitant feeling that he has the inherent right to demand obedience

[7] See Leonard Binder, "Egypt: The Integrative Revolution," in *Political Culture and Political Development*, ed. Lucian Pye and Sidney Verba, pp. 407–411.

[8] Even older children are not expected to show any sign of mature behavior. For example, a young boy may not be allowed to drink tea or coffee simply because he is young. Even when a boy reaches adulthood, it is considered impolite if a son should smoke or participate in a discussion when his father is present. A common expression that epitomizes this custom is *inta lissa sughayyar* ("you are still a little one").

[9] For an interesting analysis of the changing patterns of family life in urban Cairo, see George H. Gardner, "Social Correlates of the Transitional Phase of Change from the Traditional to the Modern Way of Life."

from those under him. Every individual in the hierarchy of traditional society is aware of the duality of his position. Resentment at
being ordered around by superiors can be relieved only on inferiors
—even if it is only the village animals. Thus, the individual who
has authority need not be anxious about the rightness of his judgments or commands; they are right because he has authority.[10]

Leadership positions and relative status in the traditional Egyptian village are based on a number of assumed value indicators based
on concepts such as age, experience, wisdom, knowledge, and skills.
In a world guided by unknown forces the longest experience was
judged the best guide. Ammar notes that one norm that governs
the social structure "is the weight and respect given to, and the
authority wielded by, the person who plays the role of the senior,
normally chosen on age basis as well as on capacity to speak and
argue well, besides other factors such as economic status and social
prestige."[11]

Thus the young fellah learns to obey without questioning, but
fails to acquire an understanding of the world that explains the
phenomena around him as elements in a rational system whose
operations are amenable to analysis or responsive to his initiative.
Instead he tends to gain two other impressions of his environment
that are overwhelmingly decisive in shaping his later behavior.
One of these is the perception of the world as arbitrary and capricious, consisting of an agglomeration of phenomena not related
to some cause-and-effect network. The second impression is that
the caprice of the world is not accidental but the play of willful
powers, far greater than his, which serve their own purposes and
disregard his own needs unless he is willing to submit to their
demands.

[10] In chapters 5–9 I will describe the implications for the political process
and administrative efficiency in a society where satisfaction in yielding to the
judgments and wishes of superiors and satisfaction in dominating inferiors are
both an integral part of the fellahin's social interrelationships.

[11] Hamed Ammar, *Growing Up in an Egyptian Village*, p. 47. While leadership positions are a function of individual characteristics, the dominant factor
in the traditional village life has been the prestige of one's family. Thus candidates for village leadership positions were generally restricted to a member of
one of the prestigious families.

There is a sense of dependency in this hierarchical system that pushes upward beyond the highest human authority to the spiritual forces believed to control the phenomena of nature. The peasant in the typical situation is entirely "rational" if "rationality" is defined as doing what is deemed necessary to satisfy needs. He understands that there is a best time for planting, a best condition of the soil, the appropriate times and methods of irrigation, of cultivation and harvesting. In all these matters he exercises with craft, skill, and high rationality a learning accumulated throughout the generations.

But other matters—storms, drought, destruction of crops, death of his cattle or family—are not only understood as the result of unknown or unseen forces, but also are perceived as the result of God's anger for certain sins, recognized or unrecognized.[12] His only hope is to appease God by prayer or by seeking to bribe the spirits (jinn) that may well have caused this disaster in his life. Thus continual prayer, combined with magic and the placating of evil or unfriendly spirits, is the major way of obtaining help.

From this perception of reality has developed a complex set of superstitions and myths. Far beyond the external reality of the person's family and village is the unknown yet real world of the jinn.[13] The jinn are a society of unpredictable, capricious, and tyrannical spirits who live under the earth, yet who in large measure provoke and stimulate the forces of nature that would do one harm. At all cost one must not antagonize the jinn. Since they are believed to be made of flame and love their native element, before you throw anything into the fire you must be careful to say aloud

[12] The common expression of grief for the loss of a child or any other similar calamity is *ghadabullah* ("the anger of God").

[13] There are several excellent works describing the fellahin's concept of the jinn (pronounced *ginn* by the fellahin). See 'Ahmad 'Amīn, *Qamūs al-'ādāt wa al-taqālīd wa al-ta 'ābīa al-miṣrīyah* [Dictionary of Egyptian Customs, Traditions, and Expressions]; M. Ghallab, *La Survivance de l'Egypte antique dans le folklore égyptien moderne*; Salīm Ḥasan, *al-'Ādāt al-miṣrīyah al-qadīma al-bākīyah 'ilā al-'an fī miṣr al-ḥadīthah* [Ancient Egyptian Customs Surviving until the Present in Modern Egypt]; Winifred S. Blackman, *The Fellahin of Upper Egypt*; Aḥmad Rushdī Ṣaliḥ, *al-'Adab al-Sha'bī* [Folklore].

"in the name of Allah, the compassionate, the merciful," thus giving the jinn due warning.

In addition to the jinn, the village supports another army of
shadowy and often malevolent creatures known as the *aqrān*
(sing. masculine: *qarīn*) the spirit double of each fellah. This
ghostly twin is born and dies with its earthly fellow and tends to
have the same characteristics. Jealousy is one of the salient features of these barren spirits and their supposedly incessant efforts
to harm or entice away the children of their living doubles causes
the fellahin endless anxiety and worry.

In such a fantastic world the magician and the medicine man
inevitably play a large part.[14] They are in fact the only allies
known to the fellah who can counteract the force of the unseen
spirits, including the occult malignity or evil eye (*'ain al-ḥasūd*)
of his fellows. "The evil eye, which is so much dreaded, especially
by women in reference to their children, usually operates if one
admires the object or child of another. To admire is thought to
imply envy, the pernicious effects of which must be counteracted,
lest some evil befall the child. If a person says, "how pretty" or
"what a darling" she ought to add "mashallah," or some other
pious ejaculation, expressive of submission to the will of God. No
ill effects are then to be apprehended: but if this is omitted, the
mother should cut off a piece of the skirt of the child's dress and
burn it; afterwards sprinkling the child with the ashes . . . or she
may prick on a paper with a needle, an outline supposed to represent the eye of the offender, and burn that . . . but whilst either
of these processes is going on, the first chapter of the Koran must
be carefully repeated. . . . During the first ten days of the month
of "Mohharram," certain individuals prepare, and dispense with

[14] A magician in rural Egypt is generally described as a religious saint who,
through the recitation of certain verses of the Koran, can heal the sick or spoil
the magic effects of the evil eye and the jinn. Not every village has its own
magician, and it is not uncommon in Upper Egypt for a peasant to travel
several miles to seek help. The medicine man (*ḥakim*) may be an individual
with some rudimentary medical training or merely a local religious *shaykh*
who can prescribe certain herbs and prayers to heal the sick.

great gravity, a mixture called the "Meyah Moo barakah" (the blessed storax). The superstitious conceive that it is in the power of these people to confer blessings upon them, and in this way to protect them from all harm during the rest of the year. This never-failing talisman is a mixture of storax, coriander seed, and dust of frankincense."[15] The magician and medicine man are therefore called in to regulate and preserve the life of the fellah and his family. In every dilemma their help is asked and paid for, and their charms and incantations are accepted with the greatest faith.

In such an environment, the dreadful, unknowable, and largely uncontrollable forces of the universe instill in man a great fear, a hesitation to use his initiative, an uncertainty concerning the quality of his own judgment, a tendency to let someone else evaluate a situation in order to avoid frustrations and anxiety. Out of these perceptions also grows uneasiness at facing unresolved or foreign situations. Rather than rely on his own analysis to solve problems of the physical world or his relations with other individuals, he avoids pain and uncertainty by falling back on traditional ways of behavior that his parents and other earlier authorities have instilled in him. Thus he tends to rely on the judgment or will of individuals superior to him in authority or power, whether political or supernatural. "The fellah preserves and repeats, but does not originate or create. What improvements and inventions have been introduced into agriculture, health and housing are imposed upon him from outside. By dint of accepting, receiving, repeating and enduring, his intelligence has become atrophied and passive."[16]

[15] William H. Yates, *The Modern History and Conditions of Egypt*, p. 340. Father Ayrout also described the functions of the rural magician or sorcerer by noting: "It is to him that the country women have recourse in order to cast out *afarit* (devils) or secure the help of the *ginns* to cast spells, counteract the evil eye, move hearts and insure conception or the birth of a male child. It would be in vain to try and persuade them that this "holy man" is only a quack or a charlatan. The more incomprehensible his magic mumble, the more firmly they believe in him. . . . Why does the written charm from the sorcerer, burned in a pot of incense, make a wish become reality? Because it is *qadim* (old). Because it holds in itself the power of the past" (H. H. Ayrout, *The Egyptian Peasant*, pp. 100–101).

[16] H. H. Ayrout, *The Egyptian Peasant*, p. 137.

Yet one should not conclude that the fellahin are dull or unintelligent. Ammar has noted that the most prominent aspect of the "*fahlawī* personality"[17] is his ability to adapt himself quickly to different situations.

Through the centuries the Egyptian peasant has easily and with little social disintegration been able to accept the Christian and then Islamic religions, a continual wave of new rulers, sultans and colonial masters. New crops such as cotton, sugar cane, fruits, and various kinds of vegetables were accepted with little delay. Modern techniques of irrigation, ploughing, and harvesting were introduced and adopted in very short time.

During several interviews with various fellahin, I was surprised by the number of village adults whose major vocal aspiration was to see their children obtain a modern education. But this tremendous flexibility must be seen as two sides of one coin. On one side there is an apparent easiness and ability to accept and live with innovation that seems so paradoxical when one reads of the difficulty that most traditional societies have in accepting change. Yet this facility with innovation has another side. For while the *fahlawī* is quick to perceive what he must do, say and believe in order to be accepted and therefore not bothered, he nevertheless accepts these values, changes, and innovations superficially—never fully convinced—and thus merely fits them into the old traditional values and behavioral norms. Emerging Christianity found a welcome place in the Nile Valley during the second and third centuries. Yet a close analysis of religious beliefs and practices among the fellahin, both Muslim and Christian, reveals a number of obvious pagan practices, beliefs, and myths that are common to both religious groups in the Egyptian village.[18]

Egyptian culture is a mixture of many cultures and traditions.

---

[17] Dr. Ḥamid 'Ammār has utilized the Arabic word *fahlawī*, which is usually defined to mean witty, clever, or tricky, to characterize a composite personality structure, which he argues is fairly common among certain segments of the Egyptian peasantry. Much of the following analysis is based on Ammar's characterization of this unique Egyptian trait. See Ḥamid 'Ammār, *Fī binā' al-bashar* [The Building of Human Beings]

[18] Otto Meinardus, *Christian Egypt: Ancient and Modern*, pp. 90–91.

Yet this adaptability is seldom perceived by the outsider. The fellah, after agreeing with the visiting agricultural engineer, the family planning expert from Cairo, or the Arab Socialist Union representative from the provincial capital, will reply to the question from other villagers—"Why did you agree?"—with the words *ahu kalām* ("these are merely words"); or he may say *fakk maglis*,[19] which suggests that the agreement was merely a way of more quickly ending the conversation and thus his words of acceptance or commitment would have no effect on his old opinions, attitudes, or behavior. This attitude of sycophancy can be extremely misleading for the aspiring party worker who receives thunderous applause after presenting a speech on Arab Socialism, or the young doctor who reports to his superior that most of the women in his village have agreed to take the "pill," or even the young agronomist convinced that the agriculture cooperatives will be well accepted by the peasants.

No doubt a political history of exploitation, deception and terror has strengthened this trait in the Egyptian personality, and through a series of historical situations the fellahin have learned to develop and preserve the appearances of goodwill and acceptance.

In a world where superficiality is the accepted behavior, no one needs ever state a final refusal to any request. The word no is seldom heard and a *fahlawī* will resort to any means of escape, including offering more than he can possibly fulfill. For him, flattery and exaggerated promises are arts to be accepted as a matter of fact. The attitude toward *tadlīs* (blandishment) is expressed in the proverbs: "If one is in need of the dog, he turns and greets him 'how are you, my sir' "; and "kiss the hand you can't bite and pray that it will be broken." The fellah will always bow to his superior, kissing his hand and caressing him with flattering words, but barely does he turn his back than the superior becomes the butt of many a stinging and bitter joke. Faced with a tradition that never allows one to openly disagree or comment in a critical

---

. [19] *Fakk maglis* means to dismiss the conference or adjourn the meeting. Used here it implies that one readily agrees in order to end the conversation without conflict.

way, the *fahlawī* satisfies his ego and frustration through the use of the joke. A careful study of these jokes and witty stories reveals the fellahin's inner fears and criticism.

A world characterized by constant pressure to conform has created frustrations and hatreds molded by the individual's desire for self-expression and development. These two contradictory aspects of the fellahin's culture have generated conflicting impulses of egotism and conformity. Egotism seeks self-esteem and personal realization and manifests itself in extreme forms of pride, boastfulness, and sensitivity to criticism. Conformity is generally explained as a function of the authoritarian family or social setting, which demands obedience to those in authority and the concomitant desire to exercise power over those in inferior roles.

Close and unchallenged group loyalty so fundamental in Egyptian village life creates a fierce sense of group identity, uniqueness, and distinctive difference. However, the fellah's fierce pride and self-esteem are under constant attack from his environment—in both political and social forms, which explicitly demonstrate his weakness, inferiority, and inadequacy.

Ammar also suggests that one of the manifestations of the *fahlawī* personality is the tendency to exaggerate one's self-importance, abilities, and control of the situation. A distinction must be made between self-confidence, which is based on one's inner feelings of security and composure, and egotism, which results from conscious or subconscious anxiety and lack of self-esteem. The egotist often cannot admit his weakness, his feelings of inadequacy and inferiority. Thus he overcompensates for these hidden feelings of insecurity with outward expressions of exaggeration, self-assertion, pride, and boastfulness, with an accompanying tendency to see the slightest skepticism or criticism from others as a grave insult.

The most common attribute of the *fahlawī* caught in the web of doubt, inferiority, and anxiety is to project an outward picture of calm, daring, carelessness, or aggressiveness. He will suggest that no problem is too great, that he can easily handle most threats or issues with no effort.

A society in which the *fahlawī* personality, with its concomitant boastfulness and hostility, is quite common requires that the society formulate detailed forms of speech and behavior in order to conceal or at least control these potentially dangerous emotions. Berger confirms this: "Hospitality and generosity (so common and famous in the Arab's way of life) are means of demonstrating friendliness; they ward off expected aggression. One has the feeling, indeed, that the hostility that becomes overt aggression is so uncontrollable that such measures as excessive politeness (a form of avoidance) or hospitality (a form of ingratiation in a situation where intimacy cannot be avoided) are at times absolutely necessary if social life is to be maintained at all.[20]

Thus from this fundamental trait of the *fahlawī* stems a lot of the excesses in proper greetings, invitations, and conversational procedures which, when coupled with an emphasis on first impressions, one's honor, and general traditions, clearly portray the *fahlawī*'s egotism. Use of the "nice word" is one of the most effective ways that the *fahlawī* manipulates direct face-to-face relations with others. But the *fahlawī* is also a master of excoriating, abusing, or ridiculing a person in his absence. Prestige is assumed to come to him who is most vicious in his private attacks on the governor, the landlord, or the village doctor. This *fahlawī* criticizes everything and everyone—emphasizing his own abilities, wisdom, and shrewd perception of the village's problems. This type of behavior is sure to obtain an audience who will listen and probably agree as only a *fahlawī* can agree, thus nurturing a sense of pride and vanity.

This attitude is clearly seen in the famous stories of the imaginary Goha. Looking into his many stories, jokes, and anecdotes,

[20] Morroe Berger, *The Arab World Today*, p. 142. While Professor Berger describes what he calls the Arab personality, one must note that Arabs and fellahin do not necessarily see themselves as identical. A true fellah tends to see the Arabs as inferior bedouins, and he would be offended if you were to call him an Arab. This would be especially true among the Christian Coptic fellahin. On the other hand, if you were to call an Arab tribesman from one of the tribes such as *al-ḥawāra* in Qena or the *ḥawitāt* in Sharqiyah a fellah, he too would be offended, for he sees himself as a descendant of the Prophet Muhammad and thus superior to the fellahin.

one recognizes that, although Goha is weak and kindhearted, he is able in the end to triumph by exposing the ignorance and stupidity of his opponents.[21]

The *fahlawī*, with his desire for self-esteem, comes to believe that equality applies to everyone but himself. Thus, while he may boast of his own merit and achievement, he feels great indignation toward anyone or anything that emphasizes difference in status—especially if it places the *fahlawī* in the inferior role. While his outer behavior toward his superiors will be marked with respect and praise, inwardly he rejects their authority. This feeling can be noted in conversations among the fellahin about the young agricultural engineers who wear "the western suits" and about whom the *fahlawī* will say *fulān 'amil rayyis* ("such a person acts like a boss").[22] Other characteristics of the *fahlawī* are his independence and individualism, traits that must be seriously considered by a regime committed to an ideology based on cooperation, sacrifice for the common good, and an unselfish attitude toward the other members of his community. The *fahlawī* does not look upon government authority as necessary to society. Power and authority are accepted only out of fear. The man in authority can never be a friend, can never be trusted, for there will always be a barrier between them. Ammar, describing leadership patterns in the village of Silwa, adds, "If one wields power, one must be powerful and forceful, the villagers say, otherwise one would not be respected and feared."[23] Thus the *fahlawī* expects the superior to be strict and firm since these are the characteristics of a good ruler. This attitude is often forgotten by bureaucrats and government workers who try to be friendly and kindhearted. Such behavior immediately creates distrust, since they are not playing the role the peasants expect of them. Even a man from the village who is given a position of authority will quickly be treated differently,

[21] For examples of the adventures of Goha see Hamed Ammar, *Growing Up in an Egyptian Village*, chapter VIII.

[22] This conflict between village leaders and government administrators will be discussed more fully in chapter 9.

[23] Hamed Ammar, *Growing Up in an Egyptian Village*, p. 80.

almost like a stranger, and he will be expected to be strict and firm. This ambivalent attitude, both accepting and rejecting authority, has resulted from a long history of unfortunate experiences for the fellahin.

Another characteristic of the *fahlawī* is his tendency to dispose of any work or responsibility by giving it to someone else and claiming the affair is outside his scope of jurisdiction. Thus he seeks to escape by any means from criticism or accusation of inefficiency. His ability to escape work and responsibility is wondrous to behold. Related to this is the *fahlawī*'s feeling that he must seek his goals through the shortest and quickest way. Thus while a goal or solution to a problem may require much work and long hours of perseverance, the *fahlawī* is looking for the trick or strategy, the "easy way." His belief in his abilities and quick wit leads him to excessive enthusiasm for a new project, improper planning for a difficult piece of work, and the complete disregard of the problems inherent in the "shortcut" way of doing things. A corollary of this attitude is a quick dissipation of enthusiasm and interest should the problem or project demand patience and continual perseverance. Thus the *fahlawī* believes he can pass his exams without going through the agony of hard study. The *fahlawī worker* thinks he can finish his job quickly and takes no time to perform the "finishing touches." In a community where the *fahlawī* personality predominates, it is easy to stimulate and attract people to the idea of starting a new school, a clinic or a youth clubhouse, but it is very difficult to make them follow through, to complete it, or, if by chance it is completed, to maintain it in good condition.

The above discussion has not been given to suggest that all peasants in Egypt are *fahlawī*s, but rather to note the kinds of personality traits personally observed among some villagers and local administrators. This cleverness, this witty and tricky approach to the outsider is common but not predominant. Far more noticeable and exasperating is the obstinate conservatism and parochialism, the suspicion and mistrust, the general apathy and unconcern. Yet the fellah is not sorrowful or gloomy, neither is he necessarily unhappy or depressed. His own few pleasures and possessions are real to him: his God, his children, his woman, his crops, and his hashish.[24] The routine of his life and his limited horizon have not, at least until recently, allowed him even a glimpse of a different or more prosperous condition. The narrowness of his experience has made possible his apparent cheerfulness and contentment and contributed to his seemingly childlike qualities—his jokes and sudden, irrepressible gaiety that can change suddenly into anger and rage. The fellah's crimes are done in the heat of uncontrolled passion and repented an hour later. The small circle of the village probably generates those personal animosities, often as irrational as schoolboy fights, that flare up so easily in an Egyptian community and that, on a larger scale, become murderous inter-village feuds. In Egyptian rural life can also be found one of the origins of that frantic jealousy which, from passionate and personal causes in the villages, saps the vitality of private enterprises and government institutions, and makes mutual confidence and cooperation almost impossible.

The circumstances of the fellah's vision, his lack of recreational and intellectual outlets, and the concentration of all his energies upon a single activity, raising and selling crops, has a further and even more vicious influence on his personality. It makes the fellah hopelessly avaricious. The objective situation in which he finds himself gives no outlet for his naturally generous instincts and impresses two objects upon his mind, the acquisition of land and money. To this thirst, his charm and his personality are subservient, and by it his whole personality is twisted. The tragedy of the situation is that this thirst is imposed by the economic situation in which he finds himself, and by the fact that the slow acquisition

[24] Since the Revolution of 1952, the Egyptian government has made a concerted effort to reduce the consumption of hashish. How successful they have been is difficult to determine. From informal discussions with Egyptians it appears that hashish is available, but is generally smoked only on Thursday evenings or on special occasions. One police officer estimated that probably 90 percent of the adult fellahin smoke hashish at least once a year, 60 percent at least once a month, and 30 percent at least once a week. The unit of hashish is the 'irsh (or nuss'irsh) and the going price for an 'irsh of hashish fluctuated between thirty-five and sixty piasters. Part of the attraction among the fellahin for hashish is the belief that it strengthens one's sexual powers.

of wealth is almost the only respectable form of self-expression open to him.

Father Ayrout argues that the soul of the fellah is best understood in terms of his preoccupation with the here and now. "The truth is that the fellah does not think outside the immediate present; he is fettered to the moment. No time and place except the present have much effect on his mind. . . . It is a fact that they do not think or act except as the occasion demands, according to the pressures of the moment. Their reactions are determined by immediate sensation. Thus they are both credulous and mistrustful, individualistic and gregarious, miserly and thriftless, long suffering and fiery tempered."[25]

From this discussion of the fellah, one might conclude that rural Egyptian society is hardly sympathetic or even amenable to change. It could be argued that the basic outlook of the fellah is, thus, fundamentally incongruent with the goal of political modernization. Yet it must be noted that the Revolution of 1952 was dedicated to the deliberate introduction of change and reform. By virtue of the authority legitimized through the Revolution, Nasser was able to effectuate a number of social and cultural changes. The basic question facing Egypt today is whether the confrontation between traditionalism and modernization will produce permanent and significant changes in the political culture.

The Egyptian government has developed during the past fifteen years a political system that provides stability but that is unable to tolerate even a small degree of autonomy in institutional, organizational, local, and specialized groups or in the actions of individuals. If a number of shared norms, created out of an intense loyalty to the "Arab cause," are developing and if part of the political infrastructure accepts the legitimacy of government control and direction, still the Egyptian elites have not felt willing to allow much autonomy or grass-roots activity in the rural areas of Egypt. The changes in attitudes and values inherent in the political culture will only take place as the peasants and rural populations

25 H. H. Ayrout, *The Egyptian Peasant*, pp. 140–141.

come to feel a part of the political process. As the United Arab
Republic moved away from a predominantly parochial political
culture, Nasser felt the need to provide some sort of political structure to maintain stability in the face of cultural fragmentation as
modernizing patterns replaced traditional patterns. Given the tena-
cious hold that tradition has over rural Egypt, Nasser felt compelled to use political structures characterized by authoritarian
centralization.

As his government programs and social services became acceptable and then expected, they soon became demands. These demands
became vocal as local leaders and active participants gained a
strong sense of national identity. Nasser's solution to this "participation crisis" was the establishment of village and popular
councils through which local demands could be articulated and
channeled to the central government.

The following chapters will analyze the party and administrative structures as they operate within the political culture so far
described. Three structures (the *'umdah* system, the party, and
local village councils) operate in the rural areas and each has
sought to monopolize the political process. The Nasser regime
sought to neutralize the old traditional *'umdah* system and strength-
en the party and the local councils. This was done not only to
assure that the so-called revolutionary clique would dominate this
process, but also to minimize the dysfunctional and disruptive
influences that traditional and "disloyal" groups might exercise
on the system.

4   Village Politics in Rural Egypt

THE DESCRIPTION of a country's political culture can be extremely valuable for the political analyst who is concerned with the problems of linking the psychological dimensions of cultural change to the large issues of modernization and political legitimization. Political culture includes the general beliefs, attitudes, and sentiments that give order and meaning to a political process and that provide the underlying assumptions and rules governing behavior in the political system. It is a general mixture of both the political ideals and the operating norms of a polity. In this sense, political culture rests on the psychological and subjective dimensions of politics, the images of politics, and the political process as perceived by the individual. As was seen, Egyptian political culture is the product of both the collective history of the Egyptian political system and the life histories of the members of that system, and thus is founded equally upon public events and individual experiences.

Stable political systems tend to have relatively homogeneous political cultures within which there is general agreement about the proper limits and functions of politics. In such a system each generation is socialized through a common cultural experience, which most agents of the socialization process (family, school, and so forth) tend to accept and strengthen.

In Egypt, as in many emerging nations, there is great confusion because the political culture appears to be fragmented between traditional and modern concepts of authority and political action. This diffuse concept of what determines appropriate political action largely hindered Nasser's attempt to introduce a new set of attitudes, values, and behavioral norms that were more conducive to the achievement of modernization. The task of communicating Nasser's ideology and cultural imperatives was primarily a process of political socialization.[1]

The socialization or learning process is closely linked with legitimization. Socialization functions to make the individual into a useful and successful member of his society by teaching him the appropriate behavior patterns and role expectations. Legitimization is the process that makes him accept the system as it is; it causes him to develop positive approving attitudes toward the system and those who exert leadership in it, as well as toward the process by which they have been selected for their prominent positions.

The universality of the socialization and legitimization processes may at times be overlooked because they are usually so spontaneous, nondeliberate, or informal that they escape the notice even of the outside observer. The insider, a member of the society, is likely to be entirely unaware of these processes. Socialization in a comparatively static or traditional society, often attracts little attention, since the very process of growing up in a traditional or stable society seems to accomplish the tasks of socialization. However, these processes may also be obscure in transitional and rapidly changing societies such as Egypt's because they abound in subcultures and separate social groups, each having its own standards of behavior and specific methods of conditioning its members. Because of this variety, the outsider can easily overlook the numerous agents of socialization.

[1] Herbert H. Hyman, *Political Socialization*.

In the previous chapter, we noted what a profound influence the family unit in rural Egypt has upon an individual's attitudes toward authority and his society in general. The fellah acquires his general beliefs and assumptions about the political process in a variety of ways. One of the earliest ways in which a child internalizes specific attitudes is by listening to his parents. One writer concerned with this process notes how children in a French village often hear their parents "referring to governments as a source of evil and to the men who run it as instruments of evil. There is nothing personal in this belief. It does not concern one particular government . . . it concerns government everywhere and at all times."[2] This same attitude is most apparent in rural Egypt and suggests some of the reasons why the vast majority of the fellahin have rather distorted and negative attitudes toward most local administration officials. This attitude, of course, is reinforced by personal observation and experience.

A child quickly learns the relative importance of different leadership positions in the village and what behavior is appropriate when dealing with them. Few children beyond the age of twelve or thirteen have not observed the efficacy of bakshish and the value of appropriate family connections. In a family situation where all outsiders must be distrusted and mutual cooperation for a common interest is all but unheard of, the development of the kind of social relationships necessary for modern institutions to function effectively is nearly impossible.

While the family and early experiences no doubt play a vital role in the political socialization process of the rural Egyptian, one must not overlook the influence of direct contact with the political system. However, the political system in Egypt is marked by "cultural dissonance" in which traditional and modern subcultures are in direct conflict. This conflict is largely caused by value differences between not only the modernized elites and the peasants but also between different generations. As generation and group needs

2 Lawrence Wylie, *Village in the Vaircluse*, p. 208.

change, values, too, will change. The whole process of modernization has created a generation gap nearly as broad as that between
the elites and the masses. The accompanying social conflict resulting from these incompatibilities increases when different socializing
agents seek to condition the same individual toward different,
mutually exclusive norms. The persistence of subcultural norms
depends upon the effectiveness of the socializing agencies. In rural
Egypt there are three major secondary political socializing structures: the traditional village leadership patterns (the *'umdah* system), the political party system (the Arab Socialist Union), and
the local administrative system (local councils and ministerial
agencies).

It will be argued that, because Nasser's regime was seeking
legitimacy in a society marked by "cultural dissonance," it could
not rely on the spontaneous process of socialization and legitimization that works on those who simply grow up in the system. The
principal reason for this unwillingness to let spontaneous socialization do its work, of course, was that the regime was committed
to replacing the inherited, traditional political culture and to promoting a completely new one. The spontaneous process working
on the growing child therefore was not to be considered merely
inadequate; it was, in fact, to be considered hostile and inimical
to the development of the kind of Egyptian citizen needed for modernization. Thus the regime embarked upon a process of resocialization through the party and a "reformed" local administration.
Since primary socialization structures such as family and peer
groups are not amenable to drastic government reformation, the
central elites were forced to rely on new secondary agencies of
socialization, namely the party and the bureaucracy.

Before describing the party and bureaucracy, which Nasser
hoped would be new mechanisms for socialization and eventually
legitimization, we must note both the countervailing influence of
the traditional leadership patterns still prominent in the villages
and the even more nebulous influence of President Nasser's charismatic leadership among the fellahin.

Traditional Leadership Patterns

The rural village is still the center of life for over 60 per cent of the thirty-three million people living in the United Arab Republic. Of the 4,012 villages only 997 have functioning local village councils. Most of the others are still largely under the traditional *'umdah* system, briefly described in chapter two. Since we are concerned with the sources of legitimacy in rural Egypt, this analysis must include a description of the leadership patterns in these villages still dominated by the *'umdah* system.

Leadership patterns in those thousands of villages, still not large enough or important enough to warrant the establishment of a village council, have not changed radically in the last fifty, maybe even one hundred years. The office of *'umdah* has been legally defined in several laws passed in 1895, 1947, 1957, and 1964.[3] These laws declare that the *'umdah* is to be the chief executive of the central government in the village. Each village area is divided into clans or family-dominated units known as *ḥiṣṣa*. Each *ḥiṣṣa* is usually headed by a *shaykh* who functions as a subordinate to the *'umdah* and also represents his family or clan in the activities of the village.

The major functions of the *'umdah* are best understood if we realize that, prior to 1947, he was chosen by the central government and not by the villagers. He is the government's man in the village. Starting with the law of 1895, the provincial government was to prepare a list of candidates for the position of *'umdah* and *shaykh*. From this list, a special commission was made up of the provincial governor (*mudīr*), a representative of the Ministry of Interior, the local prosecutor and usually four *'umdah*s specially picked by the *mudīr*. Although this commission had significant power in picking the village leaders, final selections were never

---

[3] The most detailed account of the *'umdah* system prior to 1950 is in Gabriel Baer, "The Village Shaykh in Modern Egypt (1800–1950)" *Scripta Hierosolymitama* [Studies in Islamic History and Civilization], ed. Uriel Heyd. See also Robert L. Tignor, *Modernization and British Colonial Rule in Egypt 1882–1914.*

valid until ratified by the Ministry of Interior. This law of 1895 remained in force, with only a few minor amendments, until 1947.

Because the final power of dismissal rested in the hands of the minister of interior during the turbulent years of 1920–1940, each new government made full use of its discretionary powers of appointment and dismissal. "In 1925, Ismāʿīl Ṣidḳī Pasha, Minister of Interior in the anti-Wafdist Zīwar Government, re-appointed twenty-two ʿumdas who had been dismissed a year earlier by the Zaghlul government."[4] This same Zīwar government dismissed ten other ʿumdahs a year later and then thirty-one ʿumdahs resigned in protest. When the government of ʿAdli Yeghen took office, all these dismissed ʿumdahs were reinstated. Probably the largest number of ʿumdahs ever dismissed at one time occurred in 1935 when Prime Minister Tawfik Nasim relieved some six hundred ʿumdahs appointed by the preceding government.[5]

Tawfiq al-Hakim in his most delightful novel on village life in Upper Egypt describes the solemn ceremony connected with the dismissal of one ʿumdah and the appointment of another.

I beheld a spectacle which I could not understand at first. There was the head ghafir (village policeman) and his deputy, and some others, carrying an object in their hands. Around them were crowds of men, women, and boys, reciting prayers and verses, while the women shouted as they do at joyful celebrations and beat on tambourines. I looked closely to find out what they were carrying, and the pathologist followed my gaze in stupefaction. We saw it was an official telephone! The doctor exclaimed in astonishment: "The telephone's got a procession like a bride!" One of the watchmen passed near us, and I beckoned to him. I asked what the matter was, and he replied that an order had been issued that day dismissing the umdah and appointing another in his place, a member of the rival family in the village. We understood the whole situation, and the pathologist turned to me with a grin, "It appears that the umdah's telephone is a kind of royal sceptre." He was quite right. The telephone was indeed the symbol of authority and dominion, as well as the means of communication with the government. If it was uprooted from the home of the discharged umdah, that was

4 Ibid., p. 124.
5 Ibid., p. 125.

a symbol of vanished authority. The voice of weeping with which the
telephone was escorted from the former umdah's house was a sign of
deep disaster. . . . "Like all other villages in Egypt today," I replied,
"this village has two powerful families or more which compete for
the umdah's office. Each of them belongs to one of the parties which
fight for power. How can you expect the position of the village to be
different from that of the country as a whole? This village, after all, is
only the State in miniature."[6]

This rather arbitrary way of selecting an *'umdah* led to several
individuals demanding that the *'umdah* be elected by the villagers
themselves. A repeated plea to substitute direct elections for government appointment was often voiced by the Wafd during the
period between the two World Wars, yet no government was ever
able to pass such a law in a parliament dominated by the large
landowners of the rural areas.

Dr. Muhammad 'Abd-Allah al-'Arabi, a legal adviser to the
Ministry of Interior, delivered a lecture in 1942, in which he argued that each village should elect a village council (*majlis
al-qarya*), which in turn, would be given the responsibility of selecting the *'umdah*. His compromise recommendation, while never
seriously considered by the government, influenced many individuals into championing this village reform.

The new *'umdah* law of 1947[7] did provide for the election of
the *'umdah*, but this did not affect authorities' final say in the
'umdah's appointment. Thus the *'umdah* was first elected by a
group of villagers consisting of the candidates themselves, the village *shaykh*s, anyone qualified to be a candidate for *shaykh*, and
all those in the village who paid at least three Egyptian pounds a
year in taxes.[8] The elected *'umdah* was then officially appointed by
a committee of *shaykh*s (*lajnat al-shiyākhāt*) composed of the
provincial governor (*mudīr*) or his deputy; a representative of the
Ministry of Interior; the district attorney (*wakīl niyāba*); and four
*'umdah*s, chosen by the *'umdah*s in the district (*markaz*) and then

---

[6] Tawfiq al-Hakim. *Maze of Justice*, p. 72.
[7] *Law No. 141* (August 29, 1947), *Egyptian Official Gazette*, November 30,
1947.
[8] One Egyptian pound = $2.38.

approved for membership of this committee by the minister of interior. This committee could refuse to confirm the 'umdah's election but the decision of the committee also required the final approval of the minister of interior. Once his election had been confirmed, his term of office was for life.

While the 'umdah law remained relatively unchanged during the first five years of Nasser's regime (1952–1957), the new law issued in 1957 reflected some of the fundamental changes initiated by Nasser's revolutionary government.[9]

Several noticeable changes in the selection procedure must be noted. First, the authority of the Ministry of Interior and the Committee of Shaykhs was greatly reduced. Article 16 prescribes the composition of the Committee of Shaykhs and specifies that the number of elected 'umdahs will be reduced from four to two in order to ensure that the majority of the committee will be government officials. In addition to the two 'umdahs elected from their district, the committee includes the governor, an inspector from the Ministry of Interior, and the chief prosecutor. Neither the committee nor the Ministry of Interior has any veto power over local elections, but must restrict their activities to monitoring elections in order to ensure that official procedures are followed, investigating charges of fraud or corruption in an election, and presiding over all legal proceedings involving the 'umdah's election. This diminution of authority did not, however, denote any increase of autonomy for villagers in selecting their leaders. All candidates for the office of 'umdah were submitted to an election committee presided over by the local secretary-general of Nasser's single political party, which in 1957 was the National Union. Although the law of 1957 required no landownership or tax-payment requirements in order to qualify as an elector, still, Article 9 states that if the National Union approves more than one candidate, the governor shall determine those who are eligible to vote in the election of their 'umdah.

---

[9] For a legalistic description of Law Number 106 of 1957 see Sulaymān al-Tamāwī, Mabādi' al-qanūn al-'idārī [Principles of the Administrative Law], pp. 150–155.

The new *'umdah* law of 1964[10] stipulates that every village shall have an *'umdah*. Exceptions to this rule are the governorate capitals, *markaz* (district) capitals, and towns and villages where a police station has been established.[11] Each village is divided into sections (*ḥiṣṣa*) known in Arabic by various names including: *'ezba, kafr, nazla', naj'*. Each of these sections will have a *shaykh* who is elected by the members of his section who are recorded on the electoral list.

Section two of Law Number 59 lists the requirements that all candidates for *'umdah* or *shaykh* must fulfill. To qualify he must:

(1) Be a male citizen of the United Arab Republic.

(2) Have a good reputation and not have been deprived of his political rights.

(3) Be on the electoral list of his village.

(4) Be twenty-five years or older.

(5) Be able to read and write.[12]

(6) Be a resident of the village and must own or rent cultivable land in the area or he must have a monthly salary of 20 Egyptian pounds (for *'umdah*s) and five Egyptian pounds (for *shaykh*s).[13]

[10] *Law No. 59*, Cairo: Ministry of Interior, July 11, 1964.

[11] In March 1967 one source from the Ministry of Interior indicated that, out of the 4,012 villages in Egypt, 508 now have police stations. These police stations include a police officer (usually a major), ten to fifteen policemen, and village guards (*ghafar*) hired from among the villagers. The police officer lives in the second story of the police station. In the nine police stations I visited, all were equipped with two cells, one for men and one for women, a stable containing four to eight horses, two or three duty rooms, and sleeping quarters for the policemen who were on duty. The source indicated that each police station costs approximately 36,000 Egyptian pounds ($75,000) to build and equip. He intimated that these heavy costs precluded the construction of police stations in every village, but that eventually, as the present *'umdah*s die or retire, new police stations will gradually take their place.

[12] This requirement may be waived for the *shaykh*s if there is only one candidate who fulfills this requirement.

[13] This stipulation that the *'umdah* need not own land is a sharp break with the past tradition, when the *'umdah* was always the largest or one of the largest landowners in the village. Estimates from several sources in the Ministry of Interior have indicated that well over 25 percent of the new *'umdah*s now being selected are not landowners. This is an obvious move to break the monopoly of landowners who generally hold the office of *'umdah*.

(7) Be an active member of the Arab Socialist Union.[14]

When the office of *'umdah* or *shaykh* is vacated, the governorate director of security will issue an order within thirty days after the vacancy calling for all qualified individuals in the village to submit their applications. After the director of security has verified the qualifications of all candidates, he will then issue an order calling all electors in the village to elect the new *'umdah*.[15]

Prior to 1957 the *'umdah*'s term of office was for life. In 1957 his term was limited to ten years and then in 1964 his term was again reduced to five years. Theoretically this *'umdah* system is organized in a most admirable way. The villagers were allowed, at least up to 1966, to elect from among themselves a *shaykh* or *'umdah* who is supposed to maintain order among them and to defend their interests, and all the *shaykh*s of a village are under the supervision of the *'umdah*. When a *shaykh* fails to give satisfaction to his constituents, they may complain to the governorate officials for his dismissal. If the *'umdah* neglects his duties or abuses his power, the fellahin need merely present a petition to the district or governorate representative of the Ministry of Interior. On first glance it might well seem, first in elections and second in the right of petition, that the peasants have ample guarantees against gross maladministration or serious extortion on the part of their village leaders.

In this kind of analysis three tacit assumptions have been made: (1) that the richer and more influential families in the villages, from which the *shaykh*s and *'umdah*s are drawn, contain a large

---

[14] This stipulation also differs from the 1957 law, which merely required that the party accept his candidacy.

[15] One source in the Ministry of Interior admitted that no elections for *'umdah* had been held since May 1966 due to the "Kemshish incident." Evidently a local Arab Socialist Union leader in the village of Kemshish was murdered through a conspiracy of the village *'umdah* and one of the leading landowning families in the area, the Fiki family. Since this incident, all *'umdah* elections have been suspended, and the entire *'umdah* system is presently being closely scrutinized with many leading members of the Arab Socialist Union advocating the abolishment of the system. The present pattern seems to provide for the director of security in conjunction with the governorate Arab Socialist Union secretary-general to select a replacement when an *'umdah* dies or retires.

proportion of upright, intelligent men, animated with enlightened desire to promote the welfare of their villagers; (2) that the ordinary peasant acts in the election as an intelligent, free agent, and is ever willing to challenge and complain about the present leaders in his village; and, (3) that the higher government officials are always ready to check and punish any abuses in the village leadership hierarchy. Unfortunately none of these assumptions is justified by experience.

As has been noted, the traditional Egyptian peasant society is based on family ties and family relationships. Jacques Berque points out very graphically that an individual's status and power is primarily a function of his family's power and position in the village.[16] This reliance on family-based protection rests on the fundamental fact that, in a society where agriculture is the primary means of livelihood, large families are a prerequisite for security both in terms of guarding crops and in harvesting them. The large extended family represents the most effective unit for protection and solidarity.

The traditional leaders in an Egyptian village may have a variety of personality traits, may vary in their adherence to the village's ideal moral code, and may act quite capriciously in their role as village leaders. However, they must belong to a recognized family, a family identified by its wealth, landownership, number, education, or wisdom. Kinship is the one standard no traditional leadership position can ignore.

Let me give an example of an *'umdah* in Upper Egypt.[17] This is a man to whom the villagers (Christian and Muslim) go to settle their disputes, or solve their personal problems. He may lend money to help replace a *gamoosa* (buffalo), protect a villager from police arrest, write a letter to the district director of education on behalf of a young student anxious to enter preparatory school, or

[16] Jacques Berque, *Histoire social d'un village égyptien au XXième siècle,* p. 47.
[17] The following examples of the two types of *'umdah*s come from an unpublished research paper written by Marie Assaad, a student at the American University, Cairo, in spring 1966.

act as an intermediary in business negotiations. The villagers go to him whether their disputes are among the immediate members of one family, among neighbors, or among different families. They also turn to him whenever they are in trouble with any government agency.

Following our earlier analysis, let us describe briefly the image this man evokes among the villagers in an attempt to determine the source of his authority and power. This *'umdah* has had very little education; though not completely illiterate, his proficiency in reading and writing leaves much to be desired. He dresses in the regular peasant *galabīyah*[18] and belongs to one of the ten recognized families in the village. His position is considered quite legitimate primarily because of the number of *'umdah*s who have come through his family line. From a list of eleven *'umdah*s, going back to the reign of Mohammed Ali, seven have come from the present *'umdah*'s family.

This *'umdah* started his life as a poor man, owning only two feddans (two acres). Yet he was selected as *shaykh al-ghafar* (chief of the guards) under his late cousin, who had been *'umdah* until his death in 1951. This cousin was notorious for his ruthless and cruel rule. His period is remembered by the older members of the village as a time of intrigues, blood revenge, and arbitrary demands. This earlier village *'umdah* was supported, in addition to his family, by another of the recognized families whose reputation even to this day is rather infamous for the number of criminals among its kindred. This present mayor, being his cousin's chief of guards, learned his trade well, established his own contacts, and was known for his efficiency in implementing his cousin's decisions.

When this "vicious" *'umdah* died in 1951, the power and prestige of the office were given to the eldest surviving cousin—the eldest brother of the chief of guards. He was noted for his generosity and wisdom. This older brother was also a member of the governorate council, and, because of his reputation for fairness and

---

[18] *Galabīyah* is the traditional peasant gown or dress still worn by a large majority of the fellahin in rural Egypt.

sagacity, the villagers went to him for advice concerning the general village problems. When he too died in 1961, the present *'umdah* was "elected" to his position for a ten-year term. In addition to being the oldest surviving brother in one of the leading families, he had gained much power and influence through his former position as *shaykh al-ghafar*. It is rumored that his election was ensured through the efficacious distribution of bribes.

Why do the villagers accept his authority? Why do they go to him? First, this man is recognized for his power and influence. His authority is rendered legitimate by the vast majority of the villagers, both because his family has traditionally monopolized the office of *'umdah* and also because the office of *'umdah* is perceived as an official position of the central government. His influence, therefore, rests mostly upon his wealth and family connections, although his connections with government officials and his recognized power and authority in settling disputes adds to his influence and prestige.

Of course his willingness to solve problems is not without a price. Generally he acts in terms of bribes secretly paid. These bribes are never made public as this would mar his prestige and status. His power and authority are honored, valued, even esteemed by villagers, regardless of how moral his methods may be. Thus, while they proudly admit that he is the "man of the village" they will also confide that this man has collected his wealth and land through bribery, protection of criminals, and fraudulent acquisition. (He now owns fifty feddans). "Why do you go to him, if he is such a man?" "Because of his family status, and because experience has taught us that he will solve our problems." Thus, the villagers accept their *'umdah*, even cherish him in their own way. He has the power to settle their disputes, negotiate with the outside world for them, and protect them from "the government officials."

In the vast majority of villages in Egypt, especially those still under the *'umdah* system, the *'umdah* is considered the rightful and legitimate authority in the village. In many villages he is respected and admired for his wisdom, his fairness, and his generosity. An *'umdah* is usually distinguished by his wealth, his assertiveness, and his pride. But these characteristics, in fact, are not enough. His authority rests upon his willingness to conform to village norms. Thus, while the average individual is expected to approximate the norms expected at weddings, feasts, and the arrivals of visitors, the *'umdah* is expected to exceed them. Many *'umdah*s have plunged themselves into debt, or strained their resources to make the proper impression.

Generosity is not merely an ideal, it is a concrete expectation. The typical *'umdah*, in spite of his questionable methods of ruling the village, is usually more than generous when his prestige is at stake. Their contributions to village ceremonies, collections for the repair of a mosque, and money to build a new school are apt to be very large. Yet this generosity is always a public matter. It is an advertisement of his philanthropy and encourages the idea that the village should feel indebted to him.

In an interview with the governor of Munufiyah, a newspaper reporter asked the governor if land reform and the recent sequestration of the larger landowning families had had any effect on the leadership patterns in the village. The governor answered:

Because of the social and intellectual backwardness and because of the tradition and position of the *'umdah* and the *shaykh al-ghafar*, the social (and political) relationships in the village have not changed in proportion to the revolutionary activities taken by the Committee for the Liquidation of Feudalism. The fellahin have not become politically mature. For example, if the *shaykh al-ghafar* walks into the village and asks any fellah to do something, the fellah readily complies, because he knows that the *shaykh al-ghafar* can falsely accuse him. But when the chairman of the town council or a member of the Governorate Council walks in the street, he seldom attracts much attention. . . . Another example, if I am an *'umdah* and you are a fellah—your wife must come and bake bread for me and your children must work on my land. The land of the *'umdah* will always be irrigated first. He will have first access to the seeds and fertilizer distributed by the cooperatives. And although most *'umdah*s have given up old prerogatives, some may still insist, for example, that no fellah be allowed to ride his donkey in front of the *'umdah*.[19]

[19] *al-Akhbar*, January 13, 1967, p. 8.

The reporter then asked the governor if he favored having the system of *'umdah* abolished. The governor replied:

I wish that the system of *'umdah* would be carefully studied to see how far it conforms with the system of local administration. The present system of local administration has been established to ensure that there be only one administrative power in the village (village council) which would be responsible for all the services and utilities. The *'umdah* is only supposed to represent the Ministry of Interior and not the Ministry of Local Administration. The *'umdah* should only ensure security in the village but unfortunately the office of *'umdah* for the fellahin is more than a mere administrative position—*to them he is perceived as the only person who can solve their problems.* Consequently, the existence of the *'umdah* in a village makes it extremely difficult for a village council to justify its existence.[20]

When the governor was asked to explain the strong loyalty that so many peasants seem to have toward their *'umdah*s, he noted:

It is a feeling the fellah has that the *'umdah* or one of his men can and should control his life. This feeling creates in him a kind of fearful loyalty in which the fellah tries to satisfy and comply with the orders of these people even at the expense of his own or others' interests. *This fearful respect is deemed a duty and even considered an honor* and thus he is willing to do what the *'umdah* requires—to steal for him, to beat people for him, even to murder for him. . . . Now of course the *'umdah* represents the law and to be more precise—he is the law.[21]

Not all village leaders function in such a manner. Many are the family elders who have sought to introduce change and progress into their villages. For example, I will discuss a *shaykh* (let us call him Shaykh Ibrahim) living in a large village in the governorate of Gharbiyah. Shaykh Ibrahim is quite different from the *'umdah* mentioned above. The *shaykh* would probably not consider himself a village leader, nor would the vast majority of the villagers designate him as such. But, by examining his informal influence, his interaction with other village leaders, and his activities in introducing change, we will see why he may be described as a leader.

[20] Ibid.; emphasis added.
[21] Ibid.; emphasis added.

Around the year 1800 the great-great-grandfather of Shaykh Ibrahim, a carpenter from another village, got involved in a village brawl, killed someone, and fled from the village out of fear of revenge. He moved on to a new village, pitched his tent, and proceeded to pursue his trade as a carpenter. The grandson of this man distinguished himself by his ability to read and mentally compute large figures. This attracted the attention of the local governor, who took him as his assistant to maintain the records of landownership and the collection of taxes. During the 1830's and the 1840's many people were forced to leave their land because they could not pay their taxes. Much of this deserted land eventually fell into the hands of this tax accountant. As a member of the Coptic Christian minority, his family was generally excluded from the office of 'umdah, although there are historically numerous examples of Christian 'umdahs, even in predominantly Muslim villages. Nevertheless, this Christian family resorted to other means of maintaining its position in the village. The two methods generally used included acts of charity and the introduction of new projects in the village. Village traditions state that Shaykh Ibrahim's grandfather ordered the large kitchen staff of his extended family to cook huge amounts of food and to bake a large amount of bread to spread out each night after dark so that anyone could share in the family's generosity without feeling shame. This gave the family home the nickname of "big house" or *bayt al-wassiyah*.

Although this practice seems to have stopped with the death of the grandfather, Shaykh Ibrahim and his father continued this family tradition of generosity by helping the poorer families of the village with loans of cash, seed, and farm animals, building schools and a health clinic, and providing funds for young people who wished to pursue their higher education. In addition, the family had introduced a flour mill, arranged with the central government to have a railroad station built in the village, and later in 1945, introduced a small weaving factory equipped with eight small looms powered by a diesel engine.

Shaykh Ibrahim still sponsors the projects introduced by his family. He has liberally contributed funds and land for the government's combined unit, a multi-purpose community development project recently established in the village. Today, most of his influence is through informal contacts, personal advice, and financial help.

To the question of which type of leadership, the *'umdah* or the *shaykh,* is most prevalent in rural Egypt, no simple answer can be given. Village leadership may be conceived as a power continuum, extending at one end from those leaders whose influence and power require no coercion but rest on their reputation for generosity and fairness. At the other extreme is the leadership based almost entirely on force and coercion. Political realities in rural Egypt probably rest nearer the coercion end of our power continuum, but authority and power in most situations is a complex matrix of conflicting variables, each representing in varying degrees all the sources of influence noted above. Berque also notes that the Egyptian revolution in many ways has not penetrated the rural areas of Egypt:

> But even in these rural milieux there survived, together with the increasingly unpopular institution of village chiefdom, something of the old patriarchal order. The Egyptian village preserves not only its coteries but their institutional organs, of immemorial origin: the *duwwâr* for instance, the 'great house', 'house of honour', where prevailed a way of life that was both authoritarian and generous, hospitable and tyrannical. These hierarchies are falling into decline, assuredly, and the Egyptian *'umdah* (village chief) has as bad a reputation as the Algerian *caid* (qâ'id). But it is still unwise to oppose him openly. In 1962, the Egyptian revolution still had to reckon with him.[22]

This statement still holds true today for most of the isolated rural areas, but the influence and power of local village leaders has been greatly reduced in the larger villages where the central government has managed to make its influence and power felt. The Egyptian peasants' willingness to withdraw support from traditional leaders and extend it to new government-sponsored leaders, rests primarily on their ideas of who their leaders are, what they

[22] Jacques Berque, *The Arabs,* p. 242.

ought to do and what, in fact, they actually do. As many new symbols of legitimacy are accepted and internalized by the villagers, their support and acceptance of old patterns of power and control will diminish. It is postulated that with the introduction of such concepts as land reform, social equality, antifeudalism, and government responsibility, the basis for support and legitimacy will gradually shift away from the larger landowners and traditional village leaders. The question of whether this shift of legitimacy will eventually move to the successors of President Nasser and the government officials now functioning in the villages will be considered in chapters 8–10.

Changes in rural Egypt have been largely a function of President Nasser's charismatic leadership. Many villagers identified themselves with President Nasser and thus accepted many of the regime's symbols and values which were, in fact, validating a whole new pattern of leadership and legitimacy. Thus, Egyptian rural politics may be described in terms of shifts in the basis of legitimacy from a "traditional to a legal-rational system" (to use Weber's terminology) through the instrumentality of Nasser's charismatic leadership.

Whether Nasser's charisma is eventually routinized, i.e., the villagers shift their support to the institutions established by his regime, rests primarily on the extent to which the new regime's party workers and government officials are deemed competent and dedicated to the solution of the villagers' own problems. As I have suggested, these images are established through the political socialization process predominant in rural Egypt.

Charisma and Gamal Abdel Nasser

In Arab history, the legitimate claims of authority have traditionally rested on a foundation of power and military success. The successful military chief represented the crucial political unit in Arab organization. Even a cursory study of Egypt since its Muslim conquest reveals a continuous struggle among competing military leaders. Through a series of military dynasties: the Tulunid, the

Ikhshid, the Fatimid, the Ayyubid, and finally, the Mameluke period, leadership remained primarily a function of military prowess. Even the dynasty terminated by the Egyptian Revolution of 1952 was founded by Muhammad Ali, a successful and brilliant military officer in the Ottoman army. Thus, it can be argued that a successful military leader generates a sense of legitimacy and provides a symbol of power and a mark of courage and success, which historically may explain the foundation of Nasser's charismatic appeal.

Before 1954, scarcely a soul outside Egypt had ever heard of Gamal Abdel Nasser, a lieutenant colonel in the Egyptian army, graduate of the Egyptian Officers' School, and a son of a postmaster from Upper Egypt. Abdel Nasser—his name means "slave of the victorious"—burst dramatically across the stage of history. He was the undisputed leader of the "progressive" forces in the Arab world. He gradually shifted the balance of power; he inspired and inflamed the Arab peoples to new heights of ferment and energy. Most impressive of all, he gave his name to an abstraction; today, Nasserism is one of the great political dilemmas, a constantly perplexing mixture of the noble and the despicable.

Yet, in the Arab world, few leaders possess Nasser's appeal among the masses. After five days of the most crushing defeats that any national leader could ever expect to suffer and still survive, Nasser's public acceptance of culpability on June 10, 1967, and his decision to retire to private life were treated not with relief or vengeful satisfaction, but with consternation and an immediate popular demand for his return. Not only in Egypt, but in other Arab countries, too, the popular reaction was confused but overwhelming emotion. Radio announcers wept, crowds rioted, and presidents and politicians from Morocco to Iraq encouraged him to remain.

Let no one doubt the reality of his popularity. He was respected even by his enemies, because they saw in him that quality which the Arabs know as *baraka*, or blessing, what some modern scholars call charisma. Weber wrote that charisma rests "on devotion to the specific and exceptional sanctity, heroism or exemplary character of an individual person, and of the normative patterns or order revealed or ordained by him."[23]

This definition suggests two aspects of Nasser's charisma that should be further analyzed. First, what were the sources of Nasser's charisma, and second, what "normative patterns" or ideology did Nasser create or help to establish that gave legitimacy to his charismatic appeal?

To understand the popularity of Nasser in the Arab world in general and in the Nile Valley in particular, one must turn to the past. Nasser was a real Egyptian, a genuine son of the Nile, the first "true Egyptian" to rule in Egypt in over two thousand years. This idea has only gradually taken root, yet today few fellahin are unaware of this fact. Few would say honestly that Nasser was a great orator, yet when he spoke to the crowds, his personal magnetism and his use of the simple, uncluttered language of the fellahin attracted throngs of Arabs from the lowest walks of life and kept them awake through his harangues on affairs in which they had little direct interest. For Nasser to speak to them in the *lugha 'āmmīyah* ("popular language") made him one of them.

The foundation of Nasser's charisma among the simple peasants rested on a series of successful exploits. First, he ousted the king and the pashas, instituted a measure of land reform, established real social and apparent political equality, and cleaned up the corruption and squalor that had characterized the government of Egypt for centuries.

Later, he negotiated the removal of the British base in the Suez Canal Zone and a final solution for the Anglo-Egyptian condominium in the Sudan. Next, he demonstrated his independence of the West and his determination to deal forcefully with Israel by buying large quantities of arms from the Soviet bloc, a proverbial "bombshell" that was quickly overshadowed by his nationalization of the Suez Canal. These successful attempts at defying the "old order,"

---

[23] Max Weber, *The Theory of Social and Economic Organization*, p. 328.

while never fully understood by the fellahin, generally verified in their eyes his power and influence. His success proved that *Allah ma'ah* ("Allah is with him").

In recent years, Nasser's image did not remain untarnished. In 1961 the illustrious prototype for a future United Arab States was nullified when Syria withdrew from the United Arab Republic. Nasser's support of the Yemeni Nationalist armed forces failed to recapture any of the lost brilliance of his earlier international exploits; the more recent fiasco in June 1967 signaled a most humiliating debasement for Nasser's image as the modern Salah al-Din.

Yet, these defeats did not lessen his popularity or weaken his hold on the reigns of power in Egypt. This suggests that Nasser the man had become Nasser the symbol, Nasser the myth. In his speech of resignation, Nasser proclaimed: "The forces of imperialism imagine that Abdel Nasser is their enemy. I want it to be clear to them that it is the entire Arab Nation and not Gamal Abdel Nasser. . . . Arab unity began before Gamal Abdel Nasser. It will remain after Gamal Abdel Nasser."[24]

Nasser's power and influence among the fellahin was difficult to measure. On at least fifty occasions, the author was asked to say a few words before village councils and peasant leadership groups in the cooperatives. Each time Nasser's name was mentioned, there was great clapping and cheering. Whether this is the *fahlawī* trait appearing is difficult to determine. The two most common exploits attributed to Nasser by the fellahin interviewed consisted first of his skill in removing the British from Egypt, and second, of his ability in introducing land reform.

One was constantly reminded that the fellahin sharply distinguished between Nasser and his bureaucracy. The local official may be corrupt and harsh but this was not Nasser's fault. "This would never happen, if only he knew" was a common theme in the conversations of the fellahin. In their minds, Nasser was much too preoccupied with *hagāt muhimma* ("important things") to be concerned with their problems.

[24] "Nasser's Speech of Resignation," *Foreign News and Broadcast Service*, June 10, 1967, p. 2.

It is this author's opinion that Nasser's charisma rested more on his international exploits than on his internal reforms or his recently announced domestic policies.

Charismatic authority is sharply opposed and easily defined in contradistinction to Weber's other two sources of authority: traditional authority and legal-rational authority. Both of these latter two sources specifically outline the procedures and techniques inherent in the everyday routine control of action. The traditional concept of authority, as noted in this chapter, rests on precedents handed down from the past, while the modern legal-rational authority is epitomized in the modern bureaucratic system covered by "rational rules" of administration. In opposition to these sources of power and legitimacy stands charisma. Charismatic authority tends to repudiate the past traditions and thus represents a revolutionary force. It neither rests on past commitments nor represents rules of rational behavior. The only basis for its legitimacy is the recipient of this personal charisma. This distinction between these three sources of legitimacy was especially applicable to Nasser's Egypt. Few who have observed the programs and policies inherent in Nasser's Arab Socialism would deny that their legitimacy was not a function of past traditions or of the rational norms of a bureaucratic state. Their acceptance both in ideological terms and in structural manifestations was legitimized to the extent they were perceived as the express will of President Nasser himself.

One critical question facing Egypt today is whether this charismatic leadership will now become institutionalized. Nasser as a charismatic leader championed a new set of values or cultural norms, not completely cut off from the past (as will be seen in our discussion of Arab Socialism), but reflecting a new synthesis of morality and obligation. During Nasser's early years in power he became a symbol of beliefs and sentiments which rested on his personality and not on some social structure. The belief-sentiment-morality matrix declared in Arab Socialism will eventually either be evaluated negatively, in which case it will become extinct now that Nasser has passed from the scene, or it will be evaluated positively by a large part of the Egyptian society, in which case it may become sacred. Charisma, as Weber notes, must be "routinized," made a part of the social structure, and thus pronounced legitimate. Parsons amplifies this concept by noting that "legitimacy is thus the institutional application or embodiment of charisma."[25] Charisma, by its very nature, cannot assure stability or progress but can play a crucial role in attaching legitimacy to those institutions and procedures that may well lead to stability and progress.

The regime of Nasser had in recent years established a broad system of local administration and an all pervasive political party. These two structures—the party and bureaucracy—were based upon two different aspects of legitimacy, a legitimacy which until his death rested on the charismatic appeal of President Nasser. These two aspects of legitimacy were "derived from two types of values, consummatory and instrumental. *Consummatory values* are based on a particular set of moralities. These may be expressed in a political ideology, an integrated set of cultural norms. . . . A second viability test of government involves its *instrumental values*. The adequacy of these can be judged on the basis of efficiency. When government is regarded as inefficient or powerless to deal with problems and unable to make provision for the future of the society, support is withdrawn."[26] These two value systems, one emphasizing a new ideology and the other championing efficiency and performance, tend to affiliate around two different structures in Egypt: the party system and the local administration system. While the functions of these organizations are neither mutually exclusive, nor necessarily incompatible, they too often tend to be in direct conflict with each other because of the source of legitimacy inherent in each.

One may argue that the roles and structures of these two systems were gradually being endowed with legitimacy through their charismatic relationship to Nasser. Nonetheless, as we now proceed

25 T. Parsons, *The Structure of Social Action*, p. 669.
26 David E. Apter, *Politics of Modernization*, pp. 236–237.

to a closer analysis of the party and the local administration system, we shall see that an effective institutionalization of the roles and structures of these two organizations, now that Nasser is gone, requires a genuine resolution of the value-dilemma noted above.

5   History and Ideology of the ASU

IN A MODERNIZING SOCIETY such as Egypt, the traditional way of life with its accompanying values, norms, and behavior patterns are all under severe attack not only from the present ruling elite, but also by the very introduction of modernizing structures, technologies, and reforms. Many scholars would argue that to a large degree the disintegration of this traditional way of life is a necessary and inevitable step for any society aspiring to technological and industrial development. It is self-evident that effective utilization of modern technology requires specific concomitant patterns of behavior consistent with the needs and demands of a modern, rationally oriented society. Thus, citizens must learn to pay taxes, obey laws, conform to new procedures, and engage in efficient productive economic activities if the policies generated by a modernizing political system are to function in terms of its postulated goals.

Egypt's leaders today are confronted with the need to mobilize widespread support for certain political activities, to create new nontraditional bases of legitimacy, and to provide new sets of values more appropriate to the whole process of modernization. It was for this reason that Nasser invested such a tremendous amount of time, money, and effort in the creation of a political mechanism that would provide a new basis for legitimacy, a new political culture.

Chapter five of the National Charter, under the heading "True Democracy," states: "There is a dire need to create a new political organisation, within the framework of the Arab Socialist Union, recruiting the elements fit for leadership, organising their efforts, clarifying the revolutionary motives of the masses, sounding their needs and endeavouring to satisfy them. . . . Democratic action in these fields will provide the opportunity for developing a new culture with new values."[1]

The Arab Socialist Union was introduced into the towns and villages of rural Egypt with the hope of providing the transitional fellahin with a "new culture" composed of "new values," attitudes, and aspirations more congruent with the national ideology championed by the present governing elite.

A series of conferences, speeches, projects, and programs were continually being sponsored and promoted by the Arab Socialist Union (ASU) in an attempt to strengthen and reinforce these new sources of legitimacy through a prolonged interaction between peasant and party functionaries. But if the ASU is to perform successfully the dual function of integrating the masses into the new national culture and legitimizing the activities of the ruling elite for them, it must play a positive and meaningful role in the political decision-making process. Only a political party that plugs into the critical core of national political power before it sends its interpretation of government policy out and down through the party communication network will ever be able to speak to the general citizenry in terms that make official action meaningful and acceptable as well as legitimate and binding.

Since the establishment of the ASU in October 1962, its organization, function, and ideology have been expanded and enlarged. The ASU Statute proclaims that "the Arab Socialist Union represents the socialist vanguard which leads the people, expresses their

---

[1] United Arab Republic, *The Charter*, pp. 53, 55.

will, directs national action and undertakes effective control of the progress of such action, within the framework of the principles of the National Charter."[2]

The fundamental issue for one concerned with legitimization must be to what extent does the general citizenry view and conceive the ASU as an appropriate and adequate vehicle for the protection of their interests and the satisfaction of their needs. A clear analysis of this issue requires a careful delineation of, first, the party's history and ideology; second, its organization and functions; and finally, the party's role as a socializing agent for the governing elite's "new political culture."

History of the ASU

The Arab Socialist Union was the third attempt on the part of Nasser to create a mass-based organization. Previously, the Nasser-led regime had established the Liberation Rally and the National Union. Although both organizations were allowed to die, their failures must be considered if we are to understand the present strengths and weaknesses of the ASU.

Geographical features have facilitated the establishment of a mass political party in the UAR. Certainly the concentration of Egypt's 33 million people on less than 4 percent of the country's territory—a territory limited almost entirely to the narrow Nile Valley—increases their susceptibility to organization and social communication. For centuries this geographical fact of life has created a people highly amenable to strong centralized governmental control. The Nile River has always provided the Egyptian government with a highway of domination and control.

After six months in power, the Revolutionary Command Council (RCC) led by Gamal Abdel Nasser announced the dissolution of all political parties and the confiscation of their funds. On January 23, 1953, Nasser, before a crowd of 250,000, announced the formation of Egypt's new political organization, the Liberation Rally.

Political parties, he said, had tried to divide the people in their struggle against British imperialism. Faruq "had concluded a deal

[2] United Arab Republic, *Statute of the Arab Socialist Union*, p. 4.

with the parties whereby he would close his eyes to their crimes and
they would close theirs to his." Thus had been formed a "limited company for theft and robbery in which the people had no share." It was
differences among the parties which had enabled the British to remain
so long in the country.

But now, the Colonel announced, "we have decided to put an end to
it all and to start again from the very beginning. . . . We have already
removed the hand of dishonor and torn out the root of corruption in
government." Because of the great popular support for the government
it "now needs a body to organize the people and to foster their unity,
and to coordinate the efforts of their works. In the name of the Egyptian people. . . . I announce the birth of the organization which will
build our unity." The motto of the new Liberation Rally was "unity,
discipline, and work."[3]

General Neguib, the military junta's front man, admits that this
new political organization was Nasser's idea. "I supported my
junior colleague's decision to replace the other parties with a single
united front. The purpose of the united front, which we called the
Liberation Rally, was to prepare the people to participate on a
national scale in the new political parties that we hoped to create
before the third anniversary of the revolution."[4]

Thus, while Neguib argued that the Liberation Rally was to be
a "temporary one-party system," he envisioned the eventual re-
establishment of a multiparty system within three years.

For purposes of contrast with the later ASU program, it might
be well to note the program of the Liberation Rally:

1. Complete and unconditional withdrawal of British troops from
    the Nile Valley.
2. Self determination for Sudan.
3. A new constitution expressing the fundamental aspirations of
    the Egyptian people.
4. A social system in which all citizens shall be entitled to pro-
    tection against the ravages of unemployment, illness, and old
    age—i.e., a "welfare state."
5. An economic system designed to encourage a fair distribution

---

[3] Quoted from Don Peretz, "Democracy and the Revolution in Egypt," *Middle East Journal* 13, no. 1 (Winter 1959): 30.
[4] Mohammed Neguib, *Egypt's Destiny*, p. 181.

of wealth, full exploitation of natural and human resources, and the maximum investment of new capital.

6. A political system in which all citizens shall be equal before the law and in which freedom of speech, assembly, press, and religion shall be guaranteed within the limits of the law.

7. An educational system designed to develop a sense of social responsibility by impressing youth with its duties as well as its rights and with the overriding need to increase production in order to raise Egypt's standard of living.

8. Friendly relations with all Arab states.

9. A regional pact designed to increase the influence of the Arab League.

10. Friendly relations with all friendly powers.

11. Firm adherence to the principles of the United Nations, with special emphasis on their application to subject peoples.[5]

With the creation of the Liberation Rally and its designation as the "government's party," thousands of civilians and members of the military joined, especially in the provinces. According to figures published by the government, over two million people eventually became members. Lacouture, who was in Egypt during this period, notes:

But membership in it was sought merely in order to obtain support or protection. We took the opportunity of following one of the "caravans," led by a Minister, which the Rally sent out now and again to tour the provinces. First came the speeches, which were listened to with respect, and then a kind of forum was held during which citizens could voice their complaints or suggestions. They did so, and were allowed to say as much as they liked about drains and schools. But as soon as the discussion turned toward political questions they were cut short.[6]

Nasser never envisioned that the Liberation Party was to function as the earlier parties had done, for he argued strongly that "Liberation Rally is not a political party and was never intended to be. The creation was prompted by the desire to establish a body that would organize the people's forces and overhaul the social

[5] Ibid., pp. 184–185.
[6] Jean and Simonne Lacouture, *Egypt in Transition*, p. 272.

setup. The Liberation Rally is the school where the people will be taught how to elect their representatives properly."[7]

Yet within two years this new "school" had failed, its offices had been abandoned, and its name was no longer mentioned in the government-controlled press. The reasons for the government's repudiation are worth analyzing.

General Neguib claims that the new government had actively and sincerely sought to encourage the Muslim Brotherhood to work within the framework of the government's organization. Many of the Brethren did join the party, but their motives were inimical to the success of the Rally. Neguib states that "the Moslem Brothers, instead of co-operating with the Liberation Rally, had joined it only to subvert it."[8]

Actually, many extremists, in both leftist and rightist movements, had gravitated to the government's party in an attempt to further their own aims. Internal subversion, however, was more a result rather than a cause of the Rally's ineffectiveness. Far more serious was the lack of skillful cadres committed to the revolution, trained in organizational techniques, and capable of judging men. The actual scarcity of loyal party leaders inevitably led to its subversion.

Yet even more crucial than the regime's opponents or its lack of experienced cadres was the problem of legitimacy and commitment. Unlike the FLN in Algeria or the Neo-Destour party in Tunisia, Nasser's Liberation Rally did not possess the aura of nationalist legitimacy that surrounds a party or a movement proven and tested in the struggle for independence. Nasser continually faced the challenge of creating a party without the symbols, myths, and experiences associated with a liberation movement.

Lastly, the leadership of the Liberation Rally failed to establish a clearly defined set of goals and aspirations within some meaningful ideological context. The new regime spoke in platitudes and

---

[7] *Misr Egyptian News Agency Weekly Review*, June 20, 1953, p. 2. Quoted from Keith Wheelock, *Nasser's New Egypt*, p. 23.
[8] Mohammed Neguib, *Egypt's Destiny*, p. 209.

generalizations, demanded work and sacrifice in such broad terms
that a member within the Liberation Rally could find no ideals,
no duties or obligations that set him apart from all other Egyptians.
Ideologically, the Liberation Rally was a void. Thus Keith Wheelock concludes: "As a mass organization, the Rally was a failure;
its claimed two-million membership never was realized. Nasser . . .
and others used this Falange-type organization successfully for
specific purposes—to control labor, to organize a cadre of prore-
gime youth, and to "create" demonstrations. But the government
found it impossible to impose this political organization upon the
masses of Egyptian people. Moreover, much to the chagrin of its
organizers, some of the Rally's enthusiastic participants were the
very people whom it had meant to combat: the Moslem Brethren
and the Communists."[9]

Not until 1958, after Egypt and Syria were joined together in
the United Arab Republic, did Nasser once again seek to establish
a mass movement. The new constitution of 1956 declared that a
National Union would be established to replace all the political
parties. The National Union was formally established in May
1957, but its activities generally were limited to providing some
1,171 candidates who ran for the 350 seats in the new National
Assembly. Once the union of Syria and Egypt was consummated,
Nasser sought to establish the National Union in the provinces
and in both urban and rural areas. Elections were held in each
village, and National Union committees were chosen for these
basic organization units. Egyptian officials continued to argue that
"the National Union is not a party; nor is it a one-party system.
. . .[It] is a national front which includes all the members of the
nation except the reactionaries and the opportunists and the agents
of imperialism, because it is they who controlled us in the past
and proved to be traitors."[10]

Nasser's dilemma was posed by the need to mobilize the entire
nation behind the goals and aspirations of a modernizing elite
with a political structure primarily created to prevent certain

[9] Keith Wheelock, *Nasser's New Egypt*, p. 40.
[10] Ibid., p. 54.

groups from participating in the political process. This negative role so predominated the life and functioning of both the Liberation Rally and the National Union that little spontaneous support and enthusiasm was ever allowed to germinate. There seems little doubt that the major function of Nasser's first two parties was to effectively preclude the active participation of any group opposed to the policies and programs of the ruling elite. Many will argue that Nasser's earlier parties lacked ideology, that they lacked experienced organizers and a doctrine that would generate the kind of legitimacy discussed earlier. Closer analysis may well yet reveal that these early experiments in mass mobilization rested more on Nasser's fear of the past than on his hope for the future.

Syria's secession from the United Arab Republic in September 1961 proved to be a most humiliating experience. Out of this encounter with defeat came some serious reconsideration of past mistakes and a greater desire to achieve success on the home front. This was a commitment, however, that Nasser was never able to live with or to accept. Nonetheless, on October 16, 1961, Nasser stated his determination to try a third time with a third party: "Reaction managed to infiltrate into the National Union to paralyze its revolutionary potentialities and turn it into a mere organizational façade unstirred by the forces of the masses and their genuine demands. . . . Hence, the most important task that faces us today is to reorganize the National Union to become a revolutionary instrument for the masses, who alone have a rightful interest in the revolutionary changes."[11] This third attempt is our main concern now. Will Nasser's new party also succumb to the infiltration of "reaction," and the debilitating influence of a sterile ideology or will this new structure really be a "revolutionary instrument for the masses?"

Ideology in the ASU

Since we are concerned with the Nasser regime's attempts to create a sense of legitimacy among the rural society of Egypt, we

[11] Quoted in Peter Mansfield, *Nasser's Egypt*, p. 197.

must briefly recapitulate what we mean by legitimacy. What are the sources of this legitimacy and how can these sources be strengthened and manipulated to generate this belief that the leaders have the right to rule and that members ought to obey. As Weber has pointed out, many systems achieve legitimacy as a result of tradition. The traditional, the customary, the habitual ways of doing things gradually build up an aura of rightness and justice that finds its vindication in transcendental values and truths. The traditional leadership patterns of rural Egypt rest on a series of rights and obligations identified in particular role patterns sanctified and legitimized by time and custom. The cultural milieu within which certain values and norms tend to reinforce these leadership patterns presents serious obstacles to any group seeking to introduce new values and new behavioral norms. Because of the tenacity of this traditional belief system, many emerging nations have been concerned with developing a new belief system that will not only neutralize the old but even replace it. The new belief system in Egypt is Arab Socialism. The introduction of a new ideological perspective tends to create social incompatibilities, economic strain, and political instability. Geertz argues that it is "precisely at the point at which a political system begins to free itself from the immediate governance of that received tradition, from the direct and detailed guidance of religious or philosophical canons . . . that formal ideologies tend first to emerge and take hold. . . . It is a loss of orientation that most directly gives rise to ideological activity, an inability, for lack of usable models, to comprehend the universe of civic rights and responsibilities in which one finds oneself located."[12]

While Geertz has given a perceptive analysis of ideology and its cultural sources and manifestations, we are more concerned with ideology as a device or a tool through which a particular regime may seek to arouse or maintain a minimal level of support. Thus Arab Socialism was an ideological mechanism for seeking to

[12] Clifford Geertz, "Ideology as a Cultural System," in *Ideology and Discontent*, ed. David E. Apter, pp. 63–64.

reinforce or strengthen the convictions that Nasser's rule was legitimate. Many writers have noted the efficacy of an ideology, especially in the newer nations. Almond and Powell argue that a political party is the most appropriate instrument for transmitting a new ideology. "Such an ideology defines the proper behavior of mass and elite alike, setting forth particular criteria for political legitimacy and prescribing political tactics. Adherents to the ideology are rewarded by a sense of order, a sense of identity, and a respite from the emotional confusion brought about by change. Fulfilling such needs can be a powerful factor in mobilizing support."[13]

Many scholars have even suggested that an ideology is one essential ingredient for economic and social development.[14] Daniel Bell notes: "What gives ideology its force is its passion. . . . A social movement can rouse people when it can do three things: simplify ideas, establish a claim to truth, and, in the union of the two, demand a commitment to action."[15] Thus once the "truth" of an ideology has been demonstrated or is perceived as such by individuals in the society, their commitment, so the argument goes, tends to release a tremendous force of energy, which catapults society over the obstacles to development and progress. Thus Sjoberg argues that "modernizing nations must paint an exaggerated picture of the glorious future if men are to be inspired for goals they may never attain. . . . It is for this that men will make a supreme sacrifice, will postpone or inhibit their expectations in order that their children may live more comfortably and with greater dignity."[16] Before we analyze this thesis by applying these assumptions to the problems of rural Egypt let us briefly describe the ideology that Nasser's Arab Socialist Union was seeking to prose-

[13] Gabriel A. Almond and G. Bingham Powell, *Comparative Politics*, p. 125.
[14] See Eric Hoffer, *The Ordeal of Change*; Gideon Sjoberg, "Ideology and Social Organization in Rapidly Developing Societies."
[15] Daniel Bell, "The End of Ideology in the West," *Columbia University Forum* (Winter 1960), pp. 4–7.
[16] Gideon Sjoberg, "Ideology and Social Organization in Rapidly Developing Societies," p. 5.

lyte among the fellahin. President Nasser declared in 1962 that
the new doctrine of his regime would henceforth be known as
"Arab Socialism."

Within the broad range of concepts identifiable in Nasser's new
ideology are several items especially applicable to our analysis of
politics in rural Egypt. The Charter, as the written embodiment
of a comprehensive national socialist doctrine, outlines in simple
form the historical dimensions of the Egyptian personality. The
Charter elucidates the essence of the Egyptian identity by placing
the Egyptian people in the context of world history. "This is an
established fact borne out by the study of Pharaonic history the
maker of Egyptian civilisation and the first civilisation of man
and subsequently confirmed by the events which took place during the ages of Greek and Roman domination. . . . In the history
of Islam, the Egyptian people, guided by the message of Mohamed,
assumed *the main role in defence of civilisation and mankind*."[17]
Egypt's unique role in past history has been to defend and preserve
the "heritage and wealth of Arab civilisation," first against the
Crusaders, "that first wave of European colonialism," and later
against the Tartars, "who swept over the plains of the East and
crossed its mountains bringing destruction and ruin." Within the
borders of Egypt was preserved "their noble university Al Azhar,
a stronghold of resistance against the colonialist and reactionary
factors of weakness and disintegration imposed by the Ottoman
Caliphate in the name of religion."[18]

Egypt's decline was due to foreign domination, which saw "the
whole area swept by the darkness of the Ottoman invasion." The
villain in this sweep of historical decline is the Ottoman Caliphate,
which had rejected the "genuine religious faith" and imposed a
tyranny that "cost the Egyptian people in national wealth and
vitality [but] did not shake their determination and faith."[19]

Modern history is but a continuation of this historical struggle
of the Egyptian nation. The modern Egyptian can be proud of his

[17] United Arab Republic, *The Charter*, p. 19; emphasis added.
[18] Ibid., p. 20.
[19] Ibid.

heritage—a heritage based on the endeavor to preserve social justice and freedom. No Egyptian need feel inferior before Western civilization, for "modern science [was] developed by Europe out of sciences taken over from other civilisations, foremost among which is the Pharaonic Arab civilisation."[20] Thus the past need not be rejected nor vilified, for in reality the greatness of Egypt today rests in part in this "sacred mission" of past generations. History not only establishes a sense of identity but explains most of the problems facing Egypt today. Nasser, seeking to discover the cause of the fellahin's apathy and unconcern, lamented: "My soul is torn with grief when I think as I often do, of that period in our history when a despotic feudalism was formed; a feudalism directed towards bleeding the people with and depriving them of their last vestige of power and dignity. We shall have to fight hard and long before we can rid ourselves completely from the deleterious effect of that system."[21]

Although history clarifies Egypt's positive and profound impact on the unique role of the Arab nation in world history, socialism is conceived as the key to realizing a future commensurate with the greatness of Egypt's past. "The socialist solution was a historical inevitability imposed by reality, the broad aspirations of the masses and the changing nature of the world in the second part of the 20th century."[22]

Yet this new doctrine of socialism must not be construed as a sharp break with Egypt's past, including its religion and culture. Aly Sabri declared in October 1966: "The Charter has established religion as the foundation of our surge forward to secure social justice. The Charter views the religious experience as the substance of social revolution, for the prophets always constituted a revolutionary force for social justice and against the exploitation of man by man. Consequently, all revealed religion constituted a principal factor in our socialist ideology."[23]

[20] Ibid., p. 21.
[21] Gamal Abdul Nasser, *The Philosophy of the Revolution*, pp. 40–41.
[22] United Arab Republic, *The Charter*, p. 57.
[23] *The Egyptian Gazette*, November 3, 1966, p. 4.

There is an inevitable struggle in most emerging countries between the forces of tradition and the forces of modernity. Socialism, although compatible with Egypt's past, implies a rejuvenation
of a past **Arab** characteristic—his interest in science and the scientific method as a valuable tool for man in an attempt to free
himself from the restrictions of his environment. Nasser continually sought to emphasize that "scientific socialism is the suitable
style for finding the right method leading to progress. No other
method can definitely achieve the desired progress."[24] From this
statement, as many Egyptians have argued, Arab Socialism must
be interpreted as a "style" or orientation toward national development and progress. It differs, so the argument goes, from other
kinds of Western socialism such as utopian socialism, scientific,
Fabian, national, moderate, or democratic socialism.

Arab Socialism must not be seen as springing from Western or
Marxist teachings, for its concepts and beliefs have originated in
the Arab and Islamic heritage. Dr. Muṣṭafā al-Sibāʿī[25] argues:

The essence of socialism is not nationalization, or expropriation of
capital, or the limiting of ownership, or progressive taxation. All these
things are but means, and are seen by its advocates as the right way of
reaching the goal which is socialism.

What socialism really aims at, in all the various ideologies, is to put
a stop to the individual who would exploit capital to become rich at
the expense of the misery and wretchedness of the masses; to provide
state supervision over the individual's economic potential and to
bring about social equality among all citizens so as to eliminate all
manifestations of poverty and deprivation as well as the disproportion-
ate divergence in which you have hunger, poverty, sickness and de-
gradation on the one hand—and luxury, harshness and moral disintegration on the other.

[24] United Arab Republic, *The Charter*, p. 58.
[25] Dr. Muṣṭafā al-Sibāʿī, *Ishtirākīyat al-Islam* [*The Socialism of Islam*].
Major portions of this book are translated by George H. Gardner and Sami A.
Hanna in "Islamic Socialism," *The Muslim World* 56, no. 2 (1966): 71–86.
These authors argue that Dr. al-Sibāʿī's book "is considered to be of the utmost
importance in providing form, direction, and legitimacy to the social system
emerging in present day Egypt. It is considered to be, in brief, a major statement of ideology for Egyptian Socialism." This judgment has been verified by
several sources in the ASU who admitted substantially the same as these two
authors have concluded. All page references are to the Gardner-Hanna article.

I do not believe that anyone who knows Islam and understands its spirit can properly deny that Islam clearly had these same goals.[26]

We must clearly delineate the general interpretations attributed to the concept of Arab Socialism if we are to understand the impact this ideology is having upon the rural fellahin. This tendency to equate the goals of Islam with the goals of Arab Socialism is especially significant for a regime seeking acceptance and commitment (legitimacy) from the masses.

The first part of Dr. Sabā'ī's book defines the aims of "true socialism" as the fulfillment of man's five "inherent rights" (al-ḥuqūq al-tabī'iyah):

(1) the right to life, al-ḥayāh, and the preservation of health;
(2) the right to freedom, al-ḥurrīyah, human freedom, religious freedom, academic freedom, political freedom, civic freedom, social freedom, and moral freedom;
(3) the right to education and knowledge, al-'ilm, which is of higher value than piety;
(4) the right to dignity, al-karameh, i.e., to have the right to be treated as a fellow creature and have the right to impartial social justice and to enjoy an honored position in society;
(5) the right to own property, al-tamalluk, wealth as a means of happiness, poverty being considered a social disease, labor being the means of acquiring property and a place in society.[27]

Dr. Sabā'ī, in the last half of his book, delimits the basic differences between the "Socialism of Islam" and communism.

(1) Islamic Socialism harmonizes with human nature and life's necessities in allowing individual ownership, a thing which theoretical communism forbids. . . .
(2) Islamic Socialism which permits private ownership, gives a free hand to human talents in the way of constructive competition which is undoubtedly the mainspring in cultural evolution and growth. Communism asserts that competition is the cause of social disaster and the exploitation of the masses by the capitalists. . . .

[26] Ibid., p. 75
[27] Ibid., p. 77.

(3) Islamic Socialism leads in fact not to class war, as does communism, but to cooperation among all social classes. . . .

(4) Islamic Socialism has set on foot the most imposing structure in cultural development in historical times: faith in God the giver of life. . . . The day the state parts company with this faith as communism would have it do, evil will pass all bounds, and society will commit suicide. . . .

(5) Islamic Socialism is based on morality as an integral part of faith; it urges man to seek perfection. Communism does not believe in moral and emotive values such as love and mercy, nor does it believe in such social values as truth and loyalty. It considers these values only in as much as they fit in with communist interests. . . .

(6) Islamic Socialism declares its trust in man and in his inborn goodness and nobility, believing that he is closer to good than to evil. . . . Communism does not trust man—its whole history from beginning to end is a story of despotism and a struggle for food and fortune. It does not trust his religion because that is superstition, nor does it trust his conscience because the values he believes in are false values. It has no faith in his instinctive goodness believing him to be greedy, selfish, and tyrannical.[28]

Obviously, this analysis of Arab Socialism provides some insights into the value of an ideology for a nation seeking legitimacy and acceptance by its people. Ideology can serve many functions. It outlines an interpretation of history that is gratifying and integrating for the individual lost in the moral vacuum of the transitional world. Ideology can chart the values and goals that seem "right and proper" in the modern world and suggest the means and methods most appropriate for these goals. One may see in this pattern of ideas a model that simultaneously provides for an Egyptian a sense of identity, an analysis of the current world situation, and a set of instrumental imperatives deducible from the foregoing analysis.[29] Yet in many ways Arab Socialism may more

[28] Ibid., pp. 79–84.

[29] It is not within the scope of this work to include a comprehensive analysis of all aspects of Nasser's Arab Socialism. For a fuller description see 'Iṣmat Sayf al-Dawla, Usus al-'ishtirākīyah al-'arabīyah [Bases of Arab Socialism], 'Alī Ṣabrī, Taṭbīq al-'ishtirākīyah fī miṣr [Socialist Application in Egypt]; current issues of the magazine al-Ṭalī'ah (The Vanguard), official publication

aptly be conceived as something similar to Sorel's concept of
"myth." Here I am referring not to the substantive aspects of
Sorel's myth, but rather to his analysis of how a myth may be used
in a political situation.

In the course of this study one thing has always been present in my
mind, which seems to me so evident that I did not think it worth while
to lay much stress on it—that men who are participating in great
social movements always picture their coming action as a battle in
which their cause is certain to triumph. These constructions, knowledge
of which is so important for historians, I propose to call myths. . . .
[These myths] are not descriptions of things, but expressions of a determination to act. People who are living in this world of myths, are
secure from all refutation. . . . No failure proves anything. . . . If they
are checked, it merely proves that the apprenticeship has been insufficient; they must set to work again with more courage [and] persistence than before.[30]

Sorel argues that the major function of ideology is the establishment of unity and solidarity. The essence of this unity springs
from social myths that create the moral basis of society. Ideology
as a system of myths characterized as a set of moral imperatives
may easily provide the substantive element in our concept of
legitimate authority. This approach to ideology precludes one's asking whether the ideology in question is valid or false; whether it
accurately describes the past, present, or future. This approach
merely asks for an analysis of its effectiveness and usefulness in
generating support and enthusiasm for a regime's program and
policies. The extent to which an ideology offers a means for promoting widespread acceptance and commitment will depend upon
its success in developing a close identification between government
and citizen and thus stimulating the feelings of legitimacy necessary for the effective operation of the political system.

Ideologies will vary in their effectiveness. They obviously represent means that can be controlled or manipulated to achieve given
ends. The question we must be concerned with centers around the

---

of the ASU; and Leonard Binder, *The Ideological Revolution in the Middle
East.*
  [30] George Sorel, *Reflections on Violence*, pp. 22, 32, 35, 36.

characteristics of an ideological pattern of beliefs and the conditions that determine the success or failure of these patterns in strengthening or weakening popular support. As one reads the Charter and the many descriptive analyses of Arab Socialism, it becomes apparent that not all doctrines, values, and goals in this belief structure have an equal probability of remaining an acceptable interpretation and justification for Egypt's new regime and its authorities. The acceptance of some aspects of the national ideology will depend largely upon its ability to fulfill man's psychological and material needs. Given this fundamental problem, what tactical approaches are available to the Egyptian government as it seeks to satisfy these needs in a way considered to be appropriate and legitimate? The strategies most commonly suggested by Nasser centered around two structural mechanisms for change: the party and the bureauracy—one emphasizing ideology and political culture and the other concerned with efficiency and policy implementation.

6 🔲 Organizational Structure
and Functions of the ASU

ONE INNOVATION that distinguishes the ASU from Nasser's earlier mass parties is the recruitment pattern announced in the Charter for all elective units in the ASU, including the National Assembly. The Charter states: "The popular and political organizations based on free and direct election must truly and fairly represent the powers forming the majority of the population. . . . It follows then that the new constitution must ensure that its farmers and workmen will get half the seats in the political and popular organizations at all levels, including the House of Representatives, since they form the majority of the people."[1]

Today, the ASU no longer seeks representation along the usual lines of geographic distribution, but is to be based on functional

---

[1] United Arab Republic, *The Charter*, p. 52. During the spring of 1968, workers and farmers were operationally defined as follows: (a) a worker is one who works either in industry, agriculture, or services, and his only income is from his salary. He cannot belong to a professional organization, and is not a graduate of a university, higher institute, or a military academy. (b) A farmer is one who, including his immediate family, does not own more than 10 feddans of land. He must live in a rural area and his only source of income is from the agricultural produce of his land. See *al-Ahram*, May 31, 1968, p. 4.

or employment memberships. This corporate theory of representation was imposed through the proliferation of ASU Basic Units (lowest organizational unit of the ASU) into many different kinds of institutions, organizations, and places of employment. Thus Basic Units were established in factories, professional groupings, schools and universities, banks and insurance companies, and in many government ministries and agencies. Although such a restructuring of representative units may well appear harmonious with "true democracy," many have noted that this penetration of ASU machinery provides an efficient means of control and regulation otherwise denied the central government.[2] More specifically, the government has defined the ASU as "the comprehensive political structure of national action. Its formations embrace all powers of the people—farmers, workers, soldiers, intellectuals, and holders of national capital."[3]

One common rumor heard from several different sources was that all citizens were "encouraged" to join the ASU, and that all citizens who wanted to be considered "cooperative and loyal" would pay their twelve piasters (thirty cents) each month for ASU dues. The rumors often suggested that all college graduates were encouraged to join the ASU as a precondition to receiving their degrees or certificates of graduation.

Apart from being considered "cooperative and loyal," what are the advantages of being a member of the ASU? Party membership in the rural areas tends, unfortunately for the ASU, to ensure that

[2] Leonard Binder provides a general outline of this new approach to representation as it was manifested in the 1964 National Assembly in "Political Recruitment and Participation in Egypt," *Political Parties and Political Development*, Joseph La Palombara and Myron Weiner, eds., 217–240. He provides the following breakdown of membership in the National Assembly in 1957 and 1964.

Occupational Group	1957	1964
1. Army and police	14.0%	4.4%
2. High administration	17.5	—
3. Professionals	35.4	32.1
4. Managerial and gov't employees	7.4	5.8
5. Rural middle class	19.8	38.1
6. Workers	.2	13.5
7. Urban "private sector"	3.8	4.8

[3] United Arab Republic, *Statute of the Arab Socialist Union*, pp. 7–8.

a former traditional leader will be able to maintain his position of power and authority in the village or rural community. As has been noted,[4] power and authority in an Egyptian village rest on the ability of the leader to provide services for the villagers. The village *'umdah* is respected, even honored, because he has a line of communication to government officials at the district and governorate levels. ASU membership offers additional connections to those in authority inside the village. While the villagers themselves still see the *'umdah* and the family *shaykh* as the most influential people in the village, the ASU organization is now given a prominent third place, especially in those situations where traditional leadership positions and party membership are coterminous.

Of course, maintenance of one's position of authority in the village is only one factor, but it is still a fairly common one in determining membership. Others, especially individuals previously excluded from leadership or power positions in the village, may see ASU membership as the key to an increased sense of influence and power. If such an individual should be elected to the village ASU committee, he may feel the pride of having access to the decision makers of his village. This new position offers easier access to political information and the newly elected member may feel that he is on the inside track in Egyptian politics. The new ASU leader may take considerable pride in belonging to the country's political elite, to the "decision-makers," to the vanguard of the masses, and to being a representative of the central government.

Membership in the ASU may thus appeal to a person's pride as well as to his loftiest instincts as a servant of his society. It may, at the same time, gratify his personal ambitions. The power and influence accruing from access to the ASU leadership makes itself felt in his own power and influence in the village. If he is a government official, he is more apt to be given greater responsibility and be more eligible for advanced assignments. Moreover, the ASU member in the village and small towns can deal rather strongly with other administrative agencies in the area, and with party connections he can periodically evade official channels of authority

4 See chapter 4.

more readily than a nonmember. Many of these advantages may also be used to ease the path of advancement, to break down the stringency of administrative regulations or to open doors to officials for the member's family and friends. In short, ASU membership is seen by many as an important means of securing an individual's professional and personal success.

Membership, of course, has certain obligations. The member must become familiar with the ASU's general ideology. He must keep himself informed as intimately as possible about current public issues, policies, and goal priorities. The ASU man, in addition, is expected to be an activist and a model citizen. "Political action" is the phrase most commonly used and means service in a great variety of political duties, such as election campaigns, civil defense work, or promoting special government programs and policies. As a model citizen, the ASU man is expected to lead a life above reproach. The ASU man is presumed to be more informed, more intelligent, more self-disciplined, moral, and law abiding than most of the citizenry. This idealized picture of the "new Egyptian" is, unfortunately, not what the average Egyptian himself sees when asked to describe the characteristics of a good ASU member. Many villagers see the ASU as a mutual protection society that provides a means for maintaining one's position in the village or town. It is often noted that they have more ample opportunity to conceal their lapses from moral standards, less need to violate many laws, and a good deal of protection through their political contacts, should they get into trouble.

One serious problem the ASU must face in the villages, if it is to legitimize its position, is the recruitment of new leaders. One of the most common complaints heard from practically every village official this writer contacted was the problem of the authoritarian approach of many new ASU leaders. It appears that many individuals are joining the ASU for personal rather than political reasons. Traditionally prevented from holding a position of authority or prestige because of social position, or more often because of personality traits or lack of leadership, this kind of individual mouths the socialist slogans, agitates for reform and change, and by ingratiating himself with district or governorate ASU leaders, lands himself in a position of authority in the ASU. Lacking the personal, social, and often mental qualities expected of a village leader, these new leaders resort to threats, pressure, and coercion in order to obtain compliance and respect.

The following situation is typical of many examples offered to this writer about some of the new local ASU leaders. A young doctor (let us call him Nabil), a recent graduate of the medical school in Cairo, had recently arrived in the village where he was to live for two years. The village has a new health clinic housed in a two story building, the upper portion of which is the doctor's residence. One afternoon, after Dr. Nabil had been in the village about three weeks, the ASU leader (secretary of the *lajnat al-'ish-rīn*) paid him a visit. On this particular day, the clinic was distributing *ma'ūna* (U.S. aid supplies), and Dr. Nabil was supervising the operation. Unfortunately, the ASU leader happened to arrive just when the young doctor had asked his orderly to continue the distribution while he went up to his apartment for a cup of tea.

The ASU man barged into the doctor's apartment, demanding to know why the doctor was not supervising the distribution as required. The doctor insisted that he had been performing his duties most of the morning and had taken a short break to get a cup of tea. When the ASU man refused to accept this excuse and demanded that the doctor return to his post, the doctor refused, stating that the ASU man had no authority over him and that he would return when he was good and ready. The secretary left the doctor's room with the words "we shall see about this."

Two weeks later the doctor was relieved of his position in this village, which had been only a two-hour train ride from Cairo, and was transferred to a village in Upper Egypt—a village in the governorate of Qena, often called the "Siberia of Egypt" (*al-sa'īd al-guwāni*). The charge levied against the doctor was substantiated by five witnesses—all members of the village ASU organization—and each accused him of charging bakshish for services rendered, of spending his afternoons and evenings caring for families of the wealthy landowners and of neglecting his duties in the clinic.

This story is not given to suggest that all ASU leaders act in such a manner. In fact, in the vast majority of situations where the ASU man is not only the party leader but also the "real leader," he can be a most effective agent for change and reform. Rather, the purpose of this story is to suggest two dilemmas that the ASU must face in its desire to penetrate the villages. First, the present system does not clearly define the relationship or the channels of authority between the ASU village leadership and the various administrators functioning in the village. Most village doctors, agronomists, social workers, and teachers believe their superior resides in their respective ministries. The ASU man, on the other hand, is charged with guiding, controlling, inspecting, and evaluating government programs and policies and those implementing these policies. This dual control system is alienating a lot of the village functionaries who feel caught between two authorities—both demanding compliance but neither willing to protect or defend the village bureaucrat. It is small wonder that a vast majority of all government officials working in villages are praying for the day that they can return to the big city.

Secondly, the ASU, by giving leadership positions to people perceived as unfit or unqualified in the eyes of the villagers, only alienates the villagers from the ASU. The dilemma here is that the "real leaders" are often the wealthier landowners, and therefore have no shared interest in an ideology or organization committed to their destruction. Thus the ASU, in selecting others to be the village leaders are, too often, forced to pick individuals most willing to champion the socialist ideology and the ASU's demands. These are individuals who, in the eyes of the other villagers, have no right to these positions of leadership.

In discussing the organization of the ASU it is essential to distinguish three basic types of members: the associate, the active, and "the full-timer." The ASU Statute, however, distinguishes only two kinds of members: "Active members who are entitled to candidature for membership in various organs, paying the amount of subscription fixed by the Higher Executive Committee.

Associate members whose status is to be determined by the decisions of the Higher Executive Committee organizing the system of associate members."[5]

Most members of the ASU interviewed were unable to clearly define the distinction between an active and associate member, although several felt that active members were those who had been elected to one of the committees in the ASU hierarchy.[6] Full-time party workers must be distinguished from active or associate members, since they function as a full-time cadre in the ASU organization and receive their salaries from the national ASU headquarters.

In January 1963, Aly Sabri announced that applications for membership in the ASU had reached 4,841,434 out of a total electorate of 6,417,021 members.[7] In February 1966, he noted that membership had risen to over five million.[8] To this number it might be useful, at least for certain purposes, to add the 100,000 members of the ASU's youth affiliate, the Socialist Youth Organization (SYO).[9]

General membership is open to all individuals who comply with the following requirements:

1. Be a citizen of the United Arab Republic.
2. Be at least 18 years of age holding the right to suffrage.
3. Be a good "unexploiting" citizen not previously convicted of any criminal charge.
4. Be inspired with faith in the Charter and undertake to participate in the activities of the various organs of the ASU, striving for the achievement of its objectives.
5. Should submit a written application for membership in the ASU.[10]

[5] United Arab Republic, *Statute of the Arab Socialist Union*, pp. 14–15.
[6] The ASU Statute lists some fifteen duties and seven rights for active members; see appendix A.
[7] *al-Ahram*, January 24, 1963, p. 4.
[8] "The Arab Socialist Union," *Arab Observer*, February 21, 1966, p. 6. By May 1968, the government announced that the ASU was composed of 5,135,000 old members and 710,218 new members. See *al-Ahram*, May 31, 1968, p. 4.
[9] *al-Shabāb al-'Arabī*, April 13, 1970, p. 3.
[10] United Arab Republic, *Statute of the Arab Socialist Union*, pp. 13–14.

On January 1, 1967, the Arab Socialist Union announced that active membership had been extended to members of the judiciary, the police, and the armed forces in an attempt to further integrate party membership into the local government structure.[11] This new regulation will now allow army officers and police officials presently working in local administrative positions to identify themselves with the ASU. This has also been interpreted as a move toward strengthening the "interlocking directorate" approach in local councils, which is the principal integrating mechanism between the administrators and the "popular units."[12]

The United Arab Republic is divided into twenty-five governorates (*muḥāfazāt*), twenty-two in the Nile Valley and three in the desert areas.[13] Each *muḥāfazah* is further divided into districts (*markaz*), which usually consist of one major town and several villages (*qaryah*). At each of these three levels one finds a duplicate government and party organization, each one with theoretically different functions, powers, and prerogatives.[14] At the lowest level of the ASU organization, authority supposedly rests in a Basic Unit Conference, which includes all working members in the Basic Unit. As was noted previously, the Basic Unit, as the lowest structural unit in the Arab Socialist Union, has been established in each major village. A member of the ASU can be active and vote in only one Basic Unit. In the more populated areas, Basic Units were established in residential areas, schools, government offices, labor unions, and business establishments. According to an official in the Ministry of National Guidance there were, by mid-1967, over 6,789 Basic Units with a combined membership of 5,305,191.[15]

The Basic Unit Conference (consisting of all dues-paying members) "is considered as the highest authority in the Union on the

11 *The Egyptian Gazette*, January 1, 1967, p. 3.
12 See chapter 8.
13 See appendix B.
14 See appendices C and H.
15 See appendix D. Note, however, that by 1970 the number of Basic Units had risen to nearly 8,000; interview with Egyptian government official on January 10, 1970.

level of the Unit"[16] and will be convened once every four months upon the request of the committee of the Basic Unit or at the request of one-third of the members. While a Basic Unit Conference is supposed to meet every four months, this author failed to locate a single ASU member who had ever attended such a meeting and most admitted that they had no idea what the functions of the Basic Unit Conference were supposed to be.

Executive powers are delegated by the members to the Basic Unit's committee—known as a *lajnat al-'ishrīn* ("committee of Twenty"). This committee is elected by all citizens in the village who are registered in the electoral lists for public elections. Those who are elected then select from among themselves a secretary, an assistant secretary, and various delegates to the next district level of the ASU hierarchy. Since an ASU member can serve on only one party committee, a replacement must be found for each member elected to higher-level ASU committees. The replacements at the Basic Unit level go to other candidates in the Basic Unit election in priority of the votes each received. This committee is supposed to meet every two weeks and the life of the committee is two years.[17]

Territorial ASU organizations, from town or district up to governorate are similarly organized. At the *markaz*, *qism*, or *bandar* (UAR local administrative units in rural and urban areas) level is an ASU Congress consisting of delegates elected by the basic units in its jurisdiction. The number of delegates from each unit is determined by the size of the unit. Thus a Basic Unit of less than five hundred members will have two representatives; one of

[16] United Arab Republic, *Statute of the Arab Socialist Union*, p. 22. See also appendix E for a detailed organizational chart of the ASU.

[17] Since the June war of 1967 the ASU organization has gone through some significant reorganization. On June 25, 1968, some 180,000 candidates sought membership in their village Basic Unit Committees. Under this new system, the membership of each Basic Unit Committee must include at least 50 percent workers or peasants. The only exception to this 50 percent rule are those Basic Unit Committees in government offices and higher educational institutions. In universities, for example, seats on the Basic Unit Committee are apportioned 2:2:3:3 for junior faculty, senior faculty, students, and administrators, respectively.

between five hundred and fifteen hundred, four representatives; and a Basic Unit of over fifteen hundred members will send six representatives. The 50 percent quota for workers and peasants must be observed. Each District Congress will in turn elect a twenty-member governing committee (*lajnat al-'ishrīn*) from among its members. The *lajnat al-'ishrīn* will then elect a secretary and two assistant secretaries from among its members. The District Congress has a two-year term and is supposed to meet every six months or in extraordinary sessions at the request of the *markaz* committee or one-third of the Basic Unit Committees in the *markaz*.

There is a Governorate (*muḥāfaẓah*) Congress, made up of delegates from each of the 210 District Congresses, established in each of the twenty-five *muḥāfaẓāt*. The number of delegates is determined by the size of the District Congress, with a maximum of sixteen delegates from any one district. The Governorate Congress elects a committee of not more than fifty members. These committees in turn must elect their own secretaries and assistant secretaries.

The Governorate Congress has a four-year term and meets every six months or in extraordinary sessions at the request of the Governorate Committee or one-third of the Congress members, or one-third of the ASU organizations in the *muḥāfaẓah*.

At the national level there is the National ASU Congress made up of all the members of the Governorate Congresses, plus the fifty members of a special Election Supervision Committee. The National Congress will thus have nearly two thousand members. It elects a 150-member Central Committee, which in turn elects a Higher Executive Committee of ten men and a chairman, who, until his death, was President Nasser.

Most observers would immediately notice the similarity between this party organization and the Communist party of the USSR, and thus assume all elections were rigged to ensure that candidates hand-picked by the higher levels would be elected at the lower levels. However, several different sources, both in and outside the ASU, have suggested that, in the early stages of the ASU, the elections at the village, town, and *markaz* level were often poorly managed, with little regard to the candidates elected. In fact, one of the major factors that led to the new organizational changes in 1966–1967 seems to have stemmed from the fact that many of the *lajnat al-'ishrīn* at the village, town, and markaz level were often composed of individuals who either had no interest in the aims and goals of the ASU or were actually opposed to the ASU and had joined the party in order to prevent the ASU from instituting any profound changes in their areas.[18]

Aly Sabri, former prime minister and secretary-general of the ASU, delivered a major address in July 1966 to the ASU Executive Officers' Conference in Alexandria. He noted that since he had become secretary-general (October 1964), his primary aim had been to reorganize the country's political structures so as to guarantee the "greatest possible measure of consciousness and efficiency for the UAR's political organization [in order] to provide a strong link with the popular base, which would allow for the proper guidance of the masses, help them solve their problems, and allow them a means for fulfilling their aspirations."[19] Aly Sabri further announced that candidates and party workers had to be selected more carefully and be willing to dedicate their full time and energies to the ASU.

One of the first steps in an attempt to strengthen the internal structure of the ASU was the creation of a General Secretariat composed of high-level party administrators, each responsible for a particular aspect of the ASU program.[20] Concomitant with this

[18] During the fall and winter of 1965 several evaluation teams made a tour of various villages in the Delta area and in Upper Egypt to determine the effectiveness of the ASU in these areas. The unanimous conclusion of all their reports indicates that the ASU had not penetrated to the villages, that traditional or illiterate elements generally monopolized the *lajnat al-'ishrīn*, and that most villagers believed the *lajnat al-'ishrīn* had only been established to settle disputes among the villagers. See the special edition of the ASU sponsored magazine *Shihadāt wa taqārīr wāqi'īyah 'an al-rīf al-miṣrī* [True Statements and Reports on Rural Egypt], *al-Ṭalī'ah*, September 1966.

[19] *Arab Observer*, July 18, 1966, p. 9.

[20] Some of the members of this secretariat are the secretary-general, secretary for youth affairs, secretary for the fellahin, secretary for ideology and guidance, secretary for membership, secretary for workers, and director of ASU legal affairs.

national reorganization was the creation in each governorate of an executive bureau (*maktab tanfīdhī*) made up of five to seven full-time party workers. In late February 1966 a plenary meeting of the president, the vice-presidents, the prime minister, the National Assembly speaker, the ASU secretary-general, the ASU General Secretariat, and the 170 members of the Governorate Executive Bureaus was held to initiate "a new stage of activities in which by completing its organization and finding means of working with the public, it will begin to fulfill its purpose."[21]

This "new stage" began, according to President Nasser, in October 1965 when Aly Sabri was appointed secretary-general and Executive Bureaus were established in each of the twenty-five governorates. Nasser, in his speech before these ASU leaders, noted that "everyone is criticizing the ASU harshly: who is responsible for this? Is it the president himself? Alone, I can do nothing, neither for this country nor for the State nor for the ASU. You are the ones who can do everything, and therefore, we must basically depend on the mass population and then on the various ASU leaderships in the process of founding the Union."[22] Nasser continued, emphasizing that "the first thing to do now is to acquire confidence in the ASU. For this reason, all our plans today aim at founding the ASU headquarters, at the various governorates, districts, and basic units. Then, it would become possible to form the Central Committee, and after a while to organize an ASU National Congress and from this to elect the Supreme Executive Committee."[23]

One important aspect of the new reorganization scheme implemented during the spring of 1967 was the creation of the Central Committee. Aly Sabri noted in February 1966 that the then proposed Central Committee "is bound to be quite different from the rest of the Union's units, including the General Secretariat, who represents sectors or portions of the population, such as peasants, workers, youth. . . . The Central Committee, on the other hand, represents types of activities and occupations, such as industry,

---

[21] *The Arab Observer*, February 21, 1966, p. 8.
[22] Ibid.
[23] Ibid., p. 9.

agriculture, services, including health, education, and so on."[24] Finally, in January 1967 the ASU announced the formation of the Central Committee, which was to include (1) cabinet ministers, (2) the twenty-five governors, (3) ASU leaders, (4) secretaries-general of the twenty-five governorates, and (5) distinguished professors, technicians, and administrative experts.[25]

From sources contacted within the ASU, it appears this Central Committee is to play two major roles: (1) to provide a coordinating body of top party and administrative leaders to ensure a consistent policy throughout all the provinces and at all levels of administration; and (2) to place an ASU structure at the pinnacle of the administrative hierarchy to ensure that all government policies will be interpreted as ASU sponsored, controlled, and implemented. It is envisioned that this higher ASU structure will possess the competent personnel necessary "to guide both the executive body, with its expert knowledge and experience (the Cabinet) and the legislative body, with its host of representatives and specialists (the General Assembly)."[26]

In addition to the Central Committee, full-time Executive Bureaus were established in each *markaz* during the fall of 1966 and early spring of 1967, with the hope of recruiting full-time party workers for each of the four thousand major villages by the end of 1968.[27] These Executive Bureaus were not to take the place of the *lajnat al-'ishrīn*, but were to function as an executive unit of full-time party workers. The addition of an Executive Bureau of full-

[24] *Ibid.*, p. 8.

[25] *al-Ahram*, January 21, 1967, p. 4.

[26] Ibid. One additional function of the Central Committee became apparent immediately after President Nasser's death, when the ASU Higher Executive Committee submitted a formal report to the ASU Central Committee nominating Mr. Anwar al-Sadat, Egypt's vice-president under Nasser, to be the new president. Subsequently, both the ASU Central Committee and later the 350 member National Assembly unanimously adopted Mr. al-Sadat as the single candidate for the Egyptian presidency. On October 15, 1970, some 7,143,839 Egyptians participated in the nation-wide presidential plebiscite that gave al-Sadat 90.04 percent of the total vote.

[27] The number of full-time workers in each Executive Bureau varied from *markaz* to *markaz* and suggests the difficulty of recruiting competent party administrators in all the nearly 400 *marākiz*. In six governorates of central and

time party workers to the already functioning *lajnat al-'ishrīn* of locally elected party leaders stems largely from the earlier ineffectiveness of these popularly elected committees. Aly Sabri, as early as July 1966, admitted that "the experiment of the ASU base-elections over the past few years had not served its proper purposes, for those elections were not an extension of organized political action. Further, the concept of political action was not clear to the masses who had been asked to elect their leaderships without knowing the reasons for the election."[28]

The *lajnat al-'ishrīn* ("Committee of Twenty") had been established to act as the executive organ of the ASU in the village. Unfortunately, these committees were usually dominated by traditional landowning families or government employees who had no interest in the problems of the villagers. In most of the four thousand villages that are somewhat isolated from the provincial capitals it is estimated that less than 15 percent of the adult males of the villages are even nominally associated wth the ASU.[29]

In December 1965 the evaluation teams from the national headquarters of the ASU traveled into the various rural provinces of both Upper and Lower Egypt to determine the effectiveness of the *lajnat al-'ishrīn* in the village. Ahmad Tawfiq, a member of one of these teams, described his impressions of one village (Bisindilla) in the governorate of Dakahlia[30] for the ASU magazine *al-Ṭalī'ah*.

Upper Egypt the number of members in each Executive Bureau varied as follows:

Governorate Bureau	Three Members	Four Members	Five Members	Six Members
Giza	2	3	3	1
Fayyum	2	2	2	0
Beni Suef	4	4	0	0
Sohag	2	5	5	0
Qena	4	4	2	0
Aswan	0	0	5	0

See *al-Akhbar*, March 18, 1967, p. 9.

[28] *Arab Observer*, July 18, 1966, p. 9.

[29] *al-Ṭalī'ah*, September, 1966, p. 23.

[30] Although the following information and data largely stems from Ahmad Tawfiq's article, this description of Bisindilla is by no means unique in rural

The main purpose of the ASU evaluation team was to meet with members of the *lajnat al-'ishrīn* in an attempt to gain a clearer understanding of the mentality of these elected elements in the village, their methods of operation and their procedures for meeting problems. During the first few days the atmosphere between the villagers and the "foreigners" was clouded with a "deep sense of mistrust and yet a consistent tendency to use flattering language whenever describing the ASU." The villagers, in general, denied that their village had any problems and emphasized how effective their *lajnat al-'ishrīn* was in performing its duties. As one villager commented, "If all the ASU committees of twenty were of the same standard as ours, the ASU would have achieved all of its goals." These attempts at simple flattery and saying what they think you want to hear is clearly expressive of the *fahlawī* mentality.[31] Indeed, if this evaluation team had left after a day or two, their reports would have painted the villagers' attitudes toward the ASU in glowing terms. Yet this team stayed on—insisting that the villagers speak frankly and openly.

Once rapport was established and a few individuals came forward to complain, the following description of the *lajnat al-'ishrīn* emerged. The *lajnat al-'ishrīn* had been elected some three years earlier. The secretary of this committee was a young agronomist who had graduated from an agricultural college, but who, according to the villagers, had not attended a single session of the *lajnat al-'ishrīn* since he was elected. Because he was the most educated member of the committee and had promised to build them a new school if he were elected secretary, the village chose him. Both he and his wife, who was also an elected member of the *lajnat al-'ishrīn*, now lived in Cairo and seldom visited the village. The other members of the *lajnat al-'ishrīn* included two shopkeepers, a cereal merchant, two contractors—one of whom also acts as president of the Agricultural Laborers Union—and thirteen fellahin who own

Egypt. Of the seventy-nine villages I visited, at least half could be considered carbon copies of the situation at Bisindilla. See Ahmad Tawfiq, "Bisindilla," *al-Ṭalī'ah*, September 1966, pp. 14–20.

[31] See Chapter 3.

between one-half to five feddans (acres) each. Three of these thirteen had received their land through land reform. The assistant
secretary of the *lajnat al-'ishrīn* was a *shaykh al-balad* and was
one of the three who had benefited from land reform. Seven members can neither read nor write. Except for the secretary, his wife,
and the assistant secretary, who has a primary certificate, all other
members have had less than five years of formal schooling. The
youngest member is thirty-five, and eight of the members are over
fifty.

In the process of interviewing the nonmembers of the ASU committee, the general consensus was that the *lajnat al-'ishrīn* was
"conspicuous for its inactivity." Most villagers thought the *lajnat
al-'ishrīn* had been established merely to receive complaints and
settle disputes but "even in this they were not very effective."

After several days of interviewing, discussing, and listening to
grievances, the evaluation team suggested that an "open meeting"
for all the villagers be held in order to explain what a *lajnat al-
'ishrīn* was supposed to do. The meeting was held in the evening.
After portions of the Koran had been read, the president of the
Agricultural Laborers Union requested that additional verses be
read in honor of the secretary of the *lajnat al-'ishrīn*, recently
incapacitated with an illness, "seeking God's blessings to heal him
if he were still alive and to have mercy on him if he had passed
away." The Village Council chairman was the first speaker on the
program. His speech was full of praise and satisfaction with the
workings of the Arab Socialist Union in their village, his words
being constantly interrupted by cheering and clapping. The longer
he spoke, the more the evaluation team was afraid "this meeting
would become like most conferences of the ASU in which the
major function of the people was to clap and cheer without any
attempt on their part to participate in the discussion or find solutions to their problems."[32]

The second speaker, the assistant secretary of the *lajnat al-'ishrīn* who had been briefed earlier by the evaluation team, began

[32] *al-Ṭalī'ah*, September 1966, p. 16.

his presentation with a memorized piece of Arabic poetry that "brought a more thunderous applause than all the other speeches combined." When the assistant secretary began to discuss the items recommended by the evaluation team, he merely read his prepared outline and made no attempt to elucidate the items in any detail or to bring the other villagers into a profitable two-way discussion. Ahmad Tawfiq concludes his description of this public meeting with these words:

These sessions clearly confirmed the villagers' inability to organize themselves, to express their problems coherently, and their tendency to rely on the state to find solutions to the problems they themselves cannot solve. These sessions also demonstrated the ineffectiveness of the *lajnat al-'ishrīn* which had no conception of the aims and aspirations of the Arab Socialist Union. . . . The lack of interaction and need of communication between the various levels of the ASU are the fundamental reasons for the present condition of the village committees. We must realize that most of the ASU village leaders are merely leaders in potential and thus need training and guidance.[33]

The results of these investigations by ASU evaluation teams throughout the rural provinces evoked a sharp response from the national leadership. On November 30, 1965, the Arab Socialist Union announced its intention to dismiss 2,500 members for being "reactionary, deviationist, and negative."[34]

Nasser, speaking in February 1966 on the past weaknesses and failures of the ASU in the rural areas, argued that "what has taken place so far must never intimidate us. We may go through one, two, three or maybe four experiences, and never get tired of trying. All kinds of organizations in the world had to go through hard times in the process of strengthening themselves and improving their methods of action."[35] Thus, during 1966 and early 1967, many of the *lajnat al-'ishrīn*s were dissolved, traditional leadership patterns were rooted out, and, in areas where loyal villagers were not available, village administrators were given positions in the

[33] Ibid., pp. 17–18.
[34] *Akhbar al-Yawm*, November 20, 1965, p. 3.
[35] *Arab Observer*, February 21, 1966, p. 9.

village ASU structure. In October 1966 Aly Sabri admitted that "temporarily, until we have a peasantry sufficiently enlightened to take up a leading role, we will have to depend on the cultured elite of the villages, such as the physician, the agricultural supervisor, the school headmaster, and the veterinarian."[36]

One clear innovation of this "second stage" in the restructuring of the rural ASU organization was the increased activity of the District Executive Bureau (*maktab tanfidhī*). The ASU Statute gives no indication as to the duties and functions of these new Executive Bureaus, but it is apparent that they were to assume a positive role in their respective districts, which in most cases consisted of taking over the functions and responsibilities of the *markaz lajnat al-'ishrīn*. Chapter III of the ASU Statute clearly indicates what the general duties of the *lajnat al-'ishrīn* were supposed to have been:

A) To create a political awareness among the masses insofar as the socialist, democratic and cooperative action is concerned; to strengthen the principles of Arab nationalism; to make known various rights and duties; and to practice rights and duties in various aspects of local, political, economic and social activities.

B) To work towards developing cultural, economic, and spiritual standards of the people, and to collaborate with various local authorities and organizations to this end.

C) To study requirements and problems of the working people in the area; to work towards solving such problems in collaboration with various local authorities and organizations; and to write reports to the higher formations of the Arab Socialist Union explaining, clarifying, and defending such requirements and problems.

D) To urge the people to spare no efforts in increasing the production of all units in the area of the unit.

E) To fight against all forms of exploitation; to fight against bureaucracy which prevents the people from obtaining equal opportunities in work, service, or any other rights.

F) To convey the policy and the plans of the Arab Socialist Union to the active members and the populace; and to create an awareness among them so that they will be able to participate in executing such policy and plans.

[36] Ibid., October 3, 1966, p. 12.

G) To make sure that those members working at the unit perform the duties indicated in the Statute; to make sure that the unit, as a whole, works towards creating a socialist society and realizing and practicing democracy.

H) To urge active members and help them participate and work in various organizations and councils where local, political, economic, and social activities are practiced; to see that members execute the principles and the policy of the Arab Socialist Union according to the requirements of the masses.

I) To give an opportunity to all workers to practice their rights outlined in the Statute.

J) To execute decisions taken by the conference of the Arab Socialist Union of the unit.[37]

These structural changes are an attempt to strengthen the central control over the rural areas. These bureaucratically inclined full-time ASU workers in the Executive Bureaus will no doubt seek to weed out the "dissenters," the "deviators," and the "reactionaries" who might have been willing to challenge the programs and policies of the central government. Although we do not have specific information on the social composition of these governorate and district party leaders, some indication might be gained from the occupations attributed to the new members of the Executive Bureaus in the districts of Upper Egypt announced in November 1966. They include two members of the Executive Bureau of the Beni Suef governorate, nine lawyers, eleven members of the governorate councils, thirteen teachers, three chairmen of village councils, one 'umdah, and the director of rural programs in a local broadcasting station. The article indicated that these new leaders "were chosen from among the active elements which have played a positive role in exposing and opposing the feudalists in the Governorates of Upper Egypt."[38]

In January 1967 the formation of Executive Bureaus in the marākiz of central Egypt were announced. Among the new members of these executive committees were three members of the National Assembly, eight members of the governorate councils,

[37] United Arab Republic, *Statute of the Arab Socialist Union*, pp. 25–28.
[38] *al-Akhbar*, November 27, 1966, p. 5.

two lawyers, fifteen members of labor union committees, twenty-five fellahin, sixteen youth leaders, one '*umdah*, three doctors, and one worker "recently named outstanding worker in Minya Governorate."

The secretaries-general[39] in each district had the following positions or employment:

Bandar al-Minya:	director of preparatory education in Minya Governorate
Markaz al-Minya:	member of the National Assembly
Markaz Maghagha:	director of Maghagha Loan Bank
Markaz al-'Adwa:	assistant of the Control Office of Taxation
Markaz Beni Mazār:	lawyer
Markaz Maṭai:	director of the Central Hospital
Markaz Samalūṭ:	lawyer
Markaz Abu Qurqās:	director of Education Administration
Markaz Malawi:	irrigation engineer
Markaz Dir Muwās:	member of the National Assembly
Assyut City:	
Section one (*qism*):	tax inspector
Section two:	inspector in sales department of Petroleum Cooperative
Markaz Assyut:	chairman of Committee for Tax Appeals
Markaz al-Qūssīya:	member in the governorate council
Markaz Manfalūṭ:	inspector of education
Markaz Abu Tīj:	teacher in the Teacher's Institute
Markaz Abnūb:	lawyer and member of National Assembly
Markaz al-Badāry:	agricultural inspector
Markaz Dayrūṭ:	tax controller (*murāqib*)
Markaz Sidfa:	preacher (ulema) and member of town council

The statistical information presently available is too vague and limited to be of much use in drawing generalizations, and we therefore complement our insufficient factual knowledge with personal impressions. Accordingly, the fellahin and worker leaders

[39] Ibid., January 14, 1967, p. 4.

are underrepresented in key leadership positions of the ASU, in contrast to, for example, the lawyers, doctors, or high government officials. From various conversations, it appears that these ASU workers in the Executive Bureaus, as full-time party workers, will receive salaries equal to what they would have received in the grade and position they held prior to recruitment into the Executive Bureau.

There can be little doubt that most party workers are former government officials or professional people. Entry into positions of leadership is essentially a process of co-option, in which the ASU, rather than the prospective leader, takes the initiative.

This small group of full-time party leaders works very closely with the governor and his staff. As one official suggested: "The Governor in each governorate is the real boss—he is the chief executive, the key administrator, the main representative of President Nasser in the area. The ASU General Secretary is more of an ideas man, a public relations expert, an organizer and publicity tactician."[40] While everyone knows that the governor is in charge, they also know the man standing next to him. In short, the provincial governor and the ASU secretary, working within the broad limits established by the national plan and the national laws and regulations, maintain continual close supervision over the provincial structure—socially, politically, and economically.

Functions of the ASU

One of the major themes of discussion among political leaders in Egypt since the June war of 1967 has been the role, nature, and relationship of the ASU to the formal governmental machinery of the United Arab Republic. For many, the present structures and functions of the ASU are not clear. Westerners often tend to analyze the political party systems of non-Western states in terms of their own systems. Through Western eyes it is not difficult to make statements about the role of parties in their own political systems. Many political scientists describe the American parties

[40] Interview with an official in the Ministry of Local Administration, December 17, 1966.

as machinery for the purpose of electing presidents, or more generally, as vote-getting organizations. In other words, parties are
seen as instruments for obtaining the political power that is available to those who can win an elective office. At the same time, the
elected officeholders can often reward their party followers with
appointive offices and other forms of political power. From the
point of view of the entire political system, the parties therefore
serve as recruitment agencies to provide the system with leaders.
Furthermore, commentators on the American political system note
that these parties raise issues and, in doing so, represent various
community interests. These parties often serve to articulate the
interests of specific groups, and thus function as the aggregators
and integrators of conflicting interests.

Does any of this apply to the Arab Socialist Union in the UAR?
First of all, by repudiating a two-party or multi-party system, the
ASU is precluded from operating as a vote-getting machine. The
struggle for power in Egypt was decided in the early years of the
revolution when one by one all parties, groups, and individuals
opposed to President Nasser's rule were removed.

But by having the monopoly of political power the ASU is fulfilling a familiar function of parties everywhere: through it, the
system recruits members for positions of leadership in the system.
Having no rivals in the form of other parties, the ASU may indeed perform this function very differently from a multi-party
system.

It will be argued that, in the play of conflicting interests that
do exist in the United Arab Republic, the ASU is theoretically
supposed to function much like parties in other political systems.
While this statement applies mainly to the ASU activities at the
national level, the existence of this interplay of interests has interesting implications for rural Egypt also. Thus, the ASU can serve
as an agency of aggregation and integration, as an agency from
which emerge programs and platforms, ideological positions and
policies. Hence it may well serve as an arena for political conflict.
Policy formation is primarily the result of a deliberation process
in which problems are appraised, priorities established, solutions

proposed, and alternative policies considered. In the Egyptian
political system, all these stages of policy formulation take place
within and outside the framework of the ASU. We have no information about the form these processes take. We know next to
nothing about the procedures established for bringing problems to
the central government's attention, and nothing at all about the
rules governing the subsequent steps. All that we know must be
inferred from party leaders' statements and informal comments
addressed to this writer by local party leaders.

Only one thing is clear: in a society undergoing the kind of
dynamic change one finds in Egypt, it is inevitable that there be a
never-ending need for authoritative policies regarding a myriad of
problems. Every such problem can be seen as a clash of interests
and must be decided on the basis of the regime's values and priorities. A decision is, therefore, the result of weighing the government's values and commitments (now articulated through the
ASU) and the interests of various groups, both within and outside
the ASU, which have a stake in the decision. It is a major conten-
tion of this study that the ASU is beginning to play a much more
significant role in the formulation, control, and implementation
of policy. This may be even more true now that Nasser is gone.

As this process of policy formulation shifts into the confines of
the party, the ASU will become more and more the arena within
which all conflicts of interest in the Egyptian political system must
occur. As more and more of the Egyptian leaders, both nationally
and locally, identify themselves with the ASU, the more this party
leadership will come to be concerned with formulating policies
that will not disrupt the political system itself, and their skills
will consist of steering carefully among conflicting interests,
whether they emanate from labor, student, professional, or agriculture groups. The difference between the party leaders in the
United States and Egypt is thus not so much one of function.
Rather, the difference is in the fact that the decisions made by the
party leadership in Egypt automatically become binding on the
political system.

Parties in a multi-party system, by articulating or aggregating interests emanating from the constituents, also fulfill the function of representation. Can we say the same thing about the ASU? The ASU leadership would give a positive answer to this question. They would say that the ASU knows the interests of the various classes and groups, that it articulates and promotes these interests, and that in formulating authoritative policies it acts in their behalf. The ASU thus claims to be the one and only true representative of all people in the United Arab Republic. The ASU would further strengthen its claim of true representation by noting that the National Assembly is composed of all segments of society and that the largest class groups—the peasants and workers—hold a majority of the seats.[41]

To be sure, the ASU makes use of various methods of probing into public opinion. Moreover, the regime's leaders have shown an awareness of various group interests in Egyptian society, may have taken these interests into serious consideration, and have obviously attempted to make the National Assembly representative by recruiting members from various groups and strata of the population. But at the same time the public interest is defined by the regime primarily according to its own doctrines. The representatives of the public are generally co-opted by an established oligarchy, which therefore decides for itself who is and who is not truly representative. At this point it may be well to analyze in more detail the general function of the ASU, especially as it operates in the rural areas of Egypt.

One important function might be described as political communication. Two very different, albeit related, tasks are involved here. One concerns information obtained from and about various groups in Egyptian society: the ruling elite must keep itself informed about all developments within the entire system that might affect the success or failure of its goals and policies. In delegating

[41] "In March 1964, elections for the National Assembly were held, and 360 candidates were elected. Of these, seventy-five are workers, 115 farmers, and 170 belong to other categories. Thus, workers and farmers constitute 54% of the total membership. For the first time in history, Egypt witnesses a rule of the people, by the people, for the people" (United Arab Republic, *Statistical Handbook*, April 1966, p. 263).

to the members of the ASU the function of supervising and controlling the execution of policies, the government elite can be expected to gather much of the information it needs through the ASU hierarchy. In that sense, the tasks of supervision and information gathering overlap or coincide. But the central government also wants to have information about the needs or interests of the various groups composing Egyptian society. This upward moving communication system thus includes the problem of gauging public opinion.

For our purpose, which is to survey the various functions carried out by the ASU, it does not matter whether or not these opinions or needs are taken into serious consideration when policies are actually made. The fact remains that the ASU can function as a channel of communication for making public opinion and group interests known to the policy makers.

Nasser, on many occasions, argued that the ASU must communicate with the masses, must listen to their complaints, and must understand their problems. "Should all bureau staffs remain within the walls of their offices, giving out orders and instructions, no kind of contact would have been established. . . . Any leadership that does not take over from the masses and learn from them, eventually falls into isolation. It can only express its own views and looses the privilege of being a mouthpiece of public interest since it becomes detached from it. It is gradually transformed into a bureaucracy, for its views are frozen."[42] These words express a condition that does exist today in the rural areas and a condition that must change if the ASU is to be a vehicle of communication between the villagers and the ruling elite.

The second task inherent in the ASU's function of political information is the downward flow of instructions that eventually controls the political, economic, and social policies being implemented by the local administrative agencies. Conflicting reports from newspapers, journals, party literature, and party workers make it impossible to determine the express role that the ASU

[42] *Arab Observer*, February 14, 1966, p. 9.

organization plays at the national level. Most local administrators interviewed indicated confidently that Nasser had given his party leaders the power to mold the ASU into a mechanism capable of checking and evaluating all bureaucratic agencies throughout the administrative hierarchy. The new Executive Bureaus in the governorates and districts are now very much concerned with regular and careful supervision of policies and programs issued by the various ministries. This task of supervision and evaluation, at all levels of the administrative hierarchy down to the very isolated village level, must be included as one of the new functions recently assigned to the ASU.

The forms in which decisions on these matters are transmitted to the agencies and persons concerned vary considerably. From the scant information available, it seems evident there is a steady flow of directives from the central ASU headquarters in Cairo to the lower levels in the governorates. These directives and orders are not published and are in fact restricted in their distribution. Such communiqués may take many forms, from guidelines sent out from one of the central secretaries' offices to formal instructions from the president himself. There has been a definite attempt to separate the government machinery from the party hierarchy. The cabinet reshuffling of September 1966 was interpreted as a means of shifting government people into party positions. Yet, at the same time that the party has drafted several key administrators into its ranks, the ASU organization at the governorate level finds itself closely intertwined with various local councils and bureaucratic agencies. Let us now turn to the lower level of the ASU hierarchy to study how they mesh with the formal government structure.[43]

The ASU has territorial organizations corresponding to the administrative subdivision of all the governorates.[44] Although a detailed analysis of the relationship between the ASU and gov-

---

[43] Chapters 7 and 8 will cover in greater detail the actual functions and operations of the village administrative machinery, including the village councils, combined units, and agricultural cooperatives.
[44] See appendix C.

ernorate, town, and village councils will be made later, three items
ought to be noted:

(1) By law, a majority of all governorate, town, and village
councils must be elected members of their corresponding ASU
lajnat al-'ishrin, thereby insuring ASU dominance in all local administrative councils.

(2) The governorate, town, and village council chairmen are
not to be considered ASU party workers. They are chosen by the
central government. Governors (governorate council chairmen)
and town council chairmen are usually, but not always, former
military officers personally screened by the president, and village
council chairmen are selected through the Ministry of Local Administration. These three types of council chairmen, while they
may be members of the ASU, remain outside the party's formal
leadership structure and are primarily responsible to the ministries
for the efficient implementation of state policies and programs.

(3) The governorate and district secretaries of the Executive
Bureaus are full-time party workers and play a very important
role in controlling, prodding, and evaluating the functioning of the
government machinery. The secretary of the village *lajnat al-'ishrīn*, while not a full-time party worker yet, gradually has been
given greater prestige and authority as the older traditional leadership groups have been removed or neutralized.

The ASU is organized as a command structure in which information moves up, while policies and directives are handed down.
The ASU, in an attempt to enhance its attractiveness and acceptance among the peasants, has sought to monopolize all symbols of
progress, reform, modernity, improvement and prosperity. One
symbol that has gained legitimacy in the eyes of the peasants is
government-sponsored activity that offers services and utilities. By
monopolizing the channels through which government services are
made available, the ASU has tried to enhance its own legitimacy.
Yet this kind of acceptance is negative rather than positive in its
implications for change or development. The villagers' commitment in this situation rests not upon some positive sense of personal
motivation in which the party's ideology galvanizes one into effort

or participation, but rather gravitates negatively to the ASU as a substitute structure for the traditional 'umdah, who had to be obeyed, placated, and propitiated if one's interests were to be protected or if one's dealing with the government were to be beneficial. Where before, a fellah would have turned to his 'umdah for advice or intercession, now he may turn to the ASU man, often with disastrous results for the efficiency and peace of mind of the local village administrators.

In an attempt to strengthen their image as the instrument through which change will be introduced, the governorate and district Executive Bureaus have, since the summer of 1966, played a most aggressive role in announcing, sponsoring, and implementing "reform projects."

The single-party organization in the United Arab Republic encourages political mass participation, but only within carefully controlled and prescribed limits. Perhaps participation is an inappropriate term, since the real goal of the ASU is not participation but mobilization. Thus the party leadership is more concerned with changing and developing new political attitudes and behavior in the population as a whole, and it uses the instrument of the party structure as the most effective mechanism to achieve these goals.

In order to contrast the responsibilities of the ASU with the duties and responsibilities of the administrative structure under the control of the provincial governor, I will examine the following categories of ASU activities in the rural areas: mass meetings and general conferences, programs of "political action," supply distribution, and complaint and arbitration.

Mass Meetings and General Conferences

One common ASU activity is the mass meeting and the general conference. Typical of these meetings and conferences was the Farmers' Cooperative Conference held in early September 1966. The opening sessions and ceremonies were attended by the ASU secretary-general, the ASU secretary for farmers' affairs, the ministers of agriculture and irrigation, as well as ministerial under-secretaries and the directors of the Cooperative Organization. The conference delegates included some 450 "fellahin" representing the governorate ASU executive offices, the Agricultural Development Committee of the National Assembly, agricultural cooperatives, and agricultural workers' trade unions in all the governorates.

These delegates were then divided into six subcommittees:
1. the cooperative organization committee
2. the agrarian reform committee
3. the economic and agricultural development committee
4. the committee for the development of rural communities
5. the agricultural workers and seasonal workers committee
6. the committee for rural information and political and cooperative education[45]

For twelve days these representatives were exposed to a series of lectures, rallies, committee meetings, and discussions. Although the main purpose was obviously to generate enthusiasm and popular support for the regime's rural programs and projects, a surprising amount of grass-roots criticism and complaint was allowed. Several village agronomists indicated to this writer that many changes and alterations in the cooperative organization were initiated as a direct result of the complaints and charges put forth at this Farmers' Conference. All the ASU secretaries within the General Secretariat periodically preside over conferences to discuss the problems within their scope of concern. Although complaints and comments are encouraged, the prime purpose of these meetings is to encourage acceptance and commitment to the government's new programs.

Political Action

The ASU, during recent years, has sought to recruit technical experts into the party hierarchy who will serve on ASU advisory committees. These committees may be called upon by the governorate *maktab tanfīdhī* (Executive Bureau) to provide the techni-

45 *Al-Ahram*, September 10, 1966, p. 3.

cal and scientific information needed to properly control, supervise, and evaluate administrative programs and policies within their areas. Each ASU Executive Bureau at the governorate and district level must submit quarterly reports indicating what steps have been taken to solve problems, increase production, and generate enthusiasm. Also this report must outline in detail proposed projects of "political action" to be implemented in the coming three months. As the socialist system gradually gains control of all segments of the economy, the local and provincial *maktab tanfīdhī* will concern itself with the entire economy of the area under its jurisdiction. Today there are few activities in the rural areas that are not of concern to the ASU, including price control, black-market activities, agricultural cooperatives, food distribution, irrigation projects, family planning, adult education, and youth sport programs. The eventual goal is to create specialized committees of party technicians at all levels of the governmental hierarchy to help examine and formulate the production plans and social services requirements that are to be submitted for approval by higher authorities. Since all village, town, and governorate councils now submitting budgetary requests and proposed production goals are already composed of a majority of ASU members, their economic and administrative functions are already largely controlled by the ASU.

One source of friction already noted in many villages is the conflict between a party man and the village administrators. The attempt on the part of the ASU man to establish deadlines for the implementation of ministerial programs, to inspect schools, clinics, and youth clubs, and even to evaluate the performance of these bureaucrats tends to create dissension, mistrust, and antagonism, especially since no clear delineation of power and authority has been made among the party, the council, and the bureaucrat.

One general program of "political action" announced by the ASU General Secretariat was entitled "The Unified Work Plan." During March and April 1967, leadership groups (*jamā'a qiyādīyah*) were to be established in all of the 4,000 major villages. These leadership groups were to be considered "village production councils." These councils were to be selected "from the fit elements of the *lajnat al-'ishrīn*, the Agricultural Laborer's Union Committee, the Agricultural Cooperative Council, from the suitable elements in the Socialist Youth Organization, active leaders among the fellahin who have participated in identifying feudalists, and various educated people in the village such as the *'imam*, the agronomist, the teacher, the doctor and the social worker."[46] The Executive Bureau in each governorate would nominate and select candidates for these leadership groups. The criteria for selection would include "a belief in socialism, faith in Islam, and Neutralism." Membership in this production council would not include members of the village *lajnat al-'ishrīn* or any other village organization unless "the person is a revolutionary and faithful to the Revolution, the Charter, and Socialism." Lastly he was to be required to be "cultured and know how to behave properly."[47]

The functions of these new leadership groups were to include activities "to increase agriculture production, to establish new social relations in the village, to counteract deviation and bureaucracy, to abolish illiteracy, to spread the new political culture, and to encourage greater savings and less consumption."[48]

The ASU secretary for farmers' affairs further defined the groups' general duties to include the supervision of all economic activities in their area, to control the distribution of material and supplies, to determine what crops are to be grown, what machinery would be needed, and proper distribution of irrigation water. They were to control all cooperative marketing in their village, encourage the peasants to repay their debts to loan banks, and spread the teachings of socialism. In order to fulfill this last requirement, members were to be encouraged to study and discuss the speeches of President Nasser and other printed material to be issued by the ASU central headquarters. The scope of these recommendations suggests the breadth of control envisioned by the ASU in future village programs.

[46] *al-Akhbar*, January 22, 1967, p. 6.
[47] Ibid.
[48] Ibid.

Supply Distribution

One source of power and influence that the ASU has sought to monopolize is the control and distribution of those items of supply presently being rationed. As more than one village administrator admitted, "He who controls the distribution of *maʿūna*, soap, kerosene, and other rationed foods and supplies in the village can control that village." The ASU leadership in the village, town, and governorate, as it seeks to control these supplies, often faces stiff opposition from the village doctor or the village social worker who insists on distributing these items in terms of need rather than for political expediency. On the other hand, I know of several examples where ASU representatives have been instrumental in discouraging village black-market activities by personally distributing rationed products as they were needed. The ASU sees this distribution responsibility as one significant way of gaining friends and supporters in the rural areas. Ironically, this very responsibility has resulted in more unfavorable publicity than probably any other program it controls.

Complaint and Arbitration

Although the *ʿumdah*s and family heads still maintain the role of final arbitrator in the vast majority of villages in Egypt, still the ASU is gradually taking over this responsibility. In the eyes of villagers, where the *ʿumdah* or family power has been removed, the ASU is gradually assuming the role of a court of last resort in the villages and districts. Thus the ASU committees of twenty and *markaz* Executive Bureaus are becoming a ready recipient of complaints or petitions from anyone who may feel that he has been wronged by an administrative agency or wish to call alleged mismanagement or corruption to the ASU's attention. From the evidence gathered, it appears that the ASU leadership treats such complaints and allegations quite seriously.

One of the most common causes of disputes and conflicts centers around landownership and tenant rights on land. Many of the Executive Bureaus in the Delta governorates have established committees to settle these disputes. These committees often include a judge selected by the Ministry of Justice, a public prosecutor, a member of the *markaz* Executive Bureau, a representative of the Ministry of Agriculture, and two members chosen by the governorate ASU organization from a *markaz*-level agricultural cooperative organization who represent the landowner and the tenants.[49]

The *markaz* Executive Bureau in many areas now requires all landlords to draw up their contracts in three copies: one for the landlord, one for the tenant, and one for the ASU. The newspapers *al-Akhbar* and *al-Ahram*, between September 1966 and March 1967, presented over a hundred articles describing peasants who had petitioned their local ASU organizations to settle disputes with their landowners.[50]

One issue that Egyptian leaders must face is to determine with sufficient preciseness how much control is desirable or fruitful. Egyptian leaders often seem obsessed with the need for controlling all activities and behavior within Egyptian society and to allow no autonomy whatsoever to groups or organizations. If the ASU is to be the vanguard of the people—directing, guiding, and controlling them—how much control is needed or desired? If the concept of ASU control is carried to its logical conclusion, there would be no need for any organization outside the ASU. Yet this was hardly the intention of Nasser and his compatriots. ASU officials,

[49] *al-Ahram*, November 1, 1966, p. 4.
[50] Several students at the American University in Cairo whose parents own from 50 to 100 acres pointed out that the fellahin in many areas had quickly learned that, by complaining to the ASU that their landlord was forcing them to pay rent twice, they could be released from paying rent at all. *Al-Akhbar*, March 16, 1967, ran a humorous article in which a local peasant complained to the governorate *maktab tanfīdhī* that the governorate director of agriculture had forced him to pay bakshish in order to obtain some needed fertilizer. The director of agriculture happened to be attending the meeting and asked the peasant if he could remember what the director of agriculture looked like. To this the peasant replied, "Yes sir, if I ever see him again I am sure I'll recognize him." When the director identified himself, the peasant feigned poor eyesight and quickly changed his story. While the ASU has sought to eradicate many of the abuses perpetrated against the illiterate fellahin, many of the peasants, exhibiting the *fahlawī* characteristic of trying to deceive or trick those in authority, sometimes see the ASU as an organization that they can use to exploit others.

nonetheless, do show persistent tendencies to extend their control over non-ASU institutions and agencies; the complaint from village doctors, agronomists, and village council chairmen against undue meddling and interference is equally perennial.

This close relationship between the bureaucracy and the ASU, however, gives rise to still another difficulty. It becomes almost impossible to fix responsibility for successes and failures. There is a tendency for the party and the administration to become so intertwined that credit or blame cannot be placed clearly on any agency involved in the business of carrying out the directives flowing from above.

One common result is for local party leaders and administrators to establish a "protective alliance" in which both agree to "scratch each other's back." This mutual protection agreement unfortunately breeds inefficiency, encourages traditional leadership patterns, and prevents the information necessary for efficient national planning from ever reaching those in positions responsible for that planning. Unfortunately, in villages where the ASU members and administrators are tightly controlled by family or feudal ties, there is usually a tendency to ignore laws and regulations, deceive higher authorities, and maintain the economic and political structure inherent in the traditional Egyptian village. This problem remains largely unresolved in a vast majority of the villages in Egypt.

7 ▣ Political Socialization and the ASU

▣▣ SINCE THE EGYPTIAN GOVERNMENT is committed to the
▣▣ creation of a whole new set of attitudes, values, and be-
▣▣ havioral norms, the ASU has been strengthened and reorganized to provide a mechanism for the initiation and maintenance
of these new patterns of political culture. This task of communicating the regime's ideological pronouncement is, as already noted,
primarily a process of political socialization, which is basic to the
establishment of legitimacy and commitment. By political socialization I mean the process of training the citizens for their roles in
the political system. It is the process of inculcating new attitudes,
desires, values, and cultural norms appropriate for the new social
system and political process inherent in the ideology advocated by
the regime. Of course, this process involves not only a continuous
effort to make the Egyptian citizen accept the structure of the
political system as legitimate, but also the attempt to make them
internalize the goals of the party and accept them as their own.
As a result of effective political socialization, the constituents
identify with the system so that their personal interests coincide
with the goals of the ruling elite. In short, the ASU has been organized to create a sense of identity and solidarity with the regime,

which will generate a high morale and esprit de corps among the citizenry.

We need not at this point go into details concerning the work of the provincial ASU organizations in the field of socialization and indoctrination. It must be noted, however, that the regime's control over mass media, the school system, and entertainment and other cultural activities is exercised in the same fashion as its control over administration, production, and personnel. Various secondary sources of political socialization include the public school system, governorate Higher Institutes of Socialist Studies, lectures, and seminars, as well as traveling plays and skits.

Nearly all the school headmasters interviewed denied that the secondary and primary schools were openly or directly teaching any political ideology to the village children. It was observed, however, that the children were undergoing a certain amount of political indoctrination. Usually when entering a classroom, the teacher would ask the students to stand. Rising to their feet they would shout "Nasser" or "freedom" or perhaps "independence," and when asked to sit down they again would shout, usually a word symbolizing some aspect of the regime's ideology. I made it a practice to question students as to their preference for future employment and the three most popular vocations mentioned were *thābit* (military officer), *muhandis* (engineer), and *mudarris* (schoolteacher), in that order. One inevitably sees posters on classroom walls—pictures of Nasser, short quotes from the National Charter, and often a map of Israel outlined in black with the words "Remember Palestine" written underneath. In most of the rural high schools, I noticed a bulletin board upon which many quotes from the Charter would be neatly printed in English. One English teacher proudly required several of his students to recite portions of Nasser's speeches.[1]

One memory I have of rural Egypt is waking in the morning to the loud singing of children in a nearby schoolyard, shouting praises to their "president and leader, Gamal Abdel Nasser." Their

[1] During 1966 and 1967, forty-seven different village school teachers were interviewed in both Lower and Upper Egypt.

rhythmic shout of "Nasser! Nasser! Nasser!" at the close of their song was a common sound from the broad stretches of the Delta to the narrow valley at Aswan.[2]

Although the Ministry of Education has traditionally been apolitical, greater emphasis on civic training has become a standard portion of all the grades. The degree of indoctrination varies considerably from school to school. It is my impression that most rural teachers have neither the interest nor the ability to embark on an effective program of indoctrination. The best organized programs were observed in those schools where the headmaster also happened to be the secretary of the ASU's "Committee of Twenty" in that village. This combination of two roles—the teacher and party leader—appeared to have a profound effect in the majority of cases where the village *lajnat al-'ishrīn* was functioning properly.

The ASU as a structure for political socialization, although potentially capable of involving large numbers of people in political action on a sustained and controlled basis, has probably been most effective among the youth. In fact, several ASU leaders in recent years have reiterated the fact that the youth of Egypt are the hope of its future.

Nasser, in the preface to a pamphlet describing the ASU's new youth organization, notes: "the main task we must put before our eyes in the next stage is to pave the road for a new generation which would lead the revolution in all its political, economic, and intellectual spheres. We can not say that our generation has done its duty unless we can be sure, before and after all the achievements, that progress would continue. Otherwise, all that we have accomplished would be liable to become, despite its brilliance, a mere beginning that progressed then stopped."[3]

In October 1965, the ASU formally established the Socialist

[2] One song that was often heard among the elementary students was:
> *Nasir kulina bi nihibak*
> (Nasser all of us love you)
> *Nasir wi-hanifdal gambak*
> (Nasser we will remain on your side)
> *Nasir, ya za'im al-kull, ya Nasir*
> (Nasser, leader of all, oh Nasser)

[3] United Arab Republic, *Socialist Youth Organization*, p. 3.

Youth Organization (SYO). During the preparatory stage, which ended in July 1966, over 100,000 young men and women from Basic Units in secondary schools, institutes, universities, factories, companies, and agricultural areas were given an intensive training course to teach this group of youth cadre the "history of our nation's struggle, to clarify for them historical and political facts. It has thereby sought to make them fully aware of the social, economic and political developments which have taken place since the Revolution of 1952."[4] These courses of political indoctrination were given to university students, workers, fellahin, village agronomists, doctors, and social workers. They were given to women, government employees, newspaper reporters, radio and TV workers, union leaders, and intellectuals. The courses are broken down into three stages. All lectures are given by university professors and "cultural labour experts." Those who distinguished themselves in the first course were encouraged to attend the second and third stage of "socialist instruction." In September 1966, Dr. Hussein Kamel Baha Eddin, ASU secretary for youth, announced that 250,000 young men and women would qualify for membership in SYO by July 1967. He noted that 50,000 had completed the first course, 5,500 had completed the second course, and over 2,000 had completed the three stages of "indoctrination."[5]

From all these exhortations, it is apparent that the Egyptian government is concerned with converting the youth to a new set of political values and behavioral patterns. In spite of all these training programs, indoctrination courses, and mass youth meetings, one wonders how effective such campaigns may be either in changing people's attitudes or their behavior. The following impressionistic description of a young Egyptian involved in the regime's program of political socialization is based on countless

[4] "ASU Programme for Youth—Pioneers of the Future," *Arab Observer*, February 14, 1966, p. 8.

[5] *al-Ahram*, September 22, 1966, p. 4. An announcement in early 1970 indicated that the SYO, with its new reorganization, now has 100,000 members: 10 percent are fellahin, 37 percent are workers, 38.5 percent are students, and 14.5 percent from other groups. See *al-Shabāb al-ʿArabī*, (Cairo), April 13, 1970, p. 3.

interviews, observations, and private discussions. While the principal character is fictitious, he is typical of hundreds of other young Egyptian villagers. In describing the effectiveness of these indoctrination programs in actually changing behavior or attitudes, one must distinguish between two extremes along a wide continuum. One extreme we shall call the "convert" and the other extreme is the familiar *fahlawi*."[6]

Our "convert," whom we shall call Ahmad, is a youth of nineteen. He is a member of the SYO and has been nominated by the local secretary of the village *lajnat al-'ishrīn* to attend the twelve-day indoctrination course at a nearby SYO Camp. His nomination is accepted by the governorate Executive Bureau, and early one Saturday morning he finds himself at the youth camp. The camp itself is rather isolated from public view, austere in appearance, yet neat and clean. The camp area is fitted with tents, a self-service cafeteria, an athletic field, and a space for study and lectures. Within these confines, Ahmad and two hundred other youths will live, work, and play together for twelve days. Their daily schedule will be rigorous, new friendships will be made, a sense of comradeship and pride will develop. For twelve days they will be an elite, a vanguard—students of history, politics, foreign policy, socialism, and rural development. New ideas will be thrown at them; their attitudes, assumptions, and beliefs will be challenged. They will be called on to voice their opinions; old ways and ideas will be ridiculed; and new concepts and explanations will be introduced and emphasized.

How much of this twelve-day training remains with the trainees is difficult to determine. All will leave this camp influenced to some degree, some will come away profoundly impressed, eager to embark upon a program of "political action." Many will leave with a sense of mission—but a mission easily forgotten as the overwhelming pressure of their villages' traditional life bears down upon them.

During the first day the new trainees are divided into groups

6 See chapter 3.

of between thirty and forty individuals. Each group will be required to elect a "rapporteur" who, with the other group leaders or "rapporteurs," will constitute the camp's executive committee—a committee responsible for the management, discipline, and administration of the camp's activities. In order to develop and train the participants in the working of "sound democracy and organizational collective leadership," each group elects representatives to various camp "action committees"—sports, entertainment, health and services, voluntary work, camp work details, and social activities. Their daily schedule adheres closely to the following outline:[7]

6:00 A.M. to 7:00 A.M.—reveille and preparation for the day
7:00 to 8:00 —work details, camp cleanup
8:15 to 9:00 —breakfast
9:15 to 9:30 —flag ceremony
9:30 to 1:00 P.M.—lectures and private study
2:00 P.M. to 6:00 P.M.—lunch, rest period, sports, social and cultural activities
6:00 to 10:00 —group discussions on the morning's lectures
10:00 to midnight —dinner and entertainment

This training program is centered around a series of lectures presented to stimulate "an intellectual unity based on commitment to the Revolutionary theory, philosophy, and plan of action as laid down in the Charter."[8] The instructors present lectures on different aspects of the Charter, providing both a historical and a theoretical basis for comprehending it.

The course of study includes the following lectures:

First day: general introduction and welcome
Second day: lecture on the inevitability of the Revolution
Third day: examination of the first four chapters of the Charter
  Chapter 1: general view
  Chapter 2: the necessity of the Revolution
  Chapter 3: the roots of the Egyptian struggle
  Chapter 4: the moral of the setback
Fourth day: lecture on the inevitability of the socialist solution

[7] United Arab Republic, *Socialist Youth Organization*, pp. 23–24.
[8] Ibid., p. 28.

Fifth day: examination of chapters 6, 7, and 8 of the Charter
    Chapter 6: on the inevitability of the socialist solution
    Chapter 7: production and society
    Chapter 8: the socialist application and its problems
Sixth day: lecture on democracy and popular organization
    1. Islamic Rules for Praising the Individual and Building up Society
    2. Examination of Chapter 5 of the Charter (True Democracy)
Eighth day: foreign policy
Ninth day: the Palestine problem
Tenth day: 1. examination of chapters 9 and 10 of the Charter (Arab Unity and Foreign Policy)
    2. lecture on political action and organization
Eleventh day: general debate and evaluation
Twelfth day: graduation

Of course these youth camps do not deal exclusively with lectures and study. Great emphasis is placed on morning calisthenics, and each group is organized into teams for football, basketball, volleyball, and table tennis. Competition between groups is encouraged and some time is allotted each day for these teams to compete in one or more sports.

Each camp also has an internal radio network that presents world and local news, press commentaries, extracts from the Koran and the National Charter, and past speeches made on various occasions by President Nasser. Within each group, members prepare their own wall newspaper to which the trainees are encouraged to contribute in the form of news items, comments, photographs, and drawings. Each camp is provided with a television set and a library. One such library I visited was surprisingly complete, with over two hundred books, both in Arabic and Western languages. While the majority of these books were on "socialism," "imperialism," and Egyptian history and society, several American textbooks on politics, economics, and sociology were noted.

One important aspect of their training deals primarily with rural development projects. One hour each day is set aside to study various techniques of voluntary work—methods for conducting a survey on the problems in a village, gauging public opinion, and stimulating villagers to solve their own problems. Instruction is given on village sanitation, building construction, how to organize a literacy campaign, how to pave roads, how to put up poles for electricity, or how to build a sports field.

Upon completion of the course, Ahmad is fired with enthusiasm and desire to return to his village to engage in "political action." During the graduation exercises, one of the high officials in the ASU hierarchy speaks to them with great emotion on the glories of the Revolution. No doubt the words heard were not very different from the speech given by Dr. Hussein Kamal Baha Eddin, ASU secretary for youth, on September 21, 1966.

> The Socialist Youth Organization, by virtue of its participation in solving the problems of the masses, has managed to gain their confidence. Its members have effectively provided solutions for many problems such as draining swamps, building roads and fighting the cotton worm. The saving of the cotton crop this year [1966] can largely be attributed to their incessant efforts. . . . They took part in sanitation projects in the towns of their Governorates, participated in combatting illiteracy, extinguishing fires and rebuilding such villages as Derein Makahlia, which was almost completely destroyed by fire. They helped the police to seize large amounts of fish, which some fishermen had tried to smuggle to other Governorates.[9]

With these words ringing in his ears—"you too can be a leader, a revolutionary, an activist"—Ahmad becomes a "convert."

Visiting the rural areas of Egypt, the agricultural cooperatives, schools, village councils, clinics, and social centers, one meets many young men like Ahmad. These young idealists are proud of their country, proud of their new cooperative buildings, eager to show you through the village health clinic and to explain how the High Dam will issue in a new age. Interestingly enough, some of these young men are very polite and appear obsessed with the desire to please you, to tell you what they think you want to hear; others are belligerent, even hostile, asking pointed questions about U.S. support of Israel, U.S. policy in Vietnam, and U.S. unwillingness to supply Egypt with wheat.

[9] *The Egyptian Gazette*, September 22, 1966, p. 2.

Although the polite youth is much more common than the belligerent one, both types appear committed to the regime. They have found an emotional identity that is perceived as right and therefore satisfying. Eric Erikson, a prominent psychologist, provides some extremely interesting insights into the reasons why some individuals are especially receptive to ideology. Erikson argues that an individual's personality is the culmination of a process he designates as "the search for identity." This "identity crisis" often occurs among youth in that period of life when they must forge for themselves a personal identity and a sense of purpose. This search for identity is not limited to youth. Many individuals in a transitional society are torn between traditional and modern cultural values. These people seeking a role or cultural identity are especially vulnerable to ideologies. Erikson notes that "some young individuals will succumb to this crisis in all manner of neurotic, psychotic, or delinquent behavior; others will resolve it through participation in ideological movements, passionately concerned with religion or politics, nature or art."[10]

Young Egyptians are torn between the old ways of their parents and the new ways of their leaders. Their search for a new identity is "at the most . . . a militant system with uninformed members and uniformed goals; at the least, it is a "way of life" or what Germans call a *Weltanschauung*, a world-view which is consonant with existing theory, available knowledge, and common sense, and yet is significantly more; an utopian outlook, a cosmic mood, or a doctrinal logic, all shared as self-evident beyond any need for demonstration."[11]

Thus, the youth of Egypt, like those in many other transitional societies, face the double perplexity of identifying one's role and one's cultural values. Standing between tradition and modernity, between adolescence and maturity, the ideology of Arab Socialism offers to many young Egyptians a very simple yet logically integrated set of assumptions about this world and the role they must play in it. The attractiveness of Arab Socialism for youth who

[10] Eric H. Erikson, *Young Man Luther*, p. 14.
[11] Ibid., p. 41.

stand between the past and the future, both in individual life and in society, resides in its ability to provide an authoritative ideal that satisfies an inner anxiety evolving from this personal identity dilemma.

Yet how effective is this program of youth indoctrination? True, psychologists tell us that youth are especially susceptible to the charms of ideology. The Socialist Youth Organization recruits many of the rural youth at a critical state in their maturation when their doubts and frustrations cry out for integrity and completeness. Yet, does a twelve-day course of study really change attitudes or behavior? Students of the Chinese system of thought reconstruction have outlined the necessary elements for its success: "removal from family and community and isolation from the outer-world; restriction of sensory intake and immense magnification of the power of the spoken word; lack of privacy and radical accent on the brotherhood; and, of course, joint devotion to the leaders who created and represent the brotherhood."[12]

Effective indoctrination demands that the individual be separated from his family, friends, and former associates long enough for his former values, norms, and behavioral patterns to be weakened and then dislodged from the structure of his personality. This process must develop within the individual a new set of beliefs and behavioral patterns to replace his earlier experiences and training. This indoctrination program must be almost "a kind of shock treatment, for it is expected to replace in a short time what has grown over many formative years."[13] The net result of this process must be a "new individual" with beliefs and convictions so strongly anchored in his value structure that he firmly identifies these new "truths" with the "inevitable wheel of history." However, the ASU, at least for the present, is not committed to the extreme form of indoctrination described above and this may well be one major source of ASU ineffectiveness among many

[12] Robert Lifton, "Thought Reform of Chinese Intellectuals: A Psychiatric Evaluation," *Journal of Asian Studies* 16 (November 1956): 1; quoted in Eric H. Erikson, *Young Man Luther*, p. 134.
[13] Eric H. Erikson, *Young Man Luther*, p. 134.

graduates of these twelve-day training programs. Interviews and observations show that very few of these graduates maintain their sense of mission beyond the first two or three months after gradution.

The Egyptian press is replete with examples of this "new Egyptian youth," enthusiastic for work, motivated for reform, and guided by "true organizational precepts." In one month (February 1967) I counted ninety-seven items in the Cairo press describing the activities of recent SYO graduates: paving roads, filling in swamps, starting a literary program, building a youth clubhouse, stimulating their elders to introduce electricity, cleaning out canals, and spreading the teachings of Arab Socialism. As Erikson points out: "Ideologies serve to channel youth's forceful earnestness and sincere asceticism, as well as its search for excitement and its eager indignation, toward that social frontier where the struggle between conservatism and radicalism is most alive. On that frontier, fanatic ideologists do their busy work and psychopathic leaders their dirty work; but there, also, true leaders create significant solidarities."[14]

Examples of this new enthusiasm and energy among the youth are easy to find in the press. Typical of these new graduates from SYO camps is Mahmud Fawzi, a youth of seventeen from the village of Sabtas in the governorate of Gharbia.[15] The news article described how Mahmud "filled with enthusiasm and desire to apply his newly acquired skills," went to the secretary of his village *lajnat al-'ishrīn* and asked him to call a special meeting of the ASU Basic Unit for the purpose of discussing the possibility of starting a class to abolish illiteracy among some of the youth and adults. The secretary readily agreed, but when the meeting was to have started, Mahmud was surprised to note that only two of his close friends were present—even the ASU secretary did not come. Undaunted, the young man made a special visit to the governorate ASU secretary, explained the situation, and requested guidance. The governorate secretary acknowledged the young

[14] Ibid., p. 42.
[15] *al-Akhbar*, November 4, 1966, p. 6.

man's problem and suggested that the older members of his village would be stimulated to action only if he pointed out their problems and then found a solution.

The following week Mahmud noted that many villagers were complaining that the director of the Agricultural Cooperative and his clerk were cheating the villagers—demanding bakshish for services that legally should have been free. Mahmud wrote up a detailed report to the Executive Bureau of the ASU, which promptly sent out an investigation committee to question the director and other personnel in the cooperative.

On the following Friday, Mahmud gained permission to speak at the local mosque, where he tried to explain that illiteracy was the major cause of their exploitation and abuse. Several village officials and some university students, home for the summer, agreed to help in teaching the villagers. When Mahmud had difficulty finding adequate classroom space, he went to the director of education in Gharbia and gained permission to open a three-room school. "Within a two-month period they were able to teach over ninety villagers."[16]

While articles of this type were very common in the press prior to the June war of 1967, one wonders whether all this activity among the youth has any long-range implications for change and reform in the villages of Egypt. Even this story of Mahmud, if one reads between the lines, suggests some serious obstacles to any youth-initiated village reform. One group of youth interviewed by Dr. Abas Qasaiba were very hostile toward their elders. When asked why they hadn't organized their own club instead of roaming the streets, they complained bitterly of complete apathy on the part of the village leaders: "They told several stories of corruption and bakshish even among members of the ASU *lajnat al-'ishrin*, of the robbery and theft perpetrated by the cooperative officials, and the strict control that the 'responsibles' [a wealthy family in the village] impose on the village, monopo-

16 Ibid.

lizing all the positions and forbidding any interference from anyone—especially the youth, whom they treat and think of as
children and therefore unfit for participation."[17]

The regime's present campaign to integrate village youth into
the ASU faces many problems. The general apathy of the village
elders toward their youth, the general control of some villages
by certain landowning elements who are opposed to any change,
and a shortage of financial and administrative support necessary
for a sustained program of village development and reform—all
combine to weaken the ASU.

The kind of family control present in many villages is best
suggested by the number of government posts occupied by the
Sawaylim family in one village in Dakahlia:

1. Administrative positions: *'umdah*, assistant *'umdah*, four
   shaykhs, the *shaykh al-ghafar* and his assistant
2. ASU positions: the secretary of the *lajnat al-'ishrīn*, his
   assistant, and eighteen of the members of the "Committee
   of Twenty"
3. Village Council: the chairman, the secretary, and ten of the
   twelve members of the council
4. Agricultural Cooperative: the director, the clerk, and one
   of five members on the Cooperative Board.

When families monopolize a village in this manner, even the
most dedicated graduate of an SYO camp would soon become discouraged. The evaluation teams mentioned above also noted that
in every single village they had visited, the vast majority of the
villagers thought the *'umdah* and the big landowning families
were most powerful in the village. Less than 15 percent of those
questioned felt that the ASU *lajnat al-'ishrīn* had any influence
in the village.[18] Although these conclusions were reached in late
1965, and the ASU has had several years to reorganize, it is my

---

[17] *al-Ṭalī'ah*, September 1966, p. 24.
[18] Lufti Muḥammad Hasan, "al-'Alāqāt al-'ijtimā'īyah fī qaryah Abishna"
[Social Relations in the Village of Abishna], *al-Ṭalī'ah*, September 1966, pp.
39–44.

opinion that the ASU, even today, would hold a poor third place behind the traditional leadership positions and family influence in the vast majority of villages.

It should be noted that since the summer of 1966, the Committee for the Liquidation of Feudalism has attempted to remove, by sequestration, many of the larger landowners (owning between fifty and a hundred feddans) from villages and to require their relatives to resign all village positions. In June 1966, for example, 230 'umdahs and shaykhs were removed from all economic, political, and administrative posts in some seventeen governorates. There is little doubt that these changes will have a profound impact on leadership patterns in Egyptian villages.[19] Whether these changes will stimulate and support an effective ASU program of socialization is difficult to say. As one village doctor remarked rather cynically to the author, "sequestration merely takes power away from those who own over fifty acres and gives it to those with over twenty-five acres. This will not change village life very much."

Nasser's regime was plagued with the difficult problem of establishing a new set of symbols for, and a new foundation upon which a sense of legitimacy and commitment may rest. The fellahin's proclivity toward accepting the traditional leadership patterns in their villages must be dissipated if a new political culture is to be introduced. I have suggested that the peasants' susceptibility to change is primarily predicated upon their perceptions of what village leaders are doing and what they ought to be doing. Change in the Egyptian villages will be largely a function of the gap between these two images. To the extent they are interpreted to be incongruous, the villagers' propensity for change should increase. Nasser's charisma has legitimized a whole new set of ideals that directly challenge the old patterns of dominance and control wielded by the large landowning families. Nasser's dreams and aspirations have motivated many of the fellahin. We have seen some of the problems the ASU must face

[19] *Arab Observer*, September 12, 1966, pp. 10–11.

as it seeks to inculcate the fellahin with a new set of cultural values. The basis of their commitment is primarily emotional and subjective in orientation. Few would argue that this kind of commitment can be functional for the establishment of a stable society or provide the sense of legitimacy the new regime requires.

We must now analyze the second major structure by which Nasser hoped to introduce the new values, norms, and behavioral patterns necessary for modernization—his "new bureaucracy." It is here postulated that Nasser's charisma will be "routinized" largely to the extent that the government officials operating in the village can legitimize their own position. This requires institutions and structures that have inherited the mantle of legitimacy. This process, in the immediate future, may be derived from an ideology, yet a long-term commitment requires efficient and effective governmental machinery capable of satisfying the needs and achieving the goals desired by the nation's citizenry.

8 Structure and Functions of the Combined Units and Village Councils

A SYSTEM OF LOCAL COUNCILS was first introduced into Egypt in July 1798 during the French conquest, when Napoleon decreed that each of Egypt's fourteen provinces (*mudirīyah*) was to have a "bureau" of seven members whose duty was to look after the interests of security and administration.

Under the British rule in 1883, elective provincial councils were again established. Their functions were limited to listening and "consulting." Between 1893 and 1917 some twenty to thirty town councils were created. Primarily because of a lack of funds their functions were also limited. They were prohibited from imposing a local tax, and their resources were confined to a paltry sum granted by the Central Treasury. With their restricted funds and powers, these councils' functions were limited to garbage collection, street cleaning, enforcing sanitation and building laws, and ensuring a gas and water supply. Even in these small functions, they were required to seek final approval from the central authorities prior to their acting as a council.[1]

[1] Jacob M. Landau, *Parliaments and Parties in Egypt*, chapter V.

Starting in 1910, the British sought to establish local councils in various villages that had a police station. The chief of police in the village acted as chairman of the council. These village councils had even fewer financial resources and administrative functions than the town councils. Dr. El-Araby, a leading scholar on local administration in Egypt, declared that village councils were foreign to village life and were never really understood nor accepted. "The chief of the Police Station acted as chairman of the Council. The bureaucratic attitude of the chair dampened the interest of the villagers, and this was aggravated by the scanty value they obtained and the financial burdens they had to shoulder. The result was that the villagers always loudly protested against any attempt to create a Council in their village. Only seventy villages (by 1952) had such Councils out of more than 4000."[2]

The constitution of 1923 outlined the general framework for a new system of local administration. Egypt was divided into local administrative units—provinces, towns, and villages. Article 133 declares that all provincial and municipal councils will function in terms of the following principles:

1. Councils should be elected.
2. Councils should formulate and execute local policies subject to prior sanction of higher authorities.
3. Budgets and final accounts should be published.
4. Sessions should be open to the public.

[2] Mohamed Abdullah El-Araby, *An Outline of Local Government in the United Arab Republic*, p. 7. Nearly all research on Egyptian local government that I have seen tends merely to describe the law of local administration and how the system will function in the future or how the system is supposed to function. For examples of this approach, see Muḥammad 'Abd Allāh al-'Arabī, *Nizam al-'idārah al-mahallīyah: falsafatuha wa 'ahkamuha* [The System of Local Administration: Its Philosophy and Procedures]; Harold F. Alderfer, M. Fathalla al-Khatib, and Moustafa Ahmed Fahmy, *Local Government in the United Arab Republic 1964*; Mohamed Gamal el-Din Nassouhy, "Local Autonomy under National Planning: The Egyptian Experience"; and Mohamed Ali el-Shinnawy, "Community Development and Local Government in the Developing Nations: The United Arab Republic, India, and Pakistan." Unfortunately, none of these studies attempt to analyze how, in fact, the local administration system is functioning. It is to this question that I have focused my attention.

5. Legislative and executive authorities of the National Government could veto council decisions and actions if they would endanger the public welfare of the Nation.[3]

During the 1930's and the 1940's, a number of legislative decrees were enacted further clarifying the duties, functions, financial resources, methods of election, and relationship of the local administrative units to the central government.[4] During the nineteenth and first half of the twentieth century, the local administrative units of most countries served merely as agencies of the central government. Although this pattern of local organization was systematized in France under Napoleon, it gradually spread over most of Asia, Africa, and South America. W. H. Wickar even suggests that "one reason for introducing this administrative pattern was, in fact, an effort to put an end to semi-autonomous provincial governors and substitute for them salaried agents of the central authorities. Another reason was that the creation of regular armies . . . removed the need for a feudal system under which land was held in return for the performance of military and administrative duties."[5]

Since World War II most of the developing nations have declared their intentions to seek two major goals. First was the need to build up a strong central government to form the foundation for economic development, modernization, and, in some cases, national unity (integration). The second proclaimed goal was the development of popularly elected bodies to manage local affairs, not only in the interests of political democracy, but also in order to obtain administrative efficiency. This second goal, unfortunately, has been either postponed or ignored as these nations find themselves in a "vicious circle."

In the first place, these new governments were hesitant to dele-

[3] H. F. Alderfer et al., *Local Government in the United Arab Republic 1964*, p. 3.

[4] For a detailed description of the Local Administrative Law No. 34 of 1934 and Law No. 145 of 1944, see Mohamed Gamal el-Din Nassouhy, "Local Autonomy under National Planning: The Egyptian Experience."

[5] W. Hardy Wickwar, "Notes on Local Government Administrative Areas and Local Government Units in the Middle East," *Revue internationale des sciences* 24 (1958): 148.

gate autonomy to local units because they feared that the local leaders did not have the skill and the experience to implement the policies and reforms necessary for national development. At the same time, these local leaders did lack the necessary administrative and political skills because they had previously been confined to a very narrow area of activity. But perhaps even more crucial for the deprecation of the avowed second goal of decentralization and democratization were the ever expanding forces for centralization. It was widely argued that only a centralized government could deal effectively with social, economic, and political problems facing the nation.

A further centralizing force has been the shortage of government administrators and experts skilled in the newer techniques and problems of government. These officials tend to work for the central government and generally feel that local government officials require close supervision. The effort to satisfy mass expectations and to control the influences of mass communication has also intensified this centralizing tendency. But these centralizing forces have not all been blessings. Modern systems of transportation and communication have brought all parts of the world so much closer together that even the most isolated communities have discovered that a better life prevails in the more favored areas of the world. Improperly clothed, poorly housed, undernourished, diseased, and illiterate, these people in the rural areas and the urban slums are becoming increasingly restless. Faced with the demands for reform and a better standard of living, caught in the cross fire of rural poverty and extreme urbanization, many new nations have sought relief through a planned program of decentralization and community development in an attempt to help the rural areas become more attractive places in which to live.

Dr. V. K. Menon, director of the Indian Institute of Public Administration in New Delhi, argues that the relationship between the local and central governments in new nations is one of increasing interdependence. Among the new leaders is an "increasing recognition of the importance of local government and a growing belief that no central government can supply all the services needed by the people at the local level."[6] While central governments often must perform local services because of a lack of resources at the local level "it is now being more fully recognized that human resources at the local level are also important, for ultimately they determine how effectively the centrally supplied resources will be used; it is generally recognized that effectiveness increases with the development of local self-governing institutions."[7]

Meeting the ever-increasing demands of the masses, which involves raising the economic, health, and education standards of these people, is not an easy matter. The task becomes especially difficult when undertaken among those whose society has been more or less static for hundreds of years. Traditional ways, especially among rural peoples, cannot be changed in a day. The Egyptian experience is a vivid example of this problem. How does one develop understanding, loyalty, sympathy, and a desire to cooperate between the vast majority of illiterate fellahin and their central government? What compromises must be made, what institutions would best be conducive to community development?

In late 1960 a complete new system of local government was introduced in the United Arab Republic. Dr. al-Sayyid Mahmoud Zaki of the Ministry of Local Government has declared:

1. In view of the needs of the rapidly increasing population, the provision of various services to local communities has become beyond the capacity of the Central Government. Local communities can deal better with their own problems, introduce suitable measures and secure the full participation of the people.

2. Projects executed by the Central Government are usually of a prototype nature. Projects corresponding to the varied needs of local communities could best be developed by local authorities.

---

[6] International Union of Local Authorities, *Local Government in the Twentieth Century*, no. 76, p. 113.
[7] Ibid.

3. The participation of the people in the development of their communities can be well achieved through local administration. They become more cooperative and more receptive to new ideas when they take an active part in the betterment of their communities.

4. Rendering local services through elected councils is an effective way of training the people in practicing real democracy. Efficient local councils can play an important role in the welfare of the community they serve as well as in the development of the country at large.

5. Local administration ensures a fairer and better distribution of financial resources.[8]

From these conclusions enumerated by Dr. Zaki, one could argue strongly that the Egyptian government is committed to a program of decentralization. This vocal commitment is a sharp departure from a form of government that has prevailed in Egyptian history for over three thousand years. However, an announcement of a policy is not the same as its implementation.

I shall now attempt a critical appraisal of the progress made by the Egyptian government in its program of decentralization. As has been suggested, the Egyptian government, in seeking the effective support and acceptance of its citizenry, must legitimize its programs and policies in the rural areas. The key individual in this process is the local administrator. Upon his shoulders rests the impressive task of gaining the confidence and loyalty of the rural masses.

The Egyptian government's plan reveals emphasis on certain methods of promoting local autonomy and rural development. First, there is an emphasis on strengthening the "democratic process" of problem solving through the development of local village, town, and governorate councils. These councils are by law to be the responsible local organizations for planning and promoting self-help projects. They are also the coordinating vehicle

---

[8] A. M. Zaki, *An Outline of the Local Government System in the United Arab Republic,* pp. 5–6.

for integrating the services of government with the efforts of the rural citizens.

Second, there is an emphasis on the aided self-help method of obtaining rural improvement—the local people furnish the labor, and the government supplements their efforts with equipment and material. This self-help method implies that the local fellahin should act in their own self-interest rather than depend solely on the government.

Third, there is the emphasis on the economic and social problems of the whole community rather than on those of select individuals or institutions. This approach would require that project priorities be determined at the local level instead of in Cairo, that government agents be sensitive to the needs and wishes of the local population, and that government specialists coordinate their activities sufficiently to serve the whole community.

The Egyptian programs emphasize the local unit of government —the village, town, and governorate—as the major vehicle for implementing a wide-ranging program of community development. This development plan takes into consideration the numerous governmental agencies with established programs and seeks to coordinate their activities in the way best suited to ensure a balanced development program. This new approach to local government is highly commendable.

Theoretically, this local administration system will simultaneously reform the poverty conditions of rural areas, foster "democratic" participation in the towns and villages of Egypt, discourage migration to cities, encourage savings (important both as a virtue and as the necessary condition for any significant industrialization), and generate within local political units an esprit de corps based upon the people's pride in cooperative accomplishments and upon their confidence in their capacity for self-help.

Students of cultural change universally recognize the usual disparity between intentions and consequences when a dominant group seeks to introduce innovation. All aspects of a culture are interrelated, and a change in any part of it has repercussions

throughout the rest. Even in a situation where change and innovation appear to have been accepted, one can be sure that what
has seemingly been transferred has actually become something
different in the process.

The rural development programs envisioned by the Egyptian
government are neither longed for by the vast majority of its
supposed beneficiaries, nor, at least under the Nasser regime, did
the Egyptian government forcefully impose these cultural and
structural innovations. Furthermore, these programs require
changes of immense scope—changes in values, in institutional
forms, and in economic techniques. Changes in rural Egypt are
occurring as we have already noted, but there is still a great
difference between changes resulting from disintegration and
changes that depend upon planned reorganization along prede-
termined lines. It has been suggested by many Egyptian officials
that this latter type of guided change may occur within the ideological framework of Arab Socialism, but it is painfully obvious
that the mere existence of an acceptable ideological framework
is no guarantee that such results will be forthcoming.

While the programs and projects advocated by the Egyptian
government are very commendable, still one should not forget the
serious problem that rural officials must face as they seek to transform the traditional values and moral presuppositions of rural
Egypt. Furthermore, those who are responsible for long-range
planning in rural Egypt must consider the possible contradictions
in their programs and policies, which, even if they could be effectively administered, might still fail to realize the goals projected.
The myth of spontaneous or government initiated rural development needs to be seen for what it is.

The Egyptian government publications often visualize the
"new rural Egypt" as an idyllic, sanitary, and progressive countryside, where the masses of fellahin, by their industry, are able
to solve simultaneously their own economic problems and those
of the nation. The habit of mutual cooperation would develop
within the fellahin an unselfishness and sense of the "common
good." In this ideal world, there would be no need for a peasant

to yield to any feelings of self-interest or a desire for improving his own position. His first concern must be for the common good, to a nebulous goal that abhors the practical questions of "who gets what, when, and how?"

This critical introduction to the Egyptian approach to rural development must not be interpreted as a vilification of the "Egyptian experiment" or as a suggestion that Egypt must remain stagnate and underdeveloped. To the contrary, the questions here raised must be considered if development is to be achieved. If Nasser's charisma is to be routinized, if his mystical power to motivate and generate enthusiasm among the masses is to be harnessed and utilized for economic, political, and social development, then serious concern must be directed to the system of local administration, which includes an interrelationship between the fellahin, the ASU local leadership, and the rural administrators. The structures and institutions created by Nasser's regime may well develop legitimacy in the eyes of the peasant— the actualization of this hope rests not only upon the attitude and behavior of the present regime's party workers and local bureaucrats, but even more important, upon the peasants' perception and understanding of the purposes of these structures and institutions.

The two major structures being introduced into the villages for rural development are the combined units and the village councils. The probability of the fellahin shifting their loyalties and symbols of legitimacy to those governmental structures rests upon the ability of these structures to reflect and utilize the psychological needs and economic aspirations of the fellahin.

Combined Units

In early 1953, the new revolutionary regime announced its commitment to a general program of rural reform and development. Finally, on October 17, 1953, a Permanent Council for Public Welfare Services was established. In 1954 Nasser named one of his leading administrators, Abdul Latif Baghdadi, former minister of war, as the new minister of municipal and rural affairs. By the middle of 1955 the Permanent Council for Public Welfare Services issued the results of their study. The recommendations were summarized as follows:

1. Those ministries entrusted with national services should follow the system of administrative decentralization so that there should be set up in the capital of each province or district an administration whose head supervises the work of the ministry and its staff in the district concerned and is vested with the authority of head of administration.

2. There should be set up in each province or district a coordinating council—a social services district council—in which the heads of regional districts and representatives of the citizens participate. Its competence lies in the proposal of services programmes and the supervision of their execution and coordination in the district. Thus we advance a step forward towards local government. When provincial councils are formed, they will have to shoulder that responsibility.[9]

The committee thus concluded that these recommendations would be realized primarily by stimulating local government, by the adoption of a system of decentralization, and by the close cooperation of central and local administrative units. The early pronouncements of Nasser's regime are replete with sanguine prognostications concerning rural development and the eventual establishment of local government structures. The major emphasis focused upon a team project for rural development that was to be known as a Combined Unit.[10] Each of these units, designed to serve communities of fifteen thousand, was to include:

1. A complete Health-Centre containing 10 beds for internal patients, an operating room, an outpatient's section, one for general diagnosis, one for indigenous diseases, a child-welfare centre, a

[9] The Republic of Egypt, *The Permanent Council for Public Welfare Services*, pp. 32–33.

[10] For information on the prerevolutionary government's attempts at rural development, see Mohammed Shalaby, *Rural Reconstruction in Egypt*; Beatrice Mattison, "Rural Social Centres in Egypt," *Middle East Journal* 4 (Autumn 1951); and Ahmed Hussein, *Rural Social Welfare Centers in Egypt*.

centre for expectant mothers, a dispensary and two waiting
rooms, one for men and the other for women.

2. A social service-centre comprising an assembly-hall to seat 150
persons, a library, a museum for health and agricultural extension, as well as a room for the social expert.

3. A school containing 12 class-rooms, a headmaster's room and a
teachers' room.

4. A nursery for 100 children.

5. Five villas, each consisting of 4 rooms, for married officials.

6. Dwellings for 24 bachelor officials.[11]

In 1954 each *markaz* (district) within each *muḥāfaẓah* (governorate) was divided into administrative units comprising approximately fifteen thousand inhabitants. With a rural population
of nearly thirteen million people, some 868 areas were created.
In each area, one village was to be selected for the establishment
of a combined unit. In selecting the sites for these centers the following considerations were taken into account: (1) the net of
roads and communications that render the combined unit accessible; (2) the population of the selected village as compared with
other villages; (3) the central position of the village; (4) the
supply of potable water; (5) fairness in distributing combined
units among the population; and (6) local conditions and existing
services.[12] According to the rather optimistic estimates of the
Permanent Council in 1955, not only were all 868 combined units
to be completed by 1960, but also the facilities were to be constructed for less than 50 percent of the construction costs estimated prior to the revolution.

The Council was able to bring down the essential cost to an in-
credible minimum. Credits for the construction of hospitals amounting
to £.E. 350,000 have been reduced to a third. . . . It was possible to
bring down the cost per bed from £.E. 1,300 to £.E. 300. . . . This was
indeed a miracle, a miracle in construction and planning. Whereas
each Health Unit alone used to cost at one time £.E. 55,000 the combined unit will cost in the accepted tender about £.E. 22,880 in villages in Lower Egypt, and about £.E. 31,700 in Aswan. . . . In this

[11] The Republic of Egypt, *The Permanent Council for Public Welfare Services,* p. 96.
[12] Ibid., p. 100.

way the dreams of reformers have been realized. As a result . . . the total sum needed for building 868 units in the whole country will not exceed £.E. 22,000,000.[13]

This new program was started with great fanfare and optimism. On July 13, 1955, President Nasser inaugurated the first combined unit in the village of Barnasht in the Giza Province, with these words: "Today, after we have started launching forth our social revolution, we say that our march is speedily progressing forward. We summon all our citizens to work and toil; the farmer in his land and the labourer in his factory so that we can maintain our social revolution which will improve our conditions. This is our true revolution."[14]

The government announced in 1955 that over two hundred units were being built throughout the provinces and that they would be completed by October 1955. Based upon past progress, the government announced that "within 5 years all the 868 combined units needed for the whole country will be completed."[15]

Within three years these earlier estimates were abandoned completely. In May 1958 only 210 of these combined units were reported to be in full operation,[16] and even as late as 1960 their number had reached only 250. The first five-year plan indicated that 350 units would be in operation by 1966, and that by 1970 over 500 combined units would be functioning. By the spring of 1967, I could only verify that 301 combined units had been constructed.[17] The major reasons offered for the inability of the government to fulfill its earlier plans concerning these combined units center around lack of funds and lack of qualified personnel.

[13] Ibid., p. 13.

[14] United Arabic Republic, *The Combined Units*, p. 1.

[15] The Republic of Egypt, *The Permanent Council for Public Welfare Services*, p. 100.

[16] Keith Wheelock, *Nasser's New Egypt*, p. 119.

[17] This figure was substantiated by cross-checking the number of combined units claimed by each governorate as listed in the *Government's Statistical Handbook* with governorate officials. I would ask them to indicate on the map where each unit was located in their governorate. Then an effort was made to visit as many of these units as possible. In this way, 301 combined units were located. See appendix F.

Keith Wheeler has described the inconsistency noted among government cost estimates for these units: "The cost of the 250 Combined Units has been obscured by a welter of conflicting figures . . . (between £.E. 10-16 million). Even assuming the figure of 13 million pounds to be correct, this would mean a per unit cost almost double that estimated in 1954."[18]

In 1965 Kamal Mahmud al-Husni, general director of planning in the Ministry of Social Affairs, admitted that, while the first five-year plan included a proposal for the construction of 253 rural social units, 196 health units, and 100 new combined units, "it was possible to secure the funds for only eighty-five rural social units, only twenty-one health units and only eighty combined units throughout the years of the plan."[19] Yet lack of funds is not the only problem nor even the most crucial problem of the government's attempt to introduce a new institution for rural development. Most commentaries on the rural development programs are seldom critical or evaluative in their descriptive analysis and usually accept at face value the government's optimistic reports on these rural programs.

Patrick O'Brien concludes a brief paragraph on these combined units with the words, "apparently they are in general effective and popular."[20] Doreen Warriner appears to accept the government's figures without question and announces: "The most striking sign of social change in the country-side since 1955, however, are the Combined Centres, set up in 1955-8 to provide health, educational, social, and agricultural services to the villages. In 1960 there were 250 such centres, each serving on an average 15,000 people. . . . The total of 350 centres in 1964, together with the expanded old rural health centres, will then serve about three-quarters of the rural population."[21] Perhaps one of the most opti-

[18] Keith Wheelock, *Nasser's New Egypt*, p. 120.

[19] Kamāl Maḥmūd al-Ḥusnī, "Community Development in Rural Local Communities in the United Arab Republic," *Majallat Tanmiyat al-Mujtama'* [Journal of Community Development] 12, nos. 1 & 2 (1965): 44–45.

[20] Patrick O'Brien, *The Revolution in Egypt's Economic System*, p. 299.

[21] Doreen Warriner, *Land Reform and Development in the Middle East*, pp. 197–198.

mistic descriptions was noted in a book by Georgiana Stevens. "The fellahin, despised and despaired of for centuries as incapable of improvement, could be persuaded to accept change and improve their lot under the right circumstances. The Combined Rural Centers have proved this and are therefore still being extended. By 1961 there were 528 of them serving four million people in 1,026 villages. . . . The Combined Centers are still in the process of growth. As laboratories for rural industry and for local self-government, they seem one of the most hopeful developments to come from the general welfare program."[22]

Charles Issawi acknowledges that "the Combined Units have their weaknesses, but their achievement has been impressive. To a large extent, the future of the Egyptian villages, and therefore, of the nation as a whole, is bound up with their fate."[23] Dr. Issawi, like so many writers, tends to see the solution merely in terms of more buildings constructed and more technically trained village workers. Thus, the weaknesses of the combined units are described as structural and financial deficiencies, rather than in terms of attitudes, values, and behavioral norms of the administrators or of the villagers. Issawi argues that "throughout the history of the units the limiting factor has been not the willingness of the villagers, who have put in hundreds of requests, but the lack of funds and, still more, of trained personnel."[24]

Following this approach to rural development, O'Brien suggests that "the shortage of experts willing to work in villages is the major impediment to their rapid extension, but the government should be prepared to offer high salaries or *if necessary to use its coercive power* to direct young graduates, as it does already for doctors and engineers."[25] Wheeler, after having interviewed several individuals actively engaged in the implementation of these combined units, comes close to putting his finger on the crucial aspects of this program.

[22] Georgiana Stevens, *Egypt: Yesterday and Today*, pp. 169–171.
[23] Charles Issawi, *Egypt in Revolution*, p. 108.
[24] Ibid., p. 107.
[25] Patrick O'Brien, *The Revolution in Egypt's Economic System*, p. 299; emphasis added.

The problem of personnel was not peculiar to this program, for it always has been difficult to obtain qualified persons to serve in rural provinces. Perhaps more valid criticism could be leveled at the manner in which these units were imposed on various communities. Mohamed Shalaby, widely recognized as one of Egypt's few authorities on the establishment of social centers, expressed this criticism as follows: "Before the Revolution, the government and the individual social worker sought to give confidence, then funds, to local communities, but now they build a unit, then try to obtain the people's confidence." His observation that "the fellaheen as a rule cannot be hurried into adopting new ways of doing things" seems to be correct.[26]

The confidence and optimism characteristic of much of what has been written on development programs in rural Egypt appears incongruous and even ironic when compared with comments and remarks from individuals presently working in the combined units. In theory the combined unit as an approach to rural development is a good idea. When one visits the combined units located in the governorates just outside of Cairo such as Giza or Menufia, which appear to operate primarily as a model center for visiting foreigners, one gains a completely different picture of these combined units than from a visit to combined units in Kafr al-Shaykh, Dakahlia, Sohag, or Qena.

A combined unit in theory aims at providing social, hygienic, and cultural services for rural populations. It also aims at raising economic standards through increasing agricultural and industrial production, so as to increase the income of the fellah while these services are rendered to him. Thus, it is hoped that hygienic, cultural, social and cooperative consciousness will be raised, the general conditions in rural areas considerably developed, and progress achieved in all aspects of life. This approach to rural development is to be based upon three principles:

1. *Local community is an integrated entity*: Community development should be recognized as a comprehensive and indivisible process. It aims at stimulating life in rural communities and releasing the vitality that is latent in land

26 Keith Wheelock, *Nasser's New Egypt*, pp. 119–120.

and people so they may improve their living conditions and provide for their own well being.

2. *Public welfare services are not charities or misplaced sentiments*: Public welfare services are essential for community life in order to achieve stability, progress, and fruitful living.

3. *Services and productivity are interrelated*: The higher the productivity level and consequently the economic level of a community, the more it is able to offer efficient and variegated services to its citizens. The close relationship between the public services and productivity should be realized, for one is a means to the other, and a consequence at the same time. Equilibrium in community life depends on the proper perception and application of the concept that increased production leads to a better standard of living.[27]

The first and fundamental goal of each combined unit is to pursue programs and projects best conducive to an improvement in the standard of living of the rural communities. In a memorandum prepared by the Permanent Council's secretary-general, he argues that each unit should perform a survey of the economic potential of its area and devise a program that would double the area's income within ten years. He suggests that the survey would include an estimation of the average output of the area and the average income from all the potential forms of economic activity, and "then to develop these forms of activity to the extent of achieving a double income within the prescribed period."[28]

Some activities mentioned as possible means of increasing income included increased cultivation of field crops, vegetables, fruits, and timber-trees; cattle raising, poultry breeding, and dairying; keeping of bees and silk worms; canning of honey, vegetables, jams, and fruit; spinning and weaving industry, rug and carpet industry, sewing, cutting and embroidery; building, carpentry, fitting, turnery, and plumbing.

[27] United Arab Republic, *The Combined Units*, p. 4.
[28] The Republic of Egypt, *The Permanent Council for Public Welfare Services*, p. 146.

In each combined unit, the agricultural extension services are directed by an "agricultural social worker." He is usually a graduate of a faculty of agriculture and is required to complete a three-month preservice training program. Assisting him is an "assistant agronomist" who is usually a graduate of a secondary school of agriculture. Also, there are three or four agricultural laborers. This agricultural section in the combined unit is supposed to introduce the modern methods of cultivation, irrigation, and harvesting. Special efforts are to be made to replace the native low-producing breeds of animals, poultry, vegetables, and other crops with newer strains characterized by high productivity and increased resistance to diseases. Each agricultural section is to distribute high-protein nutrients that will enable animals and plants to yield their maximum inherent capacity. Also the agricultural experts are supposed to provide training and instruction for the fellahin in farm management, techniques of marketing, and efficient production of farm products.

The health center in each combined unit is composed of:

1. A medical doctor—a graduate of a faculty of medicine—who has completed a three-month pre-science training program.
2. A chief nurse—a graduate of a four-year training program.
3. An assistant nurse—a graduate of a two-year training program.
4. Two midwives—graduates of a one-year training program.
5. A laboratory technician—a graduate of a six-month training program.
6. A public health officer—a graduate of a two-year training program.
7. A clerk.
8. Six medical workers (*tumargi*).[29]

The secretary-general, in his memorandum to the Permanent Council, states that the health center is not to be conceived as merely a place for the treatment of diseases or the distribution of medicines, but rather as:

[29] Ibid., p. 6.

. . . a centre of radiation and diffusion of health consciousness in the locality. The planning of medical treatment is easy enough, but the main point is to use the contact existing between the doctor and the patient and his family during treatment as a means to winning their confidence. . . . In order to facilitate guidance, the unit should be a centre for the demonstration of sanitation methods. . . . The relationship between doctor and community has a far reaching influence on the life of the people. The feeling that the doctor is full of sympathy and the spirit of service touches their hearts, makes their lives bright and cures them of their sense of frustration and their haunting pessimism.[30]

The educational section of the combined unit includes a headmaster and twelve teachers who must be graduates of the rural schools for teachers or other similar institutes. This section includes a rural primary school large enough to handle five hundred children, a kindergarten, and an adult education center. The combined unit executive regulations state that the school curriculum in these rural areas must be adjusted to the real needs of their pupils and their rural environmental conditions. Special hours are to be allocated weekly in the school program in an attempt to develop adequate practical skills in farming, rural handicrafts, agricultural industries, home economics and needlework. Again the memorandum noted above declare that these schools will assume "a new function, for it will be a sort of beehive throbbing with energy day and night all the year round. The pupil will be an educated farmer or worker, and his academic education will in no way be inferior to that of his equals in other schools. The curriculum of the rural school aims at preparing the pupil for a happy and productive rural life, and at tightening the ties between him and the rural community which is the backbone of our national life."[31]

The final section of each combined unit is the social center. The object of this section, according to its executive regulations, is to create better social interaction and self-help in the rural areas. This section is to select and train rural community leaders and to encourage community development projects that seek to improve the village planning, recreation, cooperation, and reformation. This

[30] Ibid., pp. 154–155.   [31] Ibid., pp. 155–156.

section is in charge of the following facilities: a public meeting hall, a movie theater, public library, local museum, public playground, and a number of handicraft workshops.

After careful analysis of some 250 interviews with officials, fellahin, and private citizens, I have come to the conclusion that in the vast majority of the combined units, health units, social centers, and other government-sponsored rural development programs, their effectiveness, their ability to stimulate change, and their success in generating enthusiasm and commitment to the goals of development and modernization have largely failed to reach their projected aims. This rather harsh statement is substantiated by several Egyptian sources who have objectively analyzed the rural programs presently functioning in Egypt. Thus, most of the evaluation teams sent out to various governorates generally reached the same conclusion as Ahmad Tawfiq, who laments over the fact that the "combined unit, which is the center of all government services for the villagers, rarely has any peasants in it for they never go there unless it is absolutely necessary."[32]

One of the most comprehensive research endeavors ever attempted in rural Egypt was conducted by the Institute of National Planning in cooperation with and under the sponsorship of the International Labor Office in Geneva, Switzerland. The avowed purpose of this research program was to analyze the "employment problem in rural areas of the UAR." Staff members of the Institute of National Planning conducted in-depth interviews from a random sample of 994 households chosen from "forty-eight typical villages" located in six different governorates: Buheira, Gharbia, Menufia, Asyut, Qena, and al-Fayyum.

The head of each household was asked whether he or his family had received any benefits from administrative services available in their village. The following indicates the percentage of positive responses in each of the various types of services:[33]

[32] Ahmad Tawfiq, "Bisindilla," *al-Ṭali'ah*, September 1966, p. 19.
[33] The United Arab Republic, *Research on Employment Problems in Rural Areas UAR*, p. 21.

Type of Service	Male%	Female%	Total%
Health	76	61	74
Education	29	12	27
Agricultural	26	13	24
Veterinary	20	6	18
Agricultural extension	18	9	17
Recreation	11	9	10
Vocational training	2	—	2
Industrial extension	1	1	1
Other services	2	5	3
No services used	18	34	20

Aside from medical help and schools, over 75 percent of the families interviewed claimed they had not received any benefits from the other categories of government service available in the village. Even more dramatic is the fact that 34 percent of the women and 18 percent of the men claimed that their families had not even received medical or educational benefits from government-sponsored programs. The tragedy of these figures becomes even more pronounced when one realizes that all the villages in this research project have government services available.[34] It is apparent that, out of more than 5,000 villages in Egypt, only 1,525 have some form of medical service available within their borders —the one service that is the most easily accepted by the fellahin.

The ineffectiveness of this institution for rural development is

---

[34] If one adds up all the various government sponsored health, social, and agricultural units presently operating in Egypt, one notes that only about one-third of all the villages have at least one government unit within their boundaries. The exceptions to this are the agricultural cooperatives. From United Arab Republic, *The Statistical Handbook*, pp. 39, 126.

Agricultural cooperatives in land Reform areas	556
Agricultural cooperatives—general	3993
Health centers	264
Combined units	304
Social centers	104
Comprehensive treatment units	71
Rural health units	782
TOTAL (excluding agricultural cooperatives)	1525

largely due to the attitudes and assumptions that both the peasant and the village official have toward each other.

The Village Council

The village council generally represents three to seven villages.[35] In theory there is to be a village council for each fifteen thousand people. In such a population block there will eventually be a council and a combined unit, with the village council administering the combined unit.

As noted before, there are three kinds of members in each council—elected, selected, and ex officio members. In each village council there are usually twelve elected members chosen from among the twenty members of the ASU *lajnat al-'ishrīn* in the village. These elected members are chosen by the director of councils in the Ministry of Local Administration in conjunction with the governor and the governorate ASU executive secretary. In the villages visited, there was a wide pattern of selection. In most village councils, the twelve elected members were those members of the *lajnat al-'ishrīn* who had received the most votes. Thus, one usually found at least one elected member from each of the villages in the village council's area of jurisdiction. However, the largest village does not necessarily obtain a majority of seats in the council, since the selection is a function of ASU acceptance rather than electoral votes received. The early councils and *lajnat al-'ishrīns* were established with little regard to the kinds of individuals chosen and elected by their villagers. Not until the middle of 1965 did the ASU play a serious role in screening and determining the fitness of the village council members. One source in the Ministry of Local Administration stated in early 1967 that all council members were now closely screened to determine suitability and that periodic evaluation reports were to be submitted by the local ASU organization.

The second category of membership in the village council is the selected member. In each village council area, the local administra-

[35] See appendix G.

tion has the discretionary power of "selecting" two local individuals to be members of the village council. The statute requires that these two selected members be active members of the ASU. Usually they are selected for their loyalty and effectiveness as ASU workers.

The third category of membership is the ex officio member. These are government administrators working in the village area, usually six individuals per village: the village school master representing the Ministry of Education, the village doctor representing the Ministry of Health, the village agronomist or the *mushrif* (overseer)[36] in the village agricultural cooperative representing the Ministry of Agriculture, the village social worker representing the Ministry of Social Affairs, the village engineer representing the Ministry of Housing and Public Utilities and the village police officer or the *'umdah* representing the Ministry of Interior. These ex officio members may by law serve on more than one council. Thus, many ex officio members are often absent from council meetings, and too often they attend village council meetings when they are totally unfamiliar with the problems and projects being discussed in the council.[37] The following table (extracted from an unfinished statistical study conducted by the Ministry of Local Administration) indicates the distribution of council members of some 563 of the 997 village councils in terms of their education and age:

Education	
College degree:	2,213
Secondary certificate:	3,134
Primary certificate or less:	6,625
Age	
25–30 years:	1,148
31–40:	2,453
41–50:	3,253
51–60:	2,960
61– :	1,483

[36] Gabriel S. Saab, *The Egyptian Agrarian Reform 1952–62*, pp. 53–56.

[37] About one-third of the doctors, agronomists, and social workers who were interviewed held memberships in a village council. Most of them claimed complete ignorance about the rules of procedure, distinction between the "three types" of members, or even the general purpose of the council. As one doctor noted: "I was notified of my membership in the village council by mail. I have

These statistics clearly show that the vast majority of the village council members have had very little education and tend to be above the age of forty. The council chairmen, however, are largely college graduates and are usually under thirty-five. In a social setting where age is equated with leadership, the younger village council chairman often finds himself at a strong disadvantage.

Law 124 declares that the village council chairman is the key position in the village council system of rural Egypt. His major functions center around his dual responsibility, first as chief representative of the central government in the village, and second as chief spokesman for the local village council, which represents the citizens of the participating villages of the area. In the vast majority of cases his influence and authority are not a function of his role as chairman of the council. Still, clearly visible is the fact that his authority, his influence, and his reputation rest on his personality and his association with the leading families and informal village leaders. The position of chairman will not, except in a few villages, develop any sense of legitimate power until the council matures and proves itself. Because of the general illiteracy and lack of experience in self-government among the villagers, the council chairman is appointed by the Ministry of Local Government for a two-year term.

Since 1961, when the first council chairmen were selected, the basis for their selection has gone through three phases. Between 1961 and 1963, the major emphasis was on technical competence and educational achievement. No attempt was made to ensure local acceptance of the chairmen and, as one official commented, "Too many of these council chairmen tend to become little tyrants." Between 1963 and the summer of 1966, the government attempted to shift their selection basis from technical competence to include local acceptance and approval. It was during this period that the government attempted to select lawyers, doctors, and professional people who had moved from their villages, and then to

---

been to two council meetings in the past year, but both of them were a complete waste of time. I have too many things to do in my own village without wasting my time attending an ineffective council meeting in some other village."

"induce" them to return to their original villages to work as village council chairmen. During 1967 the Ministry of Local Administration, while still seeking to find local people to act as village council chairmen, began to establish a regular training program at the UNESCO Arab States Training Center for Education for Community Development (ASFEC) in Sirs al-Layyan, UAR. During the period 1961–1966, council chairmen were selected because of their technical skill as doctors, agronomists, or social workers, and these officials usually considered their positions as council chairmen to be part-time duty. Today, although most chairmen are still selected from the village functionaries, the new chairmen are given a two-week formal training course on the duties and functions of a village council chairman, and their position is coming more and more to be viewed as a full-time job.[38]

While I have no specific personal data on the 997 village council chairmen in Egypt, some indications as to their experience and background may be gleaned from the 97 chairmen who completed their training at Sirs al-Layyan in September 1966:

Education:
  61 were university graduates.
  34 were high school graduates.
  1 was a primary school graduate.
  1 had no formal schooling.
Previous employment:
  29 in education—teachers, inspectors, headmasters.
  26 agronomists or cooperative supervisors.
  12 social workers.
  6 medical doctors.

---

[38] The director of village councils in the Ministry of Local Administration, on February 14, 1967, indicated that most village council chairmen were either agronomists, social workers, doctors, or headmasters, in that order. The director also noted that his motto in selecting a chairman was "no landowner is to be a council chairman—the fit man, not the rich man." I personally observed that the council chairman's former employment varied from governorate to governorate. Thus, in the governorate of Kafr al-Shaykh, the vast majority of chairmen were agronomists, while in the governorate of Giza, just outside of Cairo, it appeared that most of the chairmen were social workers.

6 farmers (two of these were village secretaries of the ASU).
3 lawyers.
2 'umdahs.
1 civil engineer.
12 former secretaries in village councils.
Experience in a village council:
14, less than one year experience.
51, one to two years experience.
8, two to four years experience.
24, over four years experience.

Some thirty or forty village council chairmen and various officials in the Ministry of Local Administration, were interviewed to determine why a person would accept the position of council chairman. The most common reasons given were as follows:

1. Many of these people have a professional background which requires that they work and live in the village. The "prestige" of the office of village council chairman is an obvious attraction for professional people who must work in the village anyway.

2. Each council chairman is usually furnished with a two-story house. Rent for this house is 10 percent of his salary, regardless of how much he makes.

3. His salary, which is equal to what his government or professional salary would be, is supplemented by a monthly expense allowance (*badal tamthīl*) of ten pounds.

4. The cost of living in rural Egypt is easily 20 percent less than in Cairo.

5. "The government selected me and I have no choice." Many village workers admitted that they were in the village only because they were forced to be there by the government. However, only a very few of the village workers who were also the council chairmen intimated they were unhappy in the village. On the whole, these chairmen seemed enthusiastic and motivated individuals.[39]

[39] Apparently, the chairmen admit being unhappy with village life only to close friends. During my first visit to a village, I seldom met a village worker who would openly admit his discontent. After my third or fourth visit, a few gave subtle hints that they would prefer to be living in Cairo, and if these

The training program now available for all prospective council chairmen suggests the kinds of skills and knowledge required to run a village council:

Lectures: A series of ninety-minute lectures from the staff of ASFEC on:

1. Aims and organization of local administration in a socialist society
2. Characteristic features of the local administrative system in the UAR
3. Explanation of the important articles of Law 124
4. Financial and administrative responsibilities
5. Preparing the budget and balance sheet of the council
6. Developing procedural skills in the council
   a) preparing an agenda
   b) methods of organizing a council session
   c) methods of discussion, debate, and decision
   d) techniques of follow-up and evaluation
   e) utilization of council committees
7. Methods of group dynamics
8. Leadership and supervision
9. Relationship between local administration and community development
   a) theory and principles of community development
   b) the role of a village council in planning and development at the local and national levels
   c) the role of a village council in increasing local participation in the financing and administration of government services
   d) the role of a village council in training local leaders and coordinating various institutions in the local community

Seminars: Seminars were organized in order to allow representatives of the Ministry of Local Administration, the ASU, and

---

same individuals were to visit me in Cairo, it was seldom that a village worker would not openly lament his misfortune at being assigned to a village.

governorate officials to present their views on the role and po-
tentiality of the village council in the development of rural
Egypt.

Debates: All council chairmen were invited to give their comments and opinions on the information they had received
through the lectures and seminars mentioned above. Also attending these "open discussions" were the governor of Menufia, the ASU general secretary, several town council chairmen,
and technical experts from various ministries. Most questions
raised centered around the relationship between village councils
and the town and governorate councils in terms of supervision,
guidance, control, and follow-up. Many questions were also
raised concerning the relationship between the village council
and the ASU organization in the village.

Field Visits: All council chairmen were given an opportunity to
attend actual village council sessions in two nearby communities—Munūf and 'Ashmūn. These chairmen were encouraged
to observe the procedures and organizations of these operating
councils, their methods of discussion and keeping minutes, and
the projects presently being administered by the village council.

Group Discussions: During the last few days all the chairmen
were divided into groups of twenty. Each group was monitored
by a staff member of the ASFEC and was given a particular
problem to discuss. Each group was encouraged to analyze all
aspects of their problem and then submit a written paper with
their recommendations. During the last day of training, all papers were further discussed in a plenary session.[40]

Internal Structures and Functions of Village Councils

Potentially, a village council can play an important role in
developing the sense of legitimacy and commitment suggested
earlier. It can provide a sense of participation for the local inhabitants of a village or rural community. A council provides an insti-

[40] *Barnāmij tadrīb sa'ādat ru'asā' majlis al-qaryah bi-muḥāfaẓatay al-sharqīyah wa-al-munūfīyah* [Training Program for the Village Council Chairmen
in the Governorates of Sharqiyah and Munufiyah], pp. 1–3.

tutional structure by which local requests, complaints, and proposals can be channeled to higher governmental authorities. The
truly effective council may develop a series of projects or programs
of such obvious local value as to be a strong inducement to the
villagers to contribute a significant portion of the financing.

Yet, for a council to function in this manner, there must be a
literate citizenry, a group of experienced and capable leaders, an
understanding of the strengths and weaknesses of a local government system, an appreciation of the need for the local community
to shoulder a larger portion of the costs, and a willingness to participate with the central government in reforming and developing
the social, economic, and political conditions in the rural areas.

The staff of the village council consists of those employees, excluding the three types of members mentioned above, who assist
the council chairman in the preparation and implementation of his
duties. The number and qualifications of these civil servants vary
according to the amount of work a council can generate. However,
the following employees were found in most of the larger villages:
chairman of the council, secretary of the council, administrative
assistant, clerk for stores and supplies, accounting clerk, tax col-
lector, clerk for administrative affairs, administrative clerk, meter
reader (water and electricity), surveyor, and chief janitor. In
addition to these employees, it was not uncommon to find several
workers, drivers, gardeners, janitors, and errand boys. The number
of employees increases considerably in those villages that also have
a combined unit.

The council chairman is required to call for a village council
session at least once each month. By law they must meet in the
designated council room and all sessions are to be open to the public
unless the chairman or one-third of the members requests a closed
session.[41] The chairman is supposed to preside over all sessions of

---

[41] 'Umar 'Amr, ed., *al-Mawsū'ah al-tashrī'īyah fī shu'ūn al-'idārah al-maḥalīyah* [Legislative Encyclopedia of Local Administration]; cited hereafter as
Legislative Encyclopedia. This is a collection of all the laws pertaining to local
administration in Egypt, including Law Number 124 (1960) (Law of Local
Administration); all amendments and explanatory notes for Law 124 (1965);

the council. If for some reason he is absent, the eldest member of the council presides during his absence. At least 50 percent of the total membership of the council must be present for a council session to be legal.[42] No member can be absent from a session of the council without permission from the council chairman. Any member who is absent more than one time will be reported to the governor.[43]

During the first session several items of business must be performed:

1. Issue the oath of office: "I swear by God the Almighty that I will faithfully protect the presidential system and the welfare of the people and the security of the nation. I will respect the law and I will perform my duties honestly and sincerely."[44]

2. Consider all cases where a member's right to sit in the council is challenged. All challenged members are prohibited from voting or attending the session until a decision has been made.[45]

3. Determine the council's internal rules of procedure. All deviations or special procedures not authorized in the Model of Internal Procedures require the approval of the governor.[46]

4. Establish the council's permanent committees. Each council is supposed to have four committees.

Executive Rules of Procedure for Law 124 (1960); and a Model of Internal Procedures for local councils (Order No. 1, 1960).

[42] Ibid., pp. 38–39. If the 50 percent are absent, the session will be postponed three to seven days. If 50 percent are absent for the second session, the Ministry of State of Local Administration must be informed. When the third session is called, at least ten days after the second session, two things are possible if the required 50 percent are not present: a presidential decree will be issued dissolving the council; or, if there is no presidential decree, the session will be considered legal, regardless of the number present.

[43] The Model of Internal Procedures states that the governor must first notify the delinquent member. After proper notification, the governor may either reprimand him, prevent him from attending future sessions temporarily, or release him from the council permanently (ibid., p. 250).

[44] Ibid., p. 38.

[45] Ibid., pp. 244–245.

[46] Ibid., p. 130.

a) Committee of Education, Youth, Welfare, and Culture
b) Committee on Agriculture, Cooperatives, Irrigation, Rural Industries, and Supply
c) Committee on Public Health and Utilities
d) Committee on Social Services, Complaints, and Suggestions.[47]

Each of these committees must have at least three members. The council may form "special committees for certain purposes when it is necessary."[48] Each member of the council nominates himself for one of the committees in which he feels he is best qualified or has the most interest. No member is allowed to be a member of more than one committee unless two-thirds of the council approve. The members in each permanent committee elect their own chairman and a secretary or reporter. The general custom appears to ensure that the village bureaucrat in charge of the items covered by each committee will be that committee's chairman. Thus, the chairmen of the four committees are usually the schoolmaster, the agronomist, the doctor, and the social worker, respectively.

In the village council, the agenda for each session is determined by the village chairman. The Model of Internal Procedures in the local councils indicates the following matters are to be included in an agenda:

1. Matters proposed by the governor and his staff and all items suggested by the various government ministries and agencies that are of interest to the village council.

2. Matters proposed by the chairman or members of the council concerning the internal activities and responsibilities of the village council.

3. Any question directed by a member to the chairman concerning the council's responsibility. The chairman may postpone an answer to these questions until the next session.[49]

All members submitting a proposal or question must submit their requests in writing at least one week prior to the session. Any

[47] Ibid., p. 40.
[48] Ibid., pp. 277–278.
[49] Ibid., p. 252.

request already rejected cannot be considered again unless forty-five days have elapsed or unless one-third of the members request it in a written statement. It is possible for a member to submit a request during the session. First, he must submit his item to the chairman in written form; second, three members have to agree that the item requires immediate discussion; and third, a majority of the council must accept the request.

The governor and his staff have the right to inform the council during its sessions of any urgent matter that requires immediate attention. According to Law 124, each item brought before the council should be preceded by a study through one of the committees. The function of the committee is to discuss and study all the implications of any proposal to be decided by the council. The committee may request the assistance of experts and interested citizens and all sessions of these committees are to be closed. The committee chairman or reporter will draw up a report for each item referred to his committee. This report must clarify and explain the discussions of the committee and should include the opinions of both the majority and minority groups of the committee.

During the discussions and debates of these items in the council itself, the council chairman plays a key role. He begins and ends all discussions. He directs the debates, gives permission to members to speak, and indicates when each member has spoken long enough. The Model of Internal Procedures suggests the following sequence for each proposal: one speaker in favor of the proposal, one speaker in opposition to the proposal, and one speaker who wishes to amend the proposal.[50] This sequence is to be repeated, each time choosing three new individuals—unless one of the members relinquishes his turn to someone who has already spoken—until all members have had an opportunity to express their opinions.

The village council secretary or his assistant must keep detailed minutes of each session to include:

[50] Ibid., p. 261.

1. The time, date, and place of the session.
2. The name of the presiding officer during the session.
3. The names of all individuals present, to include the elected, selected, and ex officio members, representatives of all government offices and agencies, and all special guests.
4. Names of all members absent with excuse, without excuse, and those who arrived late or left early.
5. Summary of all items given to the committees for discussion.
6. Summary of all items of the agenda discussed in the council, including the results of each vote.
7. List results of all items discussed and voted upon which were not on the agenda. The council chairman may request the secretary or the clerk not to register any statement in the minutes which was made by members who had violated the internal rules of procedure.[51]

It is not my purpose to provide a definitive description of all internal rules of procedure in the Egyptian village councils, but merely to suggest the kinds of procedures that the central government is attempting to introduce among these rural councils. The problem of merely outlining the many and varied rules of procedure listed in the formal law is that many may assume that these rules describe how the councils are actually functioning. Again the researcher, in analyzing rural structures, is faced with the decision either to describe what the central government official invites him to see or to reiterate what many members of these councils claim neither the central government official nor the researcher will ever see. Thus, for example, one member of the ASFEC Training Center at Sirs al-Liyyan admitted that whenever he attends a village council they function in a calm, deliberate manner, with the chairman displaying complete control over the members of the council. Yet, the chairman himself has submitted many reports indicating that the older members of the council generally ignore him, that there is constant shouting and bickering among members from different families, and that most discus-

51 Ibid., pp. 271–272.

sions in these sessions, unattended by "outsiders," completely fail
to adhere to any of the rules of procedure dictated by the Ministry
of Local Administration. Many doctors confided that their duties
as chairmen of the Committee of Public Health merely required
that they check with their superior at the governorate office. Others, especially those who became personal friends, admitted that
many village councils do not use committees, since most village
members are either unqualified or uninterested in attending committee meetings. This tendency is strengthened and reinforced in
councils, where the relationship between the peasants and village
bureaucrats is strained or nonexistent.

Law 124 delegates a wide range of functions to the village
council, including activities in the field of education, public health,
public utilities and housing, labor, agriculture, food supply, communication, security, and economic development. Within each of
these activities the law specifically delineates the functions that,
by their nature, can best be regulated at the village council level.

Education: Article 37[52] of the Executive Rules of Procedure indicates that each village council will establish, prepare, and administer the primary schools within its village and all villages
under its control and responsibility. Article 38[53] states that each
local council is specifically responsible for the following matters:

1. Select construction sites for all new school buildings.
2. Distribute and open new classrooms among the village schools
   as the demand requires.
3. Supervise the use of the syllabus set by the Ministry of
   Education, including its application, adoption, and modifi-
   cation whenever required by local differences.
4. Establish the days and times for all school vacations—to include both national holidays and special local holidays.
5. Organize and establish an adult education program.
6. Establish and prepare a village school library.
7. Establish and equip a youth sporting club.
8. Organize and provide a daily lunch program for each school.

52 Ibid., p. 186.
53 Ibid.

9. Coordinate with the village health center to provide an adequate health program in each school.

Although a detailed description of each of these functions is outside the scope of this study, I will examine one of these functions (no. 3) in an attempt to show how detailed these responsibilities have been defined. Within each council there is to be a committee of education. This committee should hold a session at least two weeks before the school year to examine and discuss the application of the state school syllabus. This meeting should consist of the district school inspector and his assistant, the headmasters of all the village schools in the area, a few teachers from each school and members of the committee and other interested citizens from the various villages. Suggestions for any modifications in the syllabus will be discussed at this meeting. A final report will be drawn up by the committee on education and then submitted to the village council. The village council will discuss the report in a general session, amending and deleting as it sees fit. The council's final report is then forwarded to the governorate council. The committee of education at the governorate level will then collect all reports submitted by the village councils. After proper consultation, the governorate-level committee then submits a report to the governorate council designing a plan that will fit the unique circumstances of the village areas within the governorate. The governorate's final decision will be distributed to each village council, which will be responsible for the supervision and execution of the amended syllabus.

This detailed outline of one educational function assigned to all village councils suggests the profound role an effective village council might well play in encouraging a diversified first-rate educational program. Unfortunately, this is not the case in a vast majority of the councils in rural Egypt. The primary schools in the villages are still closely supervised and controlled by the Ministry of Education. The headmasters still follow very closely the rules, regulations, and programs dictated by the ministry or governorate director of education. Most village schools and their teaching staffs are evaluated primarily on the basis of the extent to which they adhere to central instructions. The appointments, promotions, and transfers are still made on the same basis and are still completely in the hands of the governorate authorities. One research group commissioned by the Egyptian government to evaluate the role of the village councils in implementing the national educational program summarized its report by noting:

> The main emphasis of the central authorities has centered around the administrative aspects of education with little attention being given to the other aspects of the educational process. The most obvious result of this approach can best be verified by the fact that students in the rural areas are generally far below the required educational level. This relationship and dependence of the villages on the central authorities has greatly delayed and hindered the implementation of the law of local administration. . . . The field research team noted that the local village councils have failed to fulfill their educational duties because of several obstacles. These include:
> a) Lack of sufficient funds and credit.
> b) Lack of educational specialists as members of the village council.
> c) Lack of proper guidance and direction from the governorate authorities.
> d) The law which assigns so many responsibilities to the village councils fails to provide guidelines to facilitate the gradual development of these responsibilities.
> e) The law does not state the relationships that are to exist among the village council, the governorate and the central authorities.
> f) The villagers themselves do not have a mature awareness of their roles and responsibilities vis-à-vis the local council.[54]

Health: Article 40[55] of the Executive Rules of Procedure indicates that the village councils are authorized to look after the health and medical requirements of their communities. They are required to establish, equip, and administer all medical units within their areas, except model and training centers maintained by the Ministry of Health. From the many doctors interviewed it appears the village council's functions in the field of health services may be divided into four areas:

[54] *al-Taqārīr al-nihā'iyah lil-lijān al-farʿiyah li-shu'ūn al-dirāsāt al-madanīyah lil-majālis al-qarawīyah* [Final Reports of the Subcommittees for Field Research on Village Councils], pp. 56–57; hereafter cited as *Final Reports*.
[55] ʿUmar ʿAmr, *Legislative Encyclopedia*, pp. 187–188.

PREVENTIVE SERVICES:

a) Vaccination against contagious diseases.

b) Taking the necessary preventive actions in the case of death through an infectious disease.

c) Periodic fumigation of homes, clothing, and individuals for ticks and lice.

d) Supervision and periodic inspections of all merchants and their employees who deal in food stuffs.

e) Supervision of all sources of drinking water.

f) Supervision of all food processing plants, market areas, and slaughterhouses.

g) Inspection of all private and public buildings and places of business to ensure that sanitary conditions are being maintained.

h) Establish a program of hygienic cultural guidance and education to increase the sanitation consciousness among the fellahin.

i) Coordinate governorate programs to control the spread of endemic diseases, such as snail eradication to reduce Bilharziasis and filling in swamps to reduce malaria.

j) Encourage the improvement of sanitary conditions in the peasants' personal housing.

k) Control the disposal of garbage and refuse and the storage of natural fertilizers.

TREATMENT SERVICES: These include the establishment and administration of the village health center and the transportation of individuals who need special attention to the nearest hospital.

EMERGENCY SERVICES: Each council is to coordinate with the village doctor in developing contingency plans to handle widespread disasters, epidemics, flooding, wars, and immigrations.

ADMINISTRATIVE SERVICES: These include providing transportation of patients from all surrounding villages to the health unit in the main village, providing ambulance service to the nearest hospital, and providing telephone service between the main village and all surrounding villages. Also, the council is responsible for raising the level of medical services in the health unit, ensuring the general cleanliness of the health unit, and maintaining the proper provision of medicine and equipment not provided by the governorate medical offices.

Again, except for the few village councils where the doctor is genuinely motivated and has the active support of the leading elements in the village, the relationship between the council and the doctors is generally unsatisfactory. As one research group concluded about health services in the villages of rural Egypt:

The village council chairman is considered responsible for the general operation of the village health unit, even though the village doctor is the direct supervisor both in the unit's technical and administrative affairs. Although the health committee of the village council is supposed to transfer villagers' petitions and requests, it seldom takes an active role in the affairs of health. Excluding the previously mentioned responsibilities, it can be said that the village council has not performed fully the responsibilities assigned to it by the law for local administration . . . (therefore) the conditions of health have remained as they have always been, differing only according to the distribution, quantity, and quality of services available.[56]

Public Utilities[57]: Each village council is encouraged to plan, supervise, and implement the following projects and services to the extent that their respective resources may permit: gas and electricity, road construction and maintenance, fresh drinking water, sewage system and garbage disposal, public parks, cemeteries, marketplaces and slaughterhouses, organization of public transportation system, filling in dangerous ponds and swamps, repairs and maintenance of public buildings, enforcement of laws regulating industrial establishments, theaters, places of amusement, and business firms, and executing housing schemes in accordance with plans drawn up by the Ministry of Housing and Public Utilities.

The research committee on housing and public utilities concluded, "The committee found that the village council was not performing its responsibilities in the sector of housing and public utilities . . . for the following reasons: (1) the law assigns many

56 *Final Reports*, pp. 89–90.
57 'Umar 'Amr, *Legislative Encyclopedia*, pp. 192–197.

technical responsibilities, but because of the lack of qualified technicians the council is unable to perform these responsibilities. (2) the council does not have sufficient financial resources to implement these programs even if qualified personnel were available."[58]

Social Activities: Article 45 of the Executive Rules of Procedure[59] states that the village council shall have the power to supervise all benevolent organizations, social institutions, and private foundations; the power to dissolve or appoint a new manager for these various associations and institutions; the power to provide financial assistance and to authorize these associations to collect and dispense charitable donations; and the power to recommend the establishment of all new social projects in the village.

One village council chairman stated that he attempted to supervise the social service activities in his village by: (1) a periodic visitation to each organization, society, and private foundation in his area to determine whether they were adhering to all government regulations and to the purposes for which they were established; (2) encouraging those societies to engage in activities that will improve the social and economic conditions of the villagers; and (3) acting as coordinator for the various governmental and private programs in order to prevent duplication of service presently being rendered to the villages.

The vast majority of social workers interviewed argued that the village councils were not performing the responsibilities assigned to them by the law. Generally the social worker functions independently of the village council. All problems, questions, and matters of policy and procedure are submitted to the governorate director of social affairs with no coordination either with the council chairman or the so-called committee of social affairs in the village council. In those village council minutes that were perused, it appeared that the village councils were not encouraging or even discussing the activities, programs, and projects sponsored by these various societies and organizations.

[58] *Final Reports*, p. 105.
[59] 'Umar 'Amr, *Legislative Encyclopedia*, pp. 192–197.

The research committee assigned to evaluate the social assistance programs operating in villages with councils concluded:

The research committee, after an extensive study of the laws and ministerial orders organizing the pensions, social assistances, and responsibilities assigned to the heads of the social units and the head of the department of social affairs at the governorate level, has come to the conclusion that the local councils cannot perform the responsibilities assigned to them for the following reasons:

(1) There is no qualified person with audit accounting training at the local council level who can verify and evaluate, from a technical point of view, the applications and disbursements of assistance, and government pensions.

(2) The local councils have no allocations in their budget for assistance and pensions because this money is retained and directly disbursed from the department of social affairs at the governorate level.

(3) Various ministerial decrees and orders have been issued which effectively preclude the village council chairman from assuming any financial responsibility in these matters.[60]

Rural Economic Development: Article 49 of the Executive Rules of Procedure[61] declares that the village council should perform the following responsibilities:

1. Expand and develop rural industries.
2. Exploit the raw materials available in the village area.
3. Submit proposals to the governorate council describing projects and amount of financing the village council is willing to provide.
4. Develop and organize the marketing facilities for all locally produced products.
5. Coordinate and implement all programs and policies generated by the central government in the field of rural industries.

The research committee for rural development noted that very little development in rural industries had occurred through the efforts of the village councils because of the following problems:

[60] *Final Reports*, pp. 143–144.
[61] 'Umar 'Amr, *Legislative Encyclopedia*, pp. 201–202.

1. Instruments and means of production in the villages are inadequate and primitive.
2. The general illiteracy of those employed in rural industries.
3. Rural industries are widely dispersed and uncoordinated because the industries develop mainly through private individuals.
4. The central government's efforts in rural development have not been concentrated in one consistent direction.
5. The difficulty of marketing rural products due to the lack of craftsmanship and artistic taste.[62]

This general outline of functions delegated to village councils is not complete. To this list one could add, among others, responsibilities in the areas of labor, agriculture, the cooperatives, food supply, communication, and security. A detailed analysis of these functions, as noted with the earlier functions, would reach much the same somber conclusion. The vast majority of village councils in Egypt have been unable to play a positive role in fulfilling these functions. One conclusion is apparent from this analysis: the village councils lack the trained personnel and the financial resources to adequately handle the numerous and complex responsibilities assigned to them. What is the proper balance of control for allocating functions to local units of authority in a way that will ensure a maximum efficiency in their implementation? If the central government fails to assign a sufficient amount of power and responsibility to the village councils, commitment and acceptance for these local institutions will never develop, and the functioning but impotent village councils will merely reinforce a traditional sense of futility and cynicism so characteristic of the Egyptian fellahin.

Yet, equally perilous is the tendency to freely allocate responsibilities to institutions that, due to a lack of finances and personnel, are neither capable nor willing to assume them. The direct result of this course of action also reinforces old images of government

62 *Final Report*, pp. 347–348.

ineffectiveness, all too often interpreted by the fellahin as further proof of their government's unconcern. The implication for legitimacy in this dilemma should be self-evident.

If we are to evaluate the role and position of the village councils, careful analysis requires that some simple typology of village councils be suggested. Most of the village councils observed appear to fall into one of four categories, depending upon which leadership group or combination of leadership groups seemed to predominate. An arbitrary classification of these groups would include: (1) "feudal" landowning families, those generally uncooperative or apathetic towards the Nasser regime, (2) "progressive" landowning families, those generally considered as committed to the Nasser regime, (3) "passive" village administrators, and (4) "active" village administrators, those motivated by either ideological or professional considerations.

Reactionary Council: In those villages where the "feudal" families and the "passive" bureaucrats were found working together in the same council, the chances that this council would be functioning effectively were very slim. Certainly prior to 1966, the vast majority of village councils would have fallen into this category. All of the field research studies conducted on village councils prior to 1966 come to the same conclusion: the village councils in general are not functioning as they should because of inadequate leadership or because of the active opposition of the leading families in the area. If the newspaper accounts can be taken for truth, many of the reactionary "feudal" families have been removed from the village areas in an attempt to weaken the hold of these families on various government institutions in the rural areas. In spite of this "antifeudalism campaign," it is estimated that perhaps 40 percent of all village councils can still be classified as "reactionary."[63] In this type of council the chairman plays a negative role, either following the orders of the dominant family or spending as much time outside the village as possible.

[63] The percentage figures offered for the four different types of councils are purely conjectural and are based on impressions gained from interviews and observations in rural Egypt.

Passive Council: In those villages where pro-Nasser families are working with "passive officials," the activities of the council must still be considered ineffective. This kind of council operates in two situations: (1) those villages where landowning families have been removed and no effective local leadership has yet appeared to take their place, or (2) the council is ignored by the local villagers who prefer to operate through families who have close connections either in the upper echelons of the ASU or the governorate hierarchy. It is estimated that 30 percent of all village councils fall in this category.[64]

Revolutionary Council: A village council composed of "feudal" family representatives and a new group of ideologically oriented bureaucrats or party workers is usually torn by conflict. It appears that many of the villages recently investigated by the Committee for the Liquidation of Feudalism fall within this category. The village council chairman in these villages, especially if he happens to be a native of the village, can play a major role in developing and strengthening the village council. The new emerging social groups, once the larger landowners have been removed, generally gravitate to the newer structures, such as the ASU *lajnat al-'ishrīn* and the village council. Nevertheless, these institutions, where "feudal" family power has been recently curtailed, generally fall under the influence of the government or ASU officials. In this situation where the council appears to be functioning properly, the villagers' acceptance and loyalty to these structures must still be considered fragile and highly susceptible to failure, since the motivating power behind the council is still primarily a group of individuals considered as "outsiders." Perhaps nearly one-fourth of all village councils might be classified as "revolutionary."

Progressive Council: Last are those few councils where pro-regime landowners and "active" administrators are functioning

[64] The distinction between the "reactionary" and the "passive" councils is primarily one of emphasis and therefore difficult to distinguish in a concrete situation. Nevertheless, one can argue that 70 percent of the village councils are ineffective, primarily because the local government administrators are "passive" and fail to take an active part in developing the council as an effective village institution.

harmoniously together. This kind of council is obviously rare in rural Egypt—certainly less than 10 percent of the total. While it is admitted that very few of the functioning councils meet the standards required to be designated as "progressive," still several councils visited were on the threshold of becoming so. Legitimacy in this case rests on the firm foundation of competent village administrators and committed local leadership capable of making the council function properly. It will be in this type of council that the village chairman will eventually be elected locally by the villagers themselves. This is the long-range goal of the Egyptian government.

In one village council in Aswan the relationship between the villagers and the village officials quite adequately epitomizes one of the fundamental problems noted in rural Egypt. The village council chairman was a young agronomist. All the officials in the village (doctor, social worker, agronomist) were under thirty years of age, all were from Cairo and thus spoke a dialect somewhat different from the villagers'. During one session the doctor recommended that the main street of the village be straightened out and widened in order to allow an ambulance to reach the various sections of the village in times of emergency. One of the *shaykhs al-balad*, a prominent member of the council, announced his complete opposition to such a project. He indicated that their village had always taken care of their emergencies in the past and then argued that "the only reason the young doctor and the young agronomist want a new wide street is so they can ride their motor bikes through our village at a faster speed."

In a village in Menufia, a bright young engineer enthusiastically presented a simple proposal suggesting that the villagers work together to build a new village center and marketplace. The council chairman, an older government official who also happened to be from the village, explained to the young engineer that he would have to obtain a copy of the law on rural housing development before the council could intelligently discuss the matter. The engineer then waited six months for his headquarters to send him a copy of the law. During the next session, after having studied the law, the chairman apologized that the council's agenda was filled with more urgent matters. Finally, eight months after the engineer first suggested his project, the council, after hearing his proposal, voted to send a request to the governorate office for further information on the costs and amount of financial aid available. Four months later the governorate director of public housing sent an answer to the council's request, indicating that no exact amount of money could be allocated without a detailed study of the housing problems and needs of the village. Before the engineer was able to begin the requested study, he was transferred to another governorate.

Mohammed Hasan, describing the village of Abishna in the governorate of Beni Suef, points out that many village councils do not function properly because the traditional families still dominate:

The popular powers in the villages have no strength within the ASU because the *'umdah* and the *shaykhs* in the village dominate the village and the agricultural laborers. . . . They did not organize themselves together into an Agricultural Workers' Union because of the *'umdah* and the large families and thus they continue to accept ten piastres [twenty-three cents] a day. . . . The *'umdah* is the real head of the village's administrative machinery. . . . [His] family controls over 800 *feddans* either by owning or leasing it, and the members of the village council are all from his family with the exception of two members who are ex-officio members.[65]

An even more drastic indictment against the village councils, specifically that of Bisindilla, was voiced by Ahmad Tawfiq:

The first person we met in the village was the chairman of the village council. He is also the headmaster of the school in the village Combined Unit. The council itself consists of the chairman, twelve members from the ASU *lajnat al-'Ishrin*, two appointed members and several ex-officio members. These figures are merely paper figures since the council only meets because the law requires it and the legal number of members is rarely present. The council never meets more than once a month and even then the council fails to discuss the real problems of their village. It was quite clear that the village council had

[65] Lutfi Muḥammad Ḥasan, "Abishna," *al-Ṭali'ah*, September 1966, p. 42.

no influence in the village and it has never tried to find solutions for the problems of the villagers. It is obvious that it does not actually supervise or even appear to supervise the services of the village and this explains the low standard of services in the village and the mistreatment and exploitation so prevalent in the village. Thus, the villagers, although they knew the name of the council, had no knowledge about its formation, the members, its sessions, its functions. . . . All this should not be surprising if we know that the village council chairman does not have any close contact with the fellahin nor does he know their problems. We noted that he had not even wandered through the village streets to observe its conditions. The chairman stays in the Combined Unit and his acquaintances in the village are limited to members of the village council, leaders in the ASU, and some of the landowners. . . . This lack of activity and effectiveness in the village council forces the masses to lose all trust and confidence in these popular and executive institutions and isolates them from the educated administrators who work in the village.[66]

While it is easy to collect examples and stories from village officials who loathe their present life away from Cairo and continually speak of the fellahin as those "mental deficients," one should not be unaware of some very striking changes taking place among certain Egyptians active in their village councils. Thus, while I have collected a large number of personal exposés, anecdotes, and interesting second-hand observations, my impressions of rural councils achieved through personal observations still lead me to optimistic rather than pessimistic conclusions. Optimistic conclusions, not because great changes can be seen in the rural villages of Egypt, but because *some change* can be seen. There is something inherently incongruous, yet still inspiring, in observing a young woman doctor stand before a group of older men steeped in Islamic culture and effectively articulate her demands that the food given to the school children in their village be stored properly to preclude any further spoiled food from being served in the school lunches.

One of the most impressive scenes I observed in Egypt occurred during a debate in the village council of Kafr al-Marazka in the governorate of Kafr al-Shaykh. The question centered around the need for a school bus to carry the older children of the village to

[66] Ahmad Tawfiq, "Bisindilla," *al-Ṭalīʿah*, September 1966, p. 19.

a nearby town where preparatory and secondary schools were available. From the beginning of the debate, it was apparent that two points of view were paramount. One group was headed by a Sayyid Muntasir, a leading landowner in the village. He wore an elegant brown *galabīyah* and walked and talked with great authority. When he spoke, which was quite often, people listened. He argued that the village cooperative, with government aid, should provide a school bus so that every child, even from the poorest families, would be able to ride free to school.

The other group in the village council had two spokesmen—the head schoolmaster and the elected head of the five-man governing committee in the local agricultural cooperative. They both argued that the cooperative could not afford to buy gasoline for a school bus and thus the villagers using the bus should pay something. The head of the cooperative was a tall, strong-looking fellah, dressed in a plain striped *galabīyah*. His father had been a landless itinerant worker. In 1950 this young fellah was offered a job as a cotton-worm observer by the provincial agricultural engineer. However, the *'umdah* in his village objected and the job was given to a cousin of the *'umdah*. From 1950 to 1960 this fellah worked as an ordinary laborer. Finally, in 1960, he was made a cotton-worm observer and in 1962 was given five *feddans* and a *gamoosa* through the Ministry of Land Reform. In 1963 he joined the ASU, and in 1964 he was elected by the villagers to be the head of the cooperative in his village.

As the debate developed between these two groups, one could not help but be impressed with the fact that the question at hand was not the thirty piastres each student would be charged for using a school bus. The head of the cooperative was openly and enthusiastically championing an opposite view from that of the rich landowner. The uneducated fellah leader spoke with a rather primitive eloquence. He argued that "the fellahin are now for the first time free and can hold their heads up with pride. . . . We all remember the days before the Revolution. We remember when the king's cousin came to our village to hunt. We all know that he maliciously killed several of our animals and even accidentally killed a young girl. We all know that by the king's order, the police never even came to investigate. . . . Things have changed and we must earn our own way. Each must be required to pay something."

The council chairman called for a vote. The result was close, but the wealthy landowner had won. The final vote was nine for and seven against. The council was divided as follows:

For	*Against*
the landowner	head of the cooperative
village doctor	schoolmaster
village *shaykh*	agricultural engineer
6 fellahin	village *shaykh al-balad*
	assistant council chairman
	(oldest fellah in the council)
	2 fellahin

This story may well strengthen the earlier observation that most village councils are under the control of the traditional landowning families, and yet it also should be apparent that a new breed of fellah is emerging. This fellah is no *fahlawī*. He is proud of his position in the village council. He is free of cynicism and that dependence so common among the vast majority of the fellahin. Is he the exception or is he a preview of the future? Before we suggest a final answer to this question, let us consider the fundamental problems that the councils are facing and what if any are the possible means of eradicating the barriers presently precluding most fellahin from extending a strong commitment or sense of legitimacy to these new rural councils.

9 🔲 Egyptian Village Bureaucracy

As was suggested in an earlier chapter, this study is based on the assumption that subjective perceptions of rural institutions both from the viewpoint of the bureaucrat and the peasant must be considered if we are to understand the effectiveness and functioning of these institutions in rural Egypt. Habits of administrative behavior that are rooted in the Egyptian political culture must be considered. Bureaucratic behavior in rural Egypt may be analyzed from many different perspectives. For the purpose of this analysis, we will focus on three major problem areas: (1) historical and cultural determinants of bureaucratic practices in rural Egypt; (2) attitudes and perceptions of the rural administrator toward the peasant; and (3) attitudes and perceptions of the village peasant toward the administrator.

Historically speaking, bureaucratic centralism is perhaps the most obvious and pervasive characteristic of Egyptian administration. From the ancient rule of the pharaohs to the Roman, Arab, and Ottoman governments, all administrative power was centralized in Cairo or Alexandria. Professor Issawi notes that "the result of all this has been greatly to weaken individualistic feeling and completely to suppress the spirit of municipal enterprise. Several millennia of centralized autocracy have accustomed Egyptians to look to the government to initiate any business whatsoever. At the same time the rapacity of the governors has led to a profound distrust of the government, the effects of which are still visible."[1]

The central government, even today, is a complicated system of controls, communication procedures, and continual reports and inspection schedules. The obvious aim of this system is control, and thus it effectively precludes any meaningful delegation of authority to the lower echelons of the administrative hierarchy. This obviously places a great burden on the senior official who is often completely swamped with so many trivial questions that he has neither the time nor the inclination to concern himself with long-range policy planning or any serious evaluation of the presently functioning programs and procedures.

This centralist tradition has had a profound impact on the functioning of government administrators in rural Egypt. In general, all decisions on local matters, of both major and minor significance, are made by officials who spend very little time outside Cairo, and most local field officials are subservient and passive in their relationships with their superiors. Initiative and unauthorized action is discouraged. Too many of the local village administrators interviewed exhibited the *fahlawi* trait of refusing to accept any responsibility which could be evaded. All decisions and questions were automatically verbalized in an "official memo" and passed up to the appropriate superior.

These general attitudes toward initiative and personal responsibility reflect a series of historical and cultural factors, which have already been discussed. The oft repeated statement that bureaucracy, like any institution, is a reflection of the larger society of which it is a part is certainly not disproved by observations in Egypt. In the following paragraphs an effort is made to recreate the atmosphere in which the business of administration is conducted in rural Egypt. Many of the circumstances described below are undergoing major change. Certainly, procedures and programs

---

[1] Charles Issawi, *Egypt in Revolution*, p. 7.

are being reformed and reevaluated continually; hence, behavioral and attitudinal changes may be expected to follow. Nevertheless, the description given here is valid, at least for the rural areas I visited.

One fundamental determinant of the social environment in Egyptian bureaucracy is the great number of university graduates who must, by government decree, be hired by the various ministries. Thus, unfortunately, the supply of poorly trained, usually unsuitable recruits for employment in the rural areas generally far exceeds the work that the government has been able to effectively organize for them.

Several directors of social affairs in governorates of both Upper and Lower Egypt candidly remarked that since 1960 the various ministries have been required to hire all graduates assigned to them. One serious problem stems from the fact that young people have little or no choice in the selection of their careers. Each student must make three or four choices from among twelve available faculties. The individual student is then selected by the faculty in terms of the grades he achieved through the national examinations. As a result of this selection process, large numbers of students are drawn into government careers that they did not choose or that are forced upon them because of their lower grades.[2]

Government service is the principle form of employment for most college graduates. Since alternative means of employment at all levels are almost nonexistent, there is no beneficial competition between government and other activities for human services. Hence, the impact of competition—which would normally compel

[2] One director of social affairs in a Delta governorate stated that since the Ministry of Social Affairs must take large numbers of graduates each year, the ministry usually sends them out to the rural governorates. The governorate director has no choice but to assign these young graduates to a village social center. He pointed out that at least 50 percent of these "social workers" did not want to be social workers, have no desire to work in a village, and passively bide their time until they can get a reassignment to Cairo or Alexandria. One tragedy that often occurs is when a new social worker with a passive, often negative, attitude toward his village assignment, is sent to a village where the previous social worker had spent two or three years seeking to gain the trust and respect of the villagers. In a matter of weeks, these "misfits" can destroy all the good work of the earlier village administrators.

the public bureaucracy to improve its conditions of work to retain its employees—is totally absent. The vicious circle of this government monopoly over employment opportunities coupled with the general tendency of lower-level administrators to perform the bare minimum in the performance of their duties, primarily reflects an educational system that unfortunately has in many ways not radically changed in fifty years. Since 1892, when Lord Cromer required all candidates for appointment into the Egyptian bureaucracy to obtain a secondary school certificate, the entire educational system has been organized with this one view in mind. The certificate became the entrance ticket into the civil service. One writer has criticized this tendency in Egyptian education by noting:

It is obvious that a national system driving constantly toward such a goal, and producing successive generations of students trained for this goal must inevitably affect the national character. The nature of the training required for government posts clearly weakened Egyptian society in its total neglect of those features of education that make for personality, individuality, initiative, self-reliance, and independent thinking. Government posts offered a sheltered and secluded haven far removed from the activity and competition of ordinary life. The government employee had comparatively easy hours, a good salary, automatic promotions, periodic increases, annual leaves of absence, and a pension waiting for him at the end of the road. Once he could get his foot on the bureaucratic ladder he was ordinarily secure for the rest of his life. But preparation for such a life of security did not call for an education that would develop the sturdier qualities of personality. Centralized civil machines tend to grind down such independent qualities and to put a premium upon mechanical ability to follow orders, obedience to authority, and subservience to the ascendancy ranks of the bureaucracy.[3]

While one may criticize an educational system that seems solely concerned with preparation for government service, an even more pressing aspect of this problem needs to be considered. For while we may object to the substantive material taught in the classroom, an even greater tragedy appears to be the educational process of the educational system itself.

[3] Russell Galt, *The Effects of Centralization of Education in Modern Egypt*, pp. 53–54.

Many of the top educators in Egypt's Ministry of Education have painted glowing pictures of the progress and reform that have occurred in Egyptian education in the past ten years. From personal observations in village schools in rural Egypt, it appears that the process of education is best characterized in terms of formal and stereotyped curriculum in which rote memorization is still the chief method of instruction.

One village school in Kafr al-Shaykh is still vividly remembered. As we entered the school yard, three teachers were observed talking together while their students were in the classrooms shouting the daily recitations. When we entered the classrooms and asked for a demonstration of their reading skills, many of the students were able to read their primer without even looking at the pages. It is little wonder, as one official in the Ministry of Education admitted, that over half of those who complete primary school in rural Egypt are illiterate again within a year or two after graduation. Yet, this system is not unique to the rural areas. Most students, even at the American University in Cairo, for example, prefer "canned" lectures and specific readings. Many of the faculty at the American University admitted that the Egyptian student in general has a very difficult time with examinations that require some reflective analysis of material covered or that require the student to utilize the material covered to explain or solve an unfamiliar problem.

One incident that brought home the tendency for even university courses to rely on memorization was when a third-year medical student showed the author the neatly typed notes that his brother had used five years previously when he too had been in medical school. This student had memorized these notes, word for word, and felt assured that he would successfully pass the examination.

While these observations may seem harsh and unfair, they nevertheless reflect a situation that obviously has a profound effect upon the individuals who are graduating from the Egyptian university system and then entering positions of responsibility in the rural administration. The fundamental problem facing the bu-

reaucrat as he seeks to legitimize his position in the village is not
one of intelligence or even technical skills, but rather the obstacles
of culture and tradition. Too often the very methods of instruction
in their formal schooling have stifled innovation, initiative, and
independent thinking—the very characteristics that the rural administrator desperately needs if he is to be an agent for change
and reform.

A second major determinant of a bureaucrat's attitudes, behavior,
and values stems from his orientation toward the village itself.
Those rural administrators who were born and raised in a large
city were socialized to feel contempt and scorn for the fellahin.
Rare is the social worker, doctor, or even agronomist working in
the village who, once you gain his confidence, fails to admit his
abhorrence for his village assignment. Those administrators whose
roots are in a village also feel their assignment in a village must
be temporary. Their attitudes and behavior toward the fellahin are
cool and usually superficial. Their only desire is to return to the
"big city."

Most of these bureaucrats are college graduates and thus have
been attending school in a larger city for several years. Few of
them still have strong ties with their old villages. By tradition, a
young fellah, once in school, is expected to leave his village. His
whole school curriculum has emphasized and prepared him for a
life in the city. Any educated man living in the village is considered a failure if he does not find a career in some government
office in Cairo. In analyzing the government official still further
and noting how he perceives himself vis-à-vis the typical fellahin,
one notes the many things that emphasize their differences. He is
educated and they are illiterate; he is a government official with
power and authority and they are nothing; he has in their eyes a
high income and they live in poverty; and he dresses in Western
attire and they wear the *galabīyah*. Thus the government official
finds little in himself that he can share with the lowly fellahin.
Since his younger days in school, the rural administrator has looked
to the day when his education would free him from the ties of his

village. Now, forced to work and live in the village again because of his education, he often considers his position a tragic twist of fate.

The Village Doctor

The young village doctors proved to be a most valuable source of information. All are college graduates, most come from upper-middle-class homes, and a majority speak fairly good English. These doctors, who are required to work in a village for at least two years, usually appeared starved for an opportunity to talk to someone from Cairo. While their problems are in many ways unique, still their attitudes and behavioral patterns are quite similar to those of most officials assigned to work in the rural areas. The following stories are typical of the circumstances and situations these young doctors must face.

One extremely difficult problem for all village officials is the lack of proper facilities and a stimulating environment. One health unit in Sohag had neither electricity nor pure water. The young doctor in the village was from Alexandria. He had never lived in a village before in his life. His family was fairly well-to-do, and he was accustomed to a European standard of living. Upon graduation from medical school, he was assigned to the governorate of Sohag. After three or four weeks orientation at the general hospital in Sohag, he was shown on a map the village where he was to work. With a large trunk and his little black bag, he set out for his village. The first leg of his trip required a three-hour bus ride. He was dropped from the bus at a deserted road junction near the river that he must cross. After dragging his trunk down to the river, he discovered that no *fallūka* (river boat) was available. The temperature was 110 degrees in the shade, and finally, after waiting two hours, he wandered up the river where he met an old woman who guided him to a village with a boat—by now it was nearly three P.M. He crossed the river only to be told that the village was still three kilometers farther down the road. He hired a donkey to carry his trunk and finally arrived at his new assignment. No one was there to meet him; he found the health unit "a filthy mess—unfit for my dog to live in. The village itself was dirtier than I had ever dreamed." His orderly was asleep when he entered the health unit. The doctor was told that his room was in the back of the health unit. His first forty-eight hours in the village are best described in his own words: "My room was even dirtier than the reception portion of the health unit. There was no food in the health unit and I didn't dare eat the "baladi" food offered by the 'umdah. Being exhausted, I tried to sleep; yet when I turned back the covers, I discovered a scorpion. There was no electricity, so I spent the rest of the night pacing the floor. For the next three days it was like a nightmare—finally exhausted, nearly famished and completely defeated, I left the village." Although the director of health eventually assigned him to a village with a combined unit, any altruistic feelings that he may have had were obviously dissipated by his early introduction to village life. This doctor was completely discouraged and longed for the moment when he could return to Alexandria.

One woman doctor, who had been assigned to a village located forty minutes by train from Cairo, generally visited her village only two or three times a week. When she did go, she never stayed more than a few hours. She argued that life in the village would be impossible, and besides she had a good orderly who ran the clinic when she was not there. If an inspector should visit her clinic during her absence, her orderly would call her and she would then make it a point to be at the clinic every day for a week or two until the inspector returned. One doctor indicated that many of the village physicians make frequent trips to Cairo. When I asked him why the orderlies were willing to cover for these doctors, he laughingly pointed out that the orderlies were in charge of distributing the ma'ūna (U.S. aid supplies) and this evidently was a rather lucrative business. In many villages in both Lower and Upper Egypt, I noticed that local schoolteachers, agronomists, social workers, and doctors generally commuted each morning to their village from a nearby district or governorate capital.

These comments are not made to suggest that all village workers are discouraged and unwilling to help the villagers. Some officials are obviously dedicated, but they are the exceptions. One of the evaluation teams concluded its report on the government services offered in the village of Abishna with these words:

The only organization that was universally praised in the village is the health unit. This is due primarily to the faithfulness and sincerity of the doctor who believes in his mission and responsibility. This is the prominent difference between this organization and the other government offices which have adopted bureaucratic and passive methods. . . . [Many of these officials] require or demand a price for their services even when they know the economic circumstances of the fellahin. The veterinarian, for example, would refuse to visit a sick *gamoosa* until he was paid some *bakshish*. . . . If we take this veterinarian as an example of a government official who does not perform his duties, we will find that the larger landowners in the village are ever willing to offer him financial and material assistance so he will provide his services to them. These are the general conclusions:
(1) Most of the employees in the government organizations feel no sense of responsibility or duty for the work for which they are paid by the State.
(2) Government workers look down on the villagers and only associate with the wealthy and the educated individuals in the village. Their isolation from the fellahin has strengthened an inherited backwardness present in the village and thus has limited the positive influence of these services in the village community.
(3) Although government services are available in this village, greater concern should be emphasized for the means and methods by which these services are being performed and on the kinds of people in the village who are benefiting from the services.[4]

An Egyptian reader may well interpret this general description of rural bureaucracy in Egypt as an unsympathetic attempt to criticize an administrative system different from the Western model. This is not the aim, for the author left Egypt with the warmest respect for the efforts being made by many government officials to improve and strengthen their administration. Effectiveness, efficiency, and competence are goals that all serious Egyptian administrators are seeking to achieve. The observations here submitted merely suggest a series of problems that must be confronted

[4] Lutfi Muhammad Hasan, "Abishna," *al-Ṭali'ah*, September 1966, p. 41.

if bureaucracy in rural Egypt is to gain the acceptance and loyalty of the fellahin—a necessary step for any effective program of reform.

There is a tendency for many village officials to assume that the people with whom they are working and whom they hope to help are essentially rational, however uneducated they may seem to be. It should logically follow, given this assumption, that if the administrator or the party worker has difficulty in putting his programs across, either the fellahin are unusually stupid and cannot see the obvious advantages (to the administrator) of the change, or the official has not been as skillful as he should be in the presentation of his case.

In fact, however, these fellahin often do understand the message perfectly, but they are evaluating these new programs in terms of a hierarchy of values usually quite different from that of the official, whose training, experience, and values are primarily urban in orientation. Thus, the official may infer a stupidity on the part of the peasant or a lack of skill on his part, when in reality neither of these things has anything to do with the peasant's unwillingness to follow the village official.

Many doctors feel that their work in the village is a waste of time. "The peasants are never going to change" is an expression often heard. One doctor explained how, during his first month in a village, he tried to implement a program to clear up bilharziasis among the fellahin. The disease can now be cured through a series of twelve shots, two each week for six weeks. The life cycle of bilharziasis can be broken if the peasants will urinate on the ground away from the canals.[5] After the doctor spent many hours explaining the hazards of the disease, the fellahin readily agreed to take the shots. For weeks the doctor worked extra hours to ensure that all his patients were given their shots. Yet within three months the doctor was completely discouraged and privately admitted that all motivation he may have had in medical school

[5] Bilharziasis is a worm disease similar to hookworm. Many doctors estimate that 60 to 80 percent of all males in many of the rural areas have this disease; see Wendell Cleland, *The Population Problem in Egypt*, p. 86.

was now dissipated. Nearly all of the fellahin once cured were again infected with bilharziasis.

Where had this young doctor failed? Here are some of the excuses given by the villagers. The youth complained it was too hot not to swim in the canals; others argued they had to drink the canal water because well water was "tasteless" and impotent. (Many believe that drinking the Nile River water ensures a man's virility.) Many farmers pleaded that the work of irrigation forced them to wade in the canals. The final blow came when the doctor saw a group of the villagers bathing and urinating in the canal. To his dismay, the village elders explained that the Koran requires each man to wash and cleanse himself (this includes urinating) prior to saying his daily prayers. Therefore, these processes are inevitably carried out on the banks of a canal, where an uninfected person runs the risk of contacting the disease again. The doctor was obviously discouraged from continuing his efforts.

This sense of frustration and agony felt by so many village officials as they seek to help the fellahin is unfortunately usually interpreted by the fellahin as hostility or a feeling of superiority and a lack of understanding. These reinforcing perceptions of what the other person's motivations and thoughts are considered to be tend to result in a "self-fulfilling prophecy." The ability of the fellahin to interpret the village official's frustration as contempt and the tendency for the administrator to see peasants' unwillingness to change as stubbornness or stupidity renders any attempt on the part of the villagers or bureaucrats to communicate nearly impossible.

Many village doctors bitterly complained that the peasants were incapable of understanding the importance and value of the family planning program. One doctor, after several months of attempting to explain the need for family planning, concluded that the peasants were either deceitful or so completely apathetic that no effort to change them could ever succeed.

The cause for this lack of interest and cooperation may easily be interpreted as peasant stupidity and unconcern. Yet the peasant's reaction may well be a logical response to the cultural imperatives of his value system. In the eyes of a peasant man, his virility must be periodically verified. This reputation for manliness and virility is extremely important in the village society. The only legitimate means of substantiating his potency is for his wife to have a child each spring. How does one convince this kind of man? No arguments about the population explosion and its impact on Egypt is going to motivate or change this man. The women too are valued and respected in the village to the degree that they produce children. Any woman who fails to regularly conceive a child runs the risk of being divorced or having her husband take a second wife.

In a traditional agricultural society, where farm equipment is either unknown or unavailable, each family requires a large number of children to cultivate, plant, care for, and harvest the crops of its land. Even higher in the value system of the peasant is the idea that each child born is the will of God and that no person should interfere in this divine process. In the farmer's hierarchy of values, no material or political inducement is going to offset the value that he places on his children. In those cases where the government had offered to provide additional rations of *ma'ūna* to those women who would accept the pills or the "loop," the government failed, largely because the women interpreted this offer as a bribe and thus assumed that the birth-control devices must be harmful.

The particular way in which people classify actions and phenomena reflects the cultural orientation of their group. General attitudes in a society about what is good or bad, desirable or undesirable, right or wrong, are largely a function of the society's socialization process and value structure. A value system justifies one's behavior and activities and reassures the member of a society that he is behaving as his society expects.

Few would deny that maintaining enthusiasm and motivation among young village bureaucrats would, under these circumstances, be extremely difficult. Yet many village administrators complain that these conditions would be bearable if their superiors would support them and place reasonable requirements upon them. Many local administrators bitterly criticized their superiors for being completely unsympathetic to their problems. As one young doctor stated: "the central government does not really care about my medical work—all they want is that I perform my administrative responsibilities. I have so many administrative duties that if I did them properly I would have no time for my medical practice." Another young doctor pointed out that the governorate inspectors always side with the villagers in any argument: "these inspectors like to show off their influence by publicly castigating the doctor in front of the peasants. All the unsanitary conditions in the village are somehow attributed to the laziness or ineffectiveness of the doctor."[6] This tendency is also prevalent among the ASU members who energetically seek to increase their influence by criticizing and embarrassing the local bureaucrats.

A feature article in *al-Akhbar*, "Looking for a Needle in a Haystack in the Governor's Office,"[7] described the government's investigation into an alleged misappropriation of a quarter million Egyptian pounds worth of fuel used by irrigation pumps in the governorate of Sohag. This story describes in vivid terms the difficulties of the bureaucracy in rural Egypt. The discussion between the chairman of the investigation committee and the Sohag director of agriculture went as follows:

Chairman: Who receives the fuel used by these pumps?
Director: The director of the cooperative and sometimes by the storekeeper (*makhzangi*).
Chairman: What efforts are being exerted to fill in the gaps of this program?
Director: We have followed the instructions that are to be executed.
Chairman: How many cooperatives have executed these instructions?
Director: Most of the cooperatives.
Chairman: Would you specify one cooperative for us?

The writer of this article parenthetically adds: "It becomes clear that the director of agriculture cannot name one cooperative that has fulfilled these regulations. The truth is that these instructions

---

[6] These doctors were interviewed in January and February 1967.
[7] *al-Akhbar*, March 7, 1967, p. 4.

are not fulfilled at all. This situation is obviously embarrassing
to the director. The secretary-general of the ASU adds to his em-
barrassment by (mockingly) insisting 'come now, find us a name
or two.' "

Chairman: What is the new system that is followed?
Director: When we felt that there were gaps in the control, we made
a register for the mechanic on which he is to show the amounts of
fuel consumed.
Chairman: There was an old register—was there not?
Director: Yes, but this is like the register used in Asyut. (The director gets up from his place and takes a copy of the new register to
the chairman as if the new register would then prevent the mechanics
or the clerks from stealing the fuel. This is like the man from whom
a box of money was stolen and when the people told him of the theft,
he stated indifferently, "So what, the key is with me.")
Chairman: What is the amount of fuel that a machine uses?
Director: There is no fixed consumption rate due to the difference
in age and type of pump.
Governor: This is the major problem. The consumption rate can be
played with and this is the weakness of small machines. We must set
up proper supervision of this operation.

The investigating team discovered that some four thousand
complaints had been submitted by local villagers to the governor.
The ASU executive secretary of the Markaz Tamā admitted: "This
matter of the fuel is a mess. The agents of the cooperative steal
one-fourth of the fuel and the mechanics steal another one-fourth
and the farmers still pay the price for the total amount."[8]
In the village of Naga' Tanun near Sohag the investigating team
discovered that "most of the people in the village do not use these
pumps to irrigate their lands but are still required to pay for the
use of these pumps. The previous director of the cooperative kept
the fuel for his own use and those pumps that were inoperative
were allowed to sit out in the open where gradually all the remov-
able parts were stolen."[9] Sayyid al-Gibirti concludes his article:
"the management of the irrigation pumps brings forth a more

[8] Ibid., p. 7.
[9] Ibid.

important question, which is how can we administer or manage the Egyptian village? The importance of this question is obvious and stems from the fact that these villages now contain new institutions not present under the old regime, i.e., the cooperatives, the social and health units and state irrigation machinery. The old *'umdah* system and even the newer police stations are unsuitable for the new structures in the Egyptian villages. A new form must develop to suit the fellahin society."[10]

From our detailed description of the political socialization process found in rural Egypt, it should be easy to outline the general attitudes prevalent among the fellahin toward the government structures and employees presently found in the rural areas.

First, it must be noted that only recently has the Egyptian government actively sought an amelioration of living conditions in the rural villages. The traditional fellahin's opinion that government must be avoided is still very prevalent. Throughout Egypt's history, the government has been associated with tax collection, police force, and army conscription. Most villagers are still suspicious and unconvinced that the new government has changed. These suspicions unfortunately have been reinforced by the government's failing to consider all the ramifications of the changes they have sought to introduce.

A student at the American University told me a story of his grandfather, who had been given five feddans of land through the land reform program. When the man measured his piece of land, he found that he had only been given four and a half feddans. When the cooperative director explained to him that a certain amount of land had to be deducted for the roads, canals, and village areas, the old peasant was not convinced. In his mind, the government had cheated him and taken advantage of him. Thus, even a program implemented primarily for the benefit of the landless peasants comes to be interpreted as another example of the government's deceit and treachery. This kind of administrative blunder could easily have been avoided with proper planning and foresight.

[10] Ibid.

Yet, too often, actions of government officials are reinforcing the very attitudes, behavioral norms, and assumptions that they are trying to eradicate.

One excellent analysis of the Egyptian bureaucracy comes to much the same conclusion:

> There is still plenty of evidence especially in the villages to the effect that officials are resented as such, and are endured merely because of the necessities of the case. One does not find the same happy relations which exist between a capable businessman and a satisfied customer. . . . [All government agencies] should begin to emphasize and work on the problem of their relations with the entire citizen body. . . . But one has to recognize that a change of attitude has to take place as well as the adoption of special measures to give effect to this new attitude. *New steps must be taken to correct the present attitude of officials towards the public.*[11]

One perfect example of this problem comes from an agricultural expert in Gharbia. He explained that each peasant is given two bags of fertilizer for each feddan of land he owns. All too often the peasant will sell half of his fertilizer on the black market to a larger landowner in order to get some quick cash. At harvest time, when he takes his crops to the cooperative, he finds that his yield is so low that it does not even cover the expenses he has incurred through the cooperative for seeds, fertilizer, equipment, and marketing costs. The peasant blames the cooperative for trying to cheat him and the government agronomist thinks the farmer must either be lazy or stupid since he is unable to follow his instructions on how to increase his yield.

In al-Fayyum a doctor related a situation that obviously reinforces these old attitudes and animosities between government officials and villagers. During 1964 and 1965, the cotton crops were hit especially hard by the cotton worm. As a result, the cooperatives were forced to purchase large amounts of insecticides, which were then deducted from the peasants' profits. Many of the smaller farmers, attempting to increase their profits, would sell a quarter

---

[11] Luther Gullick and James K. Pollock, *Government Reorganization in the United Arab Republic*, p. 61; emphasis added.

or a third of their crops to the larger owners for immediate cash, their reasoning being that the cooperative would probably give them nothing whether they turned in all or only a portion of their crop. After all the crops had been turned in, the agronomist would be strongly criticized by his superiors for the low yield in his section. He in turn took it out on the fellahin. The peasant, shedding "real *fahlawi* tears" would swear that he had given his entire crop to the cooperative and that the agronomist was being unfair.

These stories, which are not uncommon, suggest some interesting characteristics of the fellah and his relationship to the new government institutions in his village:

1) The fellah still seeks to trick the "government man" whenever he can.
2) He has a strong desire to maximize his profits.
3) He is willing to fake poverty and lack of money to get sympathy.
4) He is still willing to negotiate and work through the larger landowners.
5) He has been unable to visualize the cooperatives as a beneficial institution created for his interest.

These attitudes are being reinforced and strengthened through an administrative system chained to traditional methods of control and supervision. The problems of bureaucracy in rural Egypt are complex and will not be solved merely by changing administrative organizations or bureaucratic procedures. The attitudes and behavioral norms of the peasant and the bureaucrat will not easily be changed. Yet a careful analysis of these problems suggests that a solution may be possible. In the next chapter I will describe in detail an experiment in rural development that may provide the approach needed to reverse the failures and mistakes noted in earlier programs. This experiment, known as the local savings bank project, offers a sharp contrast to earlier attempts at rural development and suggests a unique method for legitimizing a new institution in rural Egypt.

10 ▣ The Local Savings Bank

DURING THE LATE 1950's a young Egyptian graduate student, Ahmad al-Naggar, was given a fellowship to complete his Ph.D. in Germany. He began to study local savings banks and their development during the late nineteenth century. He noted their role as a financial institution but was more strongly impressed with the role these banks played in the social and political development of Germany's rural areas. It was then that he first realized what this kind of an approach could mean for rural Egypt. He returned to Egypt and attempted to present his idea to various government officials and ministries. Many officials scoffed at the idea, arguing that an independent local savings bank among the fellahin was an impossibility. Others, especially the senior officials, were not so harsh but indicated that at least twenty years would be needed before such a system could be introduced.

After several months of seeking support, one influential man, Dr. Adel Mon'im al-Qaysuni, deputy prime minister for economy and finance, did listen with a sympathetic ear and indicated his willingness to consider the possibility of such a program. In an attempt to gain some international support, Dr. al-Naggar wrote to an old friend, the president of the largest savings bank in Germany and a leading figure in the field of international finance. He invited the German banker to consider his bank's supporting a joint project to study the possibility of introducing this kind of banking program into rural Egypt. Later he convinced Dr. al-Qaysuni to invite the bank president to Egypt. This he did, and the eventual result was the signing of a German-Egyptian agreement to jointly finance and support a rural banking system in Egypt.[1]

With the signing of this agreement, Dr. al-Naggar was invited to implement the program by establishing a pilot project. After a careful preliminary investigation, the town of Mit Ghamr (population 50,000) a *markaz* capital in the governorate of Dakahlia was selected as the project site. Mit Ghamr was chosen for three reasons: first, it is located near the center of the whole Delta region and thus offers an excellent opportunity for future expansion in several directions; second, it is demographically representative of the vast majority of rural communities in Egypt; and third, both the governor and the general-secretary of the ASU in Dakahlia were personal friends of Dr. al-Naggar and had promised their support and cooperation.

During the initial stages of the development, Dr. al-Naggar and his staff postulated four conditions that would have to exist if the local bank system was to be effective in Egyptian villages:

1. Employees of the bank must be carefully selected and trained to insure that they have not only the knowledge and skills required by a bank official but also the dedication, sympathy, and desire to effectively work with the fellahin.

2. No bank is to be established until a strong bond of trust and mutual acceptance has been created between the bank workers and villagers to ensure a continuous and open line of communication between the community and the bank.

3. Every effort must be made to discover and utilize the formal and informal leaders of the community in order to ensure that all significant groups are allowed to participate and share in the functioning of the banking system.

[1] Most of the information concerning this bank program was obtained from interviews with Dr. al-Naggar and his staff.

4. National and local administrative support is vital if the banking program is to start, but equally important is the fact that
this government support must be indirect and subtle. Every
effort must be made to create the feeling that this is the villagers' bank and not the government's.

The four assumptions became the foundation upon which Dr.
al-Naggar developed a program to train future bank officials. The
author spent several months interviewing and observing these
young bank officials both in the bank's training institute and in the
villages where banks had been established. My interest in these
young men stems largely from the tremendous difference noted
in their attitudes and behavior toward the fellahin when compared
with the vast majority of bureaucrats working with the rural
peasants. Much of their devotion, dedication, and enthusiasm appears to have been generated through their training program.

Selection

In early July 1962, Dr. al-Naggar placed advertisements in two
Cairo newspapers (*al-Ahram* and *al-Akhbar*) twice a week for a
two-week period. The advertisement stressed that candidates were
needed to pioneer a project that would stimulate the rural people
to help themselves, that there would be a certain amount of risk
involved, but that, potentially, the program could be highly beneficial to the development of the country.

Also, Dr. al-Naggar contacted the heads of various departments
at the University of Cairo and 'Ain Shams University, as well as
the personal secretaries of the different ministries and invited them
to recommend prospective candidates. He requested that all applicants be either recent university graduates or employees of a ministry for not more than three years, and that they must have a
reputation for excellence.

There were some 622 applicants, who were screened through
a series of tests and interviews. Dr. al-Naggar, working closely
with Dr. al-Said Muhammad Khairy, assistant professor of industrial psychology at 'Ain Shams University, presented a series of

industrial psychology tests to measure intelligence, personality traits, leadership capabilities, integrity, and patriotism of the applicants. Second, each person was individually interviewed by Dr. al-Naggar or Dr. Khairy in an attempt to determine (1) their reasons for seeking employment with the local savings bank program, (2) how willing they were to work in the rural areas, (3) if they would accept work for three or four months without a salary and if they would be willing to take a possible salary cut from their present employment, and (4) the extent of their motivation, patriotism, and understanding of the problems facing rural Egypt.

Of the original 622 applicants, 209 were disqualified through this first stage of screening, which was conducted during a five-day period. The remaining 413 were divided into groups of six to eight individuals. They were instructed that they would be given a series of topics and that they would have one hour to discuss these topics. Some of the topics for discussion included (1) the Arab League—should this organization be encouraged or discouraged? (2) Housing—should new housing projects be built in the centers of the cities or on the outer areas of cities? (3) Sex and women— should mixed education be encouraged or discouraged? (4) Youth problems—what are the basic problems of youth today in the U.A.R. and what solutions are possible? (5) Transportation and traffic problems—what solutions can be recommended for the present crowded bus situation? (6) Rural areas—what projects are best conducive to alleviating the problems of the fellahin?

These discussion groups were not guided or directed, but were allowed to develop spontaneously. Each group was observed carefully in an attempt to measure each candidate's ability to work in a group situation.

Upon the completion of these group discussions, Dr. al-Naggar, Dr. Khairy, and their assistants made the final selection of twenty-one candidates. These candidates ranged in age from twenty-four to thirty-two, although the majority were under thirty. All had graduated with a B.A. from an Egyptian university—two in sociology, two in business administration, twelve in accounting, two in economics, and two in psychology.[2] Four of the twenty had only recently completed their university work, four had been employed in various ministries, one was in journalism, and the other eleven had been working for private companies. Six of the candidates were from a village background, while the other fourteen came from Cairo, Alexandria, or Ismailia.

Training Program

The training program started in September 1962 and ended in April 1963. The earlier portions of the training took place in a rented building in Cairo. Classes were held six days a week from 9 A.M. to 3 P.M. and from 5 P.M. to 8 or 9 P.M. The training program included the following techniques: reading assignments in Egyptian history; the culture of the Egyptian fellahin; economic history of the underdeveloped countries; economic situation in the United Arab Republic; principles of community development; leadership techniques; group dynamics; history of the savings banks; banking systems in Germany, Great Britain, the United States, and the Soviet Union; economics, with an emphasis on banking and finance; the new local government system in the U.A.R.; techniques of social research; interview techniques; survey techniques and objective reporting; and, finally, public relations and publicity.

Discussions

One of the most important and effective means of training the candidates was the informal discussion sessions. Each student would prepare a lecture or two on some phase of the training. This technique not only provided an opportunity for independent reading and research, but it also developed confidence among the trainees as they presented and explained the material they were studying. Following each lecture there would be a question and answer period. Dr. al-Naggar indicates that many of the unique aspects of the present local savings bank program were developed

2 Although twenty-one were selected, one dropped out before the training began.

during these discussion periods. During the discussion of how a new savings system could best be introduced into the villages of Egypt, the idea of a "non-interest-paying account" came into existence. Subsequent discussions broadened and conceptualized this non-interest-paying approach into a bank system with three types of savings account.[3]

Dr. al-Naggar felt that the real problems of the fellahin were questions of behavior and attitude rather than poverty or lack of intelligence. During these discussions, Dr. al-Naggar and the trainees sought to conceptualize more clearly the ways and means by which the peasant's behavior patterns could be changed. The value of this kind of approach to training cannot be overemphasized. Group participation stimulated individual creativity and initiative. Each member of the group felt that the techniques and solutions being developed through these informal exchanges of ideas belonged to them. The ability of Dr. al-Naggar to present key questions that would stimulate a broad range of responses, ideas, and solutions not only provided an intellectual growth for the trainees, but also suggested a whole new range of creative solutions to the problems of community development in Egypt.

Research Papers

Each trainee was required to write a series of research papers on some of the following topics: What is community development? How can one introduce new ideas and techniques among rural people? What problems and aspects must be considered in preparing talks or discussions with groups of peasants, women, students, etc.? How do you discover the real leaders in the village? What are the latest up-to-date bookkeeping systems for banks? What are the major problems involved in administering a local bank?

The major value of this kind of research in depth was not fully appreciated by the trainees until they actually began their work in the project itself. Within a matter of months, however, the

---

[3] See below, pp. 242–243.

value of these research papers became apparent. Not only was the information found in these training research papers applicable and valuable for a solution of the kinds of problems faced by the trainees in their new employment, but the expertise and confidence generated by an actual application of knowledge recently gained greatly reinforced their confidence and commitment to the whole banking program.

Practical Exercises

During the latter part of the training program, the trainees with Dr. al-Naggar spent a week camped outside a village in the governorate of Menufia, just north of Cairo. During the week, the trainees were encouraged to mix with the villagers. Following the age-old tradition of Arab hospitality, village *shaykh*s and heads of different families invited small groups of trainees into their homes. The primary purposes of this week's training were to:

1. Provide an opportunity for the trainees to live in a village under somewhat controlled conditions, thus allowing them to observe and participate first-hand in the lives of the rural fellahin.

2. Provide an opportunity for the trainees to apply some of the techniques of community development, such as developing a sense of who the "real leaders" are, means of cultivating their friendship, and methods of influencing and motivating these real leaders.

3. Provide an opportunity to gain through informal discussions with the villagers a clearer picture of the attitudes, behavioral patterns, group norms, common expressions (the fellahin jargon), and concepts of themselves, their families, outsiders, the government, and the outside world in general.

Once a reasonable amount of trust and friendship had developed between the villagers and the trainees, special meetings were called in which the savings bank project was explained to them. Perhaps more important than explaining the project itself was the opportunity afforded by these meetings to probe deeply into the fellahin's attitudes toward savings, development, and investment. Special meetings were held for women, students, the *shaykh*s, and the fellahin. Each group was encouraged to speak frankly, to discuss and debate their personal feelings about a village savings bank. Many assumptions, fears, and prejudices voiced by the fellahin themselves provided insights for the trainees in how the program would have to be modified when introduced into Mit Ghamr.

The goals of this training program should properly be divided into three categories:

1. Knowledge: The trainees were introduced to a general understanding of economics, rural sociology, psychology, public administration, banking and finance, community development, and the general and specific problems facing the United Arab Republic.

2. Technical and administrative skills: Although an opportunity to practice the skills listed below was not provided for in the six-month training program to the degree necessary for competence, it should be noted that during the first six months of the actual program itself, the trainees were utilizing these skills during the day and then having them evaluated, strengthened, and reinforced during the evening sessions.[4] During the training session itself each trainee was required to submit a tentative plan for introducing the bank system into a village. These plans were to be formulated in terms of planning, coordination, organization, control, reporting, and evaluation. Trainees were also introduced to the techniques of public relations, interpersonal communications, group dynamics, interviewing, and social research, which included methods for observing, conducting surveys, and presenting questionnaires. In addition, the trainees were given a refresher course in accounting skills, use of business machines, and even a driver-training course in the use of automobiles, trucks, and motorbikes. A beginning course in the German language was initiated as well as a general review of English. What proved to be a most important part of their training was a "refresher" course in the Islamic religion. Villagers are keenly aware of the "proper and improper" ways of praying and performing the rituals of a true Muslim. The

---

4 See below, p. 245.

trainees were encouraged to be aware of and practice the finer points of the Islamic faith. Also there was instruction on the use of the Koran and the various Hadīths that were applicable to the banking program. One of the most effective ways of introducing the banking program into the village was through the local religious leader. His support was often crucial in determining how readily the villagers would accept the banking project. Thus, it was extremely important that the trainees be aware of the practices, rituals, and religious teaching prevalent among the rural fellahin.

3. High morale and motivation: By far the most important factor in analyzing the effectiveness of this banking project is the individual attitudes, motives, and sense of mission of these original twenty trainees. In evaluating the training program, as well as the bank project itself, this crucial element must be taken into consideration. It is my impression that this program, devoid of personnel imbued with the motivation and desire to succeed that existed among these original twenty, would never have achieved the early success that it has. It is readily admitted by all the original twenty that their commitment to the project is primarily due to Dr. al-Naggar—his personality, his devotion to his work, and the sense of mission that he feels. This charisma, this personal relationship between Dr. al-Naggar and his trainees, must be institutionalized, impersonalized, and made a part of the program itself if the program is to succeed outside the sphere of one man's influence and personality. The crucial nature of this bond between teacher and student, however, is not easily impersonalized or made a function of an institution.

One of the major weaknesses of the program thus resides in the fact that the program is primarily the work of one man—Dr. al-Naggar. The crucial question of whether this program can expand beyond his influence must be considered. While the unique aspects of this training program are described, it is recommended that the following questions be kept in mind: What aspects of the training program cannot be duplicated? What aspects of the training program can and should be duplicated? And given these aspects that cannot be duplicated, what substitutes might be incorporated that would ensure similar results? Let us now explore the techniques, approaches, and experiences that the "original twenty" were exposed to:

Importance and Practicality of the Project

Dr. al-Naggar explained and analyzed the problems and obstacles that the Egyptian peasants must overcome if they are to enjoy a higher standard of living and the comforts and blessings of modernization. He explained the relationship between savings and development and the need to change many common attitudes and beliefs of the fellahin. He created a feeling among the trainees that the savings bank project would be one of the most effective ways of improving the condition of the fellahin. The validity of this belief (that the bank could change attitudes and conditions of the rural villagers) was not fully appreciated until the trainees actually began to introduce the project among the peasants. As the trainees saw the attitudes of villagers toward savings actually change through their own efforts and powers of persuasion, as new cottage industries were established, and as personal needs and financial problems were actually solved, the trainees gradually, probably imperceptibly, internalized a commitment to the bank that no training program could have ever developed.

Personal Relationship to the Bank Program

The trainees were constantly reminded that this was their own program, that each of them had a unique opportunity to participate in a pioneer project that would eventually have a tremendous impact on the lives and future of a majority of the Egyptian people. One aspect of this early training program that may well be extremely difficult to duplicate in future groups of trainees was the very fact that the development of the project was still mainly a loose set of generalizations in the mind of Dr. al-Naggar. Thus, in the course of this first training period, the trainees were active participants in clarifying, conceptualizing, and making operational many of the techniques, procedures, methods, and modes of operation that are now regular procedures for the entire banking staff. The very fact that these "original twenty" played such an active role in developing and implementing the new project provided an added bond to the program that will indeed be difficult for future trainees to develop or experience.

The Sense of Risk

As was noted in the pretraining interview sessions, Dr. al-Naggar probed deeply into the feelings of the candidates concerning salary and risk taking. He emphasized that members of the banking program would be paid according to their work output, that their salaries might be less than they were presently making, and that in the initial years of the project there might be months when salaries would have to be reduced. At the same time he appealed to their willingness to take a risk in a program that would fail or succeed according to their own efforts. This approach, known in Arabic as *mukāfaʾa shāmilah* emphasized that employment would be based on a free contract with no guarantees of salary, promotion, or permanency. All salaries and promotions were to be based on work performed. The common system of employment known as *daragāt*, which assumed that once a person is hired he can never be fired and whose salary and promotion depend primarily on the degree and year of graduation, was completely rejected in the banking system. Again, because of the unknown quality and future of the banking project as a basis for a meaningful career, the risk taken by the original trainees certainly strengthened their commitment to the bank program. This kind of psychological reinforcement will also be difficult to duplicate among future trainees who are already aware of the bank's success and its ability to provide a comfortable salary.

Meaningful Title and Position in the Banking Project

Upon completion of the first three months of training, the trainees were given the title *bāhith* (researcher), and upon completion of the six month program they were given the title of *khābir* (expert). The purpose of these titles was twofold: first, to encourage the trainees to believe that this training course had given them the necessary knowledge and skills in a new field of endeavor which justified and validated their new title; and second, the title provided them with a measure of prestige, which not only gave them confidence and self-esteem but also provided the villagers and townspeople with a symbol of rank so very necessary in the inter-relationships of a rural community.

Personal Relationship between Dr. al-Naggar and the Trainees

Each trainee was given special individual attention, and they were encouraged to come to Dr. al-Naggar whenever they had a problem. Dr. al-Naggar went out of his way to arrange special dispensations to meet the personal needs of his group: he arranged to have the wife of one trainee move to Mit Ghamr after the project started; he was ever ready to provide personal loans for short-term needs; and he even loaned his personal automobile for non-bank matters. These many examples of genuine personal concern for the trainees created a bond of loyalty and devotion that will be very difficult to duplicate in future training programs. One might add also that Dr. al-Naggar made it a special point to "overstimulate" their motivation and dedication to the program. During the early days of the project, they were all subject to a certain amount of pessimism and cynicism from government officials and academicians, many of whom deliberately tried to discourage the idea of a local savings bank among the fellahin. As Dr. al-Naggar admits, it was the challenge of these negative attitudes coupled with an intense loyalty for the banking project that has created these "super-motivated" individuals.

From this description it should be obvious why these young men have proven to be so enthusiastic and devoted to the project. Dr. al-Naggar himself argues: "Most of the success or failure of the educational aspects of this experiment depends to a great extent on the skill, zeal, enthusiasm, and attitudes of those working in the field—this is in addition to their capacity for influencing the atti-

tudes of the people. Actually the selection of these employees can
be considered as the corner-stone for the success of the project."[5]

When the training program was completed, the group of trainees
with Dr. al-Naggar moved to Mīt Ghamr. During the first few
weeks they made an effort to meet the formal leaders in the community: members of the town council, the government administrators such as the clinic doctors, headmasters of the schools, and
the chief social worker; also the *shaykhs* of the various mosques
and the local Coptic priest, the chief of police, the members of the
ASU *lajnat al-'ishrīn*, and influential members of the five leading
families.

At the same time the town was divided into three sections and
the twenty bank "experts" were also divided into three groups and
encouraged to get acquainted with as many people as possible within these areas. The initial reaction on the part of most of the peasants was one of great suspicion and doubt. Some argued that they
were tax collectors, others were convinced that they were seeking
information for the ASU, others suggested that they must be Communist agents, while some thought they were members of the Muslim Brotherhood. The bank workers seldom discussed savings or
banking but merely encouraged the peasants to talk about their
problems and ways in which these problems might be solved.

Once the curiosity of the villagers had been aroused sufficiently,
Dr. al-Naggar asked the town council chairman to call a series
of formal meetings with various leadership groups in the community. In these formal meetings with the members of the leading
families, the ASU, the schoolteachers, the labor union, the youth
clubs, and women's organizations, Dr. al-Naggar explained the
purpose of the banking program and the procedures that would be
used. In order to appeal to a broad class of people, the bank provided three kinds of accounts:

1. *Savings account*: This account would pay no interest. The
minimum deposit was five piasters (twelve cents), and withdrawal
was possible at any time. An interest-free savings account was a

---

[5] Aḥmad al-Naggar, *Bunūk al-'iddikhār al-maḥallīyah*, p. 40.

unique innovation developed during the training session, and proved to be a key factor in gaining supporters from among the conservative Muslim population. The Koran prohibits usury, and this new approach to banking galvanized a large number of Muslim religious leaders to openly support the banking project.

2. *Social services fund*: Each pious Muslim is supposed to give a portion of his income as a donation to the poor. Working with the local religious leaders, Dr. al-Naggar suggested that this religious tax (*zakat*) be collected and allowed to accumulate in the bank. A committee of local leaders would meet periodically to determine how this money could be distributed as charitable gifts. Surprisingly enough, many people contributed to this fund who had never before given *zakat*. All bank depositors were eligible for this "disaster insurance." While I was staying in Mit Ghamr, a local horse-drawn taxi was in an accident in which the driver's horse, his sole means of livelihood, was killed. Within two days the bank, through the social services fund, replaced his horse. It is obvious how this kind of activity would greatly add to the reputation and acceptance of the bank.

3. *Investment accounts*: This account requires a minimum of one Egyptian pound and can be withdrawn only after one year. Once a year each depositor is given a share in the bank's profits earned from the projects financed and supported through investment funds.

After these formal meetings with specific leadership groups, the bank experts moved out among the people. They spent many hours in the coffee houses talking with the elder members of the town, they visited homes, and they followed the fellahin out to their fields. Special attempts were made to suggest goals that the fellah might achieve if he saved a little each week. Farmers were shown they might have a new plough or a *gamoosa*. Students were encouraged to save for a bicycle or a new soccer ball. Women were urged to consider the value of a kerosene lamp or a sewing machine. Many group discussions were held in the local factories, the schools, public buildings, and in local clubhouses.

Gradually a few peasants would give ten or fifteen piasters to one of the bank experts and then a few hours later they would demand their money back. As their confidence in the bank officials grew, more and more people began to bring their money in. A temporary bank office was set up in one of the central buildings of the town. Within the first year, over a thousand individuals became depositors, and after three years, there were fifty thousand in the area of Mit Ghamr alone. Finally, in August 1964, the bank moved into its own building constructed on land donated by the governorate.

As the idea spread throughout the governorate, several communities requested that a bank be established in their area. By the spring of 1967, there were nine branches of this bank in Mit Ghamr, Bilqas, Sherbin, Mansura, Dakirnas, Zifla, Heliopolis, Kasr Aini Hospital, and Cairo Municipal Railroad Station. In early 1967 there were over 200,000 depositors with deposits in the three accounts exceeding 500,000 Egyptian pounds. The bank staff included over 300 employees, all recruited, selected, and trained in the same way as the original twenty.

The major purpose of the bank is to finance local projects that will stimulate economic growth. The bank will not extend loans to any individual until he has been a depositor for at least six months. The bank extends two kinds of loans: non-investment loans are extended to individuals who need a quick short-term loan to cover some emergency or to replace some item required for their livelihood. The borrower is required to repay only the amount borrowed (no interest charged) and may repay the loan at his convenience; investment loans are offered to depositors who wish to invest in some local industry or commercial endeavor. During the first year loans were made to start a brick factory, a shoe factory, a bamboo basket factory, a bakery, and several other cottage-type industries. In each instance, the bank gives technical assistance on how to buy raw materials, internal procedures of production, record keeping, and efficient marketing of their products. The bank has one employee whose major function is to locate customers in Cairo for the products of these bank investors. The loans are repayable over a reasonable period of time, based upon costs, rate of growth expected, and profits to be earned. Each borrower agrees to share a portion of the profits earned during the term of the loan. Again it should be noted that the borrower is not paying interest—he is only sharing his profits with the bank.

One bank official proudly indicated that during the bank's first year about 80 percent of the depositors put their money in the savings account. At the end of the year, when those who had their money in the investment account were given a 6 percent dividend for their invested money, about half the savings account depositors shifted their money to the investment account. The peasant quickly learned the advantage of long-term savings and investments.

One aspect of the program that needs to be noted is the "evening session." Each evening all the bank experts met with Dr. al-Naggar for two or three hours to discuss their day's experience and to plan for the next day's work. All of the twenty officials were asked to describe their daily experience—people they met, what new approaches they had discovered for gaining "new converts," what were people saying, who are the "real leaders," and what were their recommendations for improving the program. Thus, each evening these bank workers came together as a board of directors, each was treated as an equal, and many new ideas were generated through these "brainstorming sessions."

Dr. al-Naggar concludes a report on the results of the new bank program after its first two years of operation: "The question now is, what does it mean when 33,000 persons become savers. . . . This is an important social operation which includes three aspects: a) the people have moved out of their seclusion, b) they have expanded and widened the circle of their social contacts, and c) confidence and trust have been created, thus making the people move away from the fatal effects of passivism. Response and activity were thus stimulated because the piastre means much to these people."[6]

One point that Dr. al-Naggar has consistently emphasized is the fact that the bank has more than just an economic function in so-

[6] Ibid., p. 27.

ciety. True, the bank was created to encourage savings, to limit consumption, and to provide capital investment for local development projects, but there are other functions just as important. The bank has a social and political role, and, in the long run, these may well be more significant, at least in terms of the various organizations and institutions that the government is trying to create in the rural areas.

In one government program established to increase egg production, an administrative agency wanted to give away some prize chickens to various villagers scattered throughout the Delta. But the fellahin refused to accept a free chicken from the government because they feared they would have to pay a fine if anything happened to the "government's chicken." Dr. al-Naggar made arrangements to distribute the chickens for the government free of charge. He then announced through a meeting of the depositors that the bank had some chickens it would sell for a nominal fee. The depositors purchased 27,000 of these prize chickens.

The doctor of a village health unit went to the director of the local bank branch and complained that he had tried for six months to bring the women of the village together for a lecture on the methods and values of family planning. The bank director merely called a meeting of all the women depositors in the village, giving the doctor an audience of over three hundred women.

The education committee of the Mit Ghamr Town Council invited several members of the bank's board of directors to their monthly meeting to discuss the question of building a secondary school. The bank officials suggested that the bank finance the project with the stipulation that all students be required to pay a certain fee until the school is paid for.

In one village outside Mit Ghamr, the branch bank director had developed, in conjunction with the local social worker, a rather successful family planning project. Two new ideas were incorporated in their program. First, prior to announcing the family planning program, the bank director and the social worker visited all the midwives in the village. From past experience it was known that these women had vigorously opposed the government's family planning program in other areas. From casual conversation, it was learned that the midwives earn about three and a half Egyptian pounds a month for their services. The bank director asked them if they would support the family planning program if the bank paid them four pounds a month, to which they readily agreed. In addition, these midwives were given an official title and sent to a nearby combined unit for a few days training. This made a tremendous impression. The salaries for the midwives were allocated from the Ministry of Social Affairs, but disbursed by the bank director whom all the midwives greatly trusted.

Second, instead of giving the doctor or the social worker one pound for each woman converted to family planning, it was agreed that the person bringing the woman to the clinic would take fifty piasters and the other fifty piasters would be placed in a community fund. When I visited this village, they were saving money for a youth clubhouse, and the director mentioned that many of the teenagers were taking their mothers to the clinic so that fifty piasters could be put in the community fund.

These examples suggest the tremendous potential that the banks have in rural Egypt. Even more significant is the lesson this experiment suggests for future rural development in Egypt. The obvious source of this new institution's success lies first in its leadership—men with knowledge, skill, but even more, men with initiative and a deep sense of mission. But equally important is the fact that the villagers trust and accept this new structure in their midst. The bank is legitimate in their eyes because it seeks to satisfy their needs and is gradually fulfilling their emerging aspirations.

Dr. al-Naggar suggests further that "the political effect of this program is mainly centered in strengthening the system of local administration and in finding a common solution to the problems facing the villagers. The process of encouraging people to move out of their isolation and seclusion, and to participate in public fields of interest has significant political effects. The process of finding and creating new aspirations and interests is, in itself, a political task."[7]

[7] Ibid., p. 50.

The obvious contracts between this "new institution" and the earlier government organizations discussed is significant enough to warrant a broader discussion of the causes for the bank's success.

While the following are merely tentative suggestions, they may offer some insights into the process by which individuals come to accept and support an alien institution. First, the bank, as a new institution, is not incompatible with the needs and behavioral patterns of the villagers. The fellahin have traditionally saved, yet their savings were usually hidden in jars under the earthen floors of their homes or invested in golden ornaments worn by their wives. Often these savings were unwisely spent on a wedding or a funeral or other uneconomic consumption. Also, the fellahin have frequently been forced to borrow, but seldom were loans contracted through a bank. Most fellahin borrowed from a local money changer at exorbitant rates. Given these obvious needs (a place to save their money and an institution through which fair and convenient loans could be obtained), the bank was certainly not inconsistent with their needs. However, government banks had existed in Egypt for many years. The local post office, after seventy years of encouraging a savings program, had only seven thousand depositors in all of Mit Ghamr prior to the establishment of the savings bank. In the late 1950's, the government instituted an agricultural credit bank, yet after ten years experience more than 60 percent of the loans were never paid back. In contrast, 100 percent of all loans made to the people in Mit Ghamr by the savings bank had been repaid. One fellah explained to me that money from a government bank did not have to be repaid because "they have lots of money." When asked why he would repay his loan to the local savings bank, he pointed out that "the money in the savings bank belongs to my neighbors, my relatives, my friends—if I didn't repay that loan I would be stealing from them."

Another important generalization that can be gleaned from this project is that traditional values are not necessarily inimical to the introduction of new structures or institutions.[8] To the contrary, the

8 This point has been argued before. See Bert F. Hoselitz, "Tradition and Economic Growth," in *Tradition, Values, and Socio-Economic Development*, ed.

most readily accepted new institutions are those defined in terms of traditional values. The "non-interest account" is a perfect example of how a traditional value can be efficacious in stimulating innovation.

Dr. al-Naggar notes also: "The people are still clinging to the intellectual and spiritual aspects that are closely related to the values in which they believe. Interest, for the people is prohibited and unlawful, and the people believe that God will bless this project because it fulfills the teachings of religion. This simple but deep belief has been the motive driving thousands of people to deposit their few piastres in full trust and confidence, without having any material benefits drawing or attracting them to it."[9]

One unique aspect of this bank program that creates an advantage over most government institutions operating in rural Egypt is its ability to measure success. How does one go about measuring trust between the villagers and a village council, or between the farmer and the cooperatives or social units. Each bank can easily measure its progress in a community by the number of depositors and by the amount of money they are willing to deposit. Thus, while a doctor or a council chairman may become discouraged and fail to see that his efforts have resulted in any progress, the local bank employee has a constant motivation to see how many people he can "convert." His efforts are quickly measured and his sense of success more easily activated. The same motivating factor works for the depositors themselves. The more they deposit, the more the institution gains acceptance and becomes legitimate.

An eminent psychologist, Leon Festinger, has developed a concept that helps explain the process by which individuals shift legitimacy from one structure to another. When a peasant must choose between two alternatives, one of which is clearly superior, his decision entails no doubts and conflicts. Thus, most traditional villagers have little trouble in deciding to follow their old 'umdah rather than the new village council chairman. But if the two alter-

Ralph Braibanti and Joseph J. Spengler; and David E. Apter, *The Gold Coast in Transition.*

[9] Ahmad al-Naggar, *Bunūk al-'iddikhār al-maḥallīyah*, p. 27.

natives are both attractive, the choice creates what Festinger calls "cognitive dissonance."[10] In psychological terms, the anxiety created from rejecting an accepted method or a traditional procedure for some equally acceptable method or procedure produces a certain amount of mental anguish over the decision made. In such a state of anxiety, the individual seeks to reduce this dissonance by changing his evaluations of the two alternatives after having committed himself to one. Thus he reduces these disturbing doubts by increasing the value of the chosen course of action and decreasing the value of the rejected course of action.

Cognitive dissonance does not arise in a situation where a superior enforces compliance for a particular action by virtue of his position with its concomitant assortment of sanctions. If a cooperative director uses his coercive power to force the fellahin to adopt a particular seed or utilize a new piece of equipment, the obvious consequences make obedience unequivocally the preferable alternative. Although the peasant acknowledges that submission is unpleasant, there is little doubt in his mind that the consequences of noncompliance would be worse. In this situation there can be no cognitive dissonance and, hence, little opportunity for the director of the cooperative and his orders to become legitimate through a process of "dissonance reduction."

How is legitimization generated through this process of dissonance reduction? Let us take the local banks again. When the bank offers services to a fellah either to hold his money or to provide him with a loan, there is no obligation to accept, and in reality there are various alternatives available by which these services might well be satisfied. If, through the effective encouragement of the bank officials or his friends and neighbors, he decides to deposit his money, a certain amount of cognitive dissonance is bound to arise. Is the bank really dependable? Is my money safer in their vault than in the floor of my own home? To resolve this cognitive dissonance, he will be compelled to rationalize his decision. Soon he inflates the value of the bank and deflates the value of hoarding money in his

[10] Leon Festinger, *A Theory of Cognitive Dissonance*, pp. 61–68.

home. One interesting development noted among the new bank depositors was the tendency to justify their decision to support the bank not only in terms of personal motivation, but also to suggest they were doing this for the good of Mit Ghamr, their country, and the revolution. Although these justifications for one's action may easily be seen as rationalizations, they quickly become a social phenomenon as more and more people adopt the same ideas. The members of a village who have deposited in the bank are often found sitting together discussing the values of the bank and actively seeking to encourage others to follow their example. Social communication gradually transfers these individual rationalizations into common values. As these values become widespread and generally identifiable with the functioning of the local bank, its existence, its structures, and its methods of procedure gradually gain legitimacy. The common belief that the bank does offer superior services becomes the basis of many normative restraints that are reinforced by social values that justify compliance and discourage nonconformity. These norms, like social norms generally, are internalized by the group members and socially enforced, with the result that even the potential deviant who for some reason may not feel personally obligated, for example, to repay his loan to the bank, is now under social pressure to comply lest he incur the disapproval of his friends and neighbors.

If this analysis proves to be correct, the same process would hold true in the operation of any structure of society. The new village council chairman, the ASU secretary-general, the doctor, the social worker, or the agronomist would all become legitimate to the extent that compliance to their requests rests not upon coercion or administrative obligation, but upon the villagers' own social norms and system of values. This, as I have suggested several times, rests on the perceived images that the villagers and bureaucrats have toward the structures operating in their community. To the extent that these structures can be identified with the benevolent fulfillment of some need or value, they will become legitimate. In most cases our feelings of loyalty and acceptance develop through a process of socialization in which the values and the institutionalized structure of these values are internalized and made a part of our conscious attitudes and assumptions. Festinger's concept of cognitive dissonance adds a new dimension to the process of legitimization inherent in the transitional society where new institutions and structures are rapidly being introduced. Those who are determined to see the ASU gain legitimacy or the village council gain an accepted position in the village might well consider the implications of this process.

"How are we to evaluate the spiritual achievements and the noble motives that have once again been brought to life? How are we going to evaluate the changes in our society—its values, its morals, and behavior? If we seek to evaluate them now, we shall fail. For despite all of these achievements we must admit that all we see are buds, but in the future these buds will yield their fruits to us."[11]

[11] Ahmad al-Naggar, *Bunūk al-'iddikhār al-maḥallīyah*, p. 27.

11 ◨ Conclusions

POVERTY IS A WAY OF LIFE for nearly two-thirds of the people in Egypt. Poverty means hunger and malnutrition. Malnutrition leads to sickness and general ill-health. Disease, in turn, debilitates and reduces human output, which then aggravates the tendency toward greater poverty. To break this vicious circle requires energy and knowledge and change, aspects of development that unfortunately are lacking in most of the rural villages of Egypt.

To remedy this situation requires a prodigious effort—for Egypt must tackle ill-health and ignorance, increase agricultural and industrial production, provide welfare services, and emancipate the rural communities from the habits and social structures of bygone centuries. The size of such a task is tremendous, for it requires the government to go into the villages, to awaken, inspire, and, in the early stages, to lead. The central government must enlist the enthusiastic support of the village communities to provide the labor for self-help projects and to participate in the introduction of services such as education and health.

Development is primarily a form of communication and persuasion. The fundamental purpose of community development in

Egypt is to generate within the fellahin a burning desire for change, which, through progressive adaptation of modern techniques, will lead to their achieving a higher standard of living. Of course, it must be emphasized that the problem is not simply one of the fellahin adopting modern ideas and techniques offered to them by the ministerial agencies of the central government. It is much more a question of adapting these ideas and techniques to suit the culture and values of the people. Somehow a communication bridge has to be constructed between Cairo and the villages to span not only the physical distance but also the centuries that often separate the rural areas from the capital in ideas, values, and patterns of living.

The traditional political structure of rural Egypt is under attack from the central government. Nasser's charismatic appeal and his new political ideology have challenged the peasant village structure of authority. Ancient patterns of power and control that centered in family relationships are now being questioned by many fellahin and even rejected by a few. The inroads of modernization have weakened the foundation of rural traditionalism. Many peasants are shifting their loyalties from the 'umdah and the old landowning families. Legitimization as a function of traditional concepts of authority is gradually decreasing as the predominant political fact of rural Egypt. New structures, institutions, and organizations have been introduced. It is obvious that these new structures, such as the ASU *lajnat al-'ishrīn*, the combined units, and the village councils have generally failed to generate a strong commitment or sense of loyalty among the rural peasants.

The crucial problem facing rural Egypt is the fact that new values are being introduced, but only a part of the citizenry is accepting them. Thus, Egyptian society is characterized by cultural fragmentation. The fellahin in transition have not fully accepted the ideology that was promulgated by the Nasser regime. In many of the institutions being introduced, traditional attitudes, values, and behavioral norms, rather than being neutralized or weakened, are in fact being strengthened. The fellahin thus have little if any sense of loyalty or commitment to the ASU committees, the combined units, or the village councils. Acceptance is still largely a matter of personal relationships. The popular village doctor, the influential ASU leader, or the respected council chairman wield power and authority because of personal, face-to-face relationships that they have developed. Put in a new doctor, a new ASU leader, or a new council chairman, and he will have to start all over. Given the attitudes of a vast majority of the peasants and the village officials living in rural Egypt, it appears that the structures herein outlined, described, and analyzed have little chance of gaining wide legitimacy or acceptance in the near future. The solution to this problem must not be conceived as merely a question of administrative reorganization or the establishment of new procedures, laws, or regulations. A long-range solution will require a gradual process. Innovation or change is not necessarily resisted by the Egyptian peasant. Opposition develops only when a traditional value is directly attacked or repudiated. From the bank project, it appears that new ideas, values, and behavioral traits will largely be accepted to the degree that the innovations are defined and identified in terms of traditional values or at least shown to hold a higher position in the value hierarchy claimed by the individual.

Nasser's planned program of resocialization through the institutional mechanism of a single political party has been defended by various scholars as the most effective means of introducing a new political culture. Ideology, so the argument runs, is a vital element necessary if the masses are to generate the enthusiasm and commitment necessary for rapid development. Yet, a careful analysis of the ASU and its impact upon the fellahin suggests that ideology usually appeals to but a small segment of the rural population. While many people are stimulated and motivated over the short run, it appears that long-term commitments from the vast majority of the people require more than mass rallies and impassioned speeches. Experience in rural Egypt forces me to go one step further. Not only is ideology ineffective in developing the kinds of attitudes and motivations necessary for growth and development, it may actually be a detriment to this development. Following Professor La Palombara's advice:

[One should] be extremely wary about the dynamic potential of the so-called 'ideology of development,' attributed to many of the leaders of developing countries. Presumably, such strong, normative commitments to economic or political change offer strong reason to suppose that obstacles or resistance to change will be overcome. Yet, such ideologies themselves constitute obstacles to the successful resolution of several crises. For example, a genuine commitment to economic and social change at all cost may quickly lead to decisions to ride roughshod over traditional institutions, thus creating conditions that surely aggravate problems of integration and legitimacy.[1]

Rural affairs have until only very recently been largely controlled by local leaders. The Nasser regime sought to introduce several major socioeconomic reforms in the Egyptian society. In this effort, they uniformly met resistance from traditional leaders and groups at the local levels. When the modernizing goals were limited, the central government permitted traditional leaders to run village affairs in the age-old fashion. However, since 1960 the Egyptian government has sought to extend the domain and speed of development. The result of this increased effort is the paradoxical situation in which an earlier administrative system, largely left to the control of local leaders, is now attacked for being too centralized. The irony of this criticism rests on the fact that the government now appears to be establishing a local administrative system much more tightly controlled by central government officials than in any earlier period in Egyptian history and this effective penetration of the rural areas is justified and defended in terms of the government's new commitment to local autonomy and decentralization.

Of course local government is the avowed aim of the present regime in Egypt. Interestingly enough, significant numbers of local leaders, especially in the larger, more populous rural communities, have come not only to accept but even to demand the fruits of modernization and progress. Many local leaders interviewed indicated

[1] Joseph La Palombara, *Alternative Strategies for Developing Administrative Capabilities in Emerging Nations*, p. 20.

a strong commitment to the goals and aspirations of the central government, such as extension of roads and bridges, increased literacy, improved sanitation and health measures, more efficient agricultural production, and a further expansion of rural industries. The more one talks with these local leaders, however, the more one realizes that they are not especially eager to raise the money to finance them. They want the central government to pay for development programs, but not to staff and control them. This problem must be recognized by those who would criticize the central government for failure to accept the full implications of its call for decentralization and local government.

Although Nasser's government imposed some taxes on the rural population, most of the revenue came from the more productive sectors located in the major urban areas and from customs imposed on international trade. Hence, the cost of local improvements has been largely financed from the center. Indeed, it is these urban sources of financial support that have allowed the central government to provide the limited services now available in the rural areas. If the central government had merely advocated change and reform, requiring local structures to finance their own development, it is doubtful if the modernization of the rural areas would have penetrated as deeply as it has.

The weakness of local self-government in rural Egypt means, of course, that the bulk of the citizenry is denied meaningful participation and thus lacks one of the most effective means of generating the acceptance and feelings of legitimacy necessary to institutionalize the new processes of decision making and political control. Thus traditional forms of local decision making appear to persist in the vast majority of village communities. Even where village councils are functioning and local elections are held, they too often tend to be of limited significance. They may, of course, become the focus of great local excitement, and certainly they can have an impact on the local scene.[2] Obviously locally elected officials can play

---

[2] Generally the function of a local election is ceremonial. Village elections

only a minor role in a decision-making process dominated, at least financially, by the central government.

One crucial problem facing the effective functioning of local government is the lack of qualified local people. As central government services are offered to the villagers, the more energetic and intelligent young people leave the villages to seek better education and employment opportunities in the urban centers. The frailty of local politics and employment opportunities precludes the rural areas from holding the more competent members of their communities. Instead of contributing to the vigorous growth of a locality, centrally based development deprives it of its best potential leadership, leaving a residue of partially educated men and women whose level of aspiration has risen more rapidly than their capabilities. Hence, the bitterness and frustration of such a system decreases the likelihood that the local citizen will accept or consider as legitimate the political process that controls his life.

One can strongly argue that the sense of commitment and identification implicit in our earlier defined concept of legitimacy will not gain long-term support until local self-government is strengthened and broadened—not only as a means of providing a truly significant political experience to large sectors of the rural population, but also as a means of controlling and challenging the local functionaries into improving and expanding their services in the village. This growth of locally independent bases of political power requires village institutions financially independent of the bureaucracy and composed of a body of local leaders, not only intellectually competent and reform minded, but more important, genuinely tied to the rural area through solid economic and political interests.

Such comments should not be construed as an argument for immediate self-government for rural communities. Quite the contrary, I believe such a policy would lead to stagnation in most villages of rural Egypt. Obviously, the first stages of political, economic, and social development in these traditionally oriented vil-

---

in Egypt tend to reflect the relative prestige rating of different families and thus are seldom based on programs or public issues.

lages require the infusion of external stimulus from the central government. Nevertheless, Egypt's experiment in local savings banks suggests that various alternatives are available.

Nasser's regime was plagued with the difficult task of establishing a new set of symbols for and a new foundation upon which a sense of legitimacy and commitment could rest. Whether the fellahin come to accept the ideology and institutions presently being introduced into rural Egypt depends in the long run on the extent to which the new regime's party workers and government officials are competent and dedicated to a solution of the peasant's own problems. Although the peasant may eventually perceive their government representatives in this light, the lasting impression of this study should suggest the difficulty of such a development.

Today the Egyptian leaders appear committed to pursuing those programs and policies for rural development initiated by President Nasser. Armed with the powerful memory of Nasser's goals and aspirations, the new regime must now seek to channel this memory into domestic programs that will stimulate development and reform in the rural areas. Nasser's charisma was real and his influence will long be felt in Egypt. The extent to which Nasser's successors will now build upon his achievements and also learn from his mistakes will largely determine the degree to which the institutions and ideals espoused by Nasser will be institutionalized and legitimized by the Egyptian people.

APPENDIX A

Duties of the Active Members of the Arab Socialist Union[1]

a) To adhere to spiritual and human values.
b) To apply the statute of the Arab Socialist Union.
c) Always to maintain and safeguard the unity and cohesion of the Arab Socialist Union.
d) To endeavour to execute the decisions of the Arab Socialist Union and the duties entrusted to the active members by it.
e) To study continually the decisions of the Arab Socialist Union's organisations and explain them to the people.
f) To accept the decision of the majority even if it is contrary to personal opinions and to try to carry it out with sincerity and devotion.
g) To set a good example to others and to socialist citizens, in the sphere of work and in behavior.
h) To try continually to raise their own intellectual and ideological standards and to fully understand the principles of the National Charter and explain them to others.
i) To sacrifice continually personal interests for the interest of the Arab Socialist Union and the people.
j) To practice criticism and self-criticism and try to rectify their own mistakes in a good spirit.
k) Not to ask any privileges or exceptional treatments for themselves or for others.
l) To try to acquaint themselves with their local environment and to raise the standard of awareness and culture of the people in their environment, in a practical and successful manner.
m) To try to be always in contact with members of the public within their own sphere to find out their wishes and needs. Also to explain the views of the people to the Arab Socialist Union.

[1] United Arab Republic, *Statute of the Arab Socialist Union* (Cairo: Ministry of National Guidance, 1966), pp. 15–19.

n) To try to discover the leading elements in their local society, have them join his subsidiary organization and give them the necessary advice.

o) To resist with all his power the enemies of the social revolution, Arab nationalism and our liberty and independence. He should consider himself as the owner of the Revolution and the Socialist Union.

The active member of the A.S.U. shall have the right:

a) To elect and to nominate himself for election to positions of leadership in the A.S.U.

b) To take part in discussions and express his opinion at meetings of the A.S.U.

c) To have his opinion heard by any leadership body in the A.S.U. if that opinion conflicts with any decision taken by the Union. He shall, however, be bound to execute such decision until his objection is considered.

d) To pose questions and put forward proposals to the formations of the A.S.U. and to make such criticisms as he may consider instrumental in raising the level of the A.S.U. and its formation.

e) To make any request or complaint to any formation of the A.S.U.

f) To debate factors affecting the raising of the social, economic and cultural standards of his basic unit; and to take part in investigation and study committees leading to appropriate solutions.

g) To debate in the press questions relating to the policy of the A.S.U. and to the realisation of its objectives.

APPENDIX B

Provinces of the United Arab Republic

	Province	Arabic Name	Area sq. kilometers	Capital
1.	Cairo	al-Qāhirah	214,000	Cairo
2.	Alexandria	al-Iskandarīyah	290,000	Alexandria
3.	Suez	Suways	307,000	Suez
4.	Port Said	Būr Saʿīd	397,000	Port Said
5.	Ismailia	al-Ismaʿīlīyah	829,000	Ismailia
6.	Kalyubia	al-Qalyūbīyah	944,000	Benha
7.	Sharkia	al-Sharqīyah	4,702,000	al-Zuqaziq
8.	Dakahlia	al-Diqahlīyah	3,462,000	al-Mansura
9.	Damietta	Dimyāt	599,000	Damietta
10.	Menufia	al-Munūfīyah	1,514,000	Shibin al-Kom
11.	Gharbia	al-Gharbīyah	1,995,000	Tanta
12.	Kafr al-Shaykh	Kafr al-Shaykh	3,492,000	Kafr al-Shaykh
13.	Buheira	al-Biḥarah	4,593,000	Damanhur
14.	Giza	al-Jīzah	1,079,000	Giza
15.	al-Fayyum	al-Fayyūm	1,792,000	al-Fayyum
16.	Beni Suef	Banī Suwayf	1,313,000	Beni Suef
17.	Minya	al-Minyā	2,274,000	Minya
18.	Asyut	Asyūt	1,553,000	Asyut
19.	Sohag	Sūhāj	1,540,000	Sohag
20.	Qena	Qinā	1,811,000	Qena
21.	Aswan	Aswān	882,000	Aswan
22.	Matruh	Matrūḥ	710,000,000	Mersa Matruh
23.	New Valley	al-Wadī al-Jadīd	30,000,000	al-Kharja
24.	Red Sea	al-Baḥr al-Aḥmar	165,000,000	Hurgada
25.	Sinai	Sīnāʾ	61,000,000	al-Arish

APPENDIX C
The ASU-Local Government Structure (Sept. 1967)

Local Government Structure

Governorate Council

(1) Elected Members
(2) 10 Selected Members
(3) Ex Officio Members

Town Council

(1) 20 Elected Members
(2) Up to 5 Selected Members
(3) Ex Officio Members

Village Council

(1) 12 Elected Members
(2) 2 Selected Members
(3) Ex Officio Members

Arab Socialist Union Structure

Governorate Committee of 50

Town Committee of 20

Committee of 20.

Governorate Conference

Town Conference

Basic Unit Conference

Formal Election - - -
Dual Membership

APPENDIX D

Basic Units of the ASU in Each Governorate (1967)

	Number	Member
Cairo	889	412,298
Alexandria	413	258,575
Port Said	63	48,519
Ismailia	49	45,655
Suez	58	39,969
Buheira	527	853,704
Damietta	79	89,874
Kafr al-Shaykh	234	199,162
Sharkia	526	434,333
Gharbia	441	366,302
Dakahlia	553	424,884
Menufia	336	303,000
Kalyubia	378	218,773
Giza	336	265,235
al-Fayyum	187	177,091
Beni Suef	258	177,056
Minya	409	33,294
Asyut	314	259,412
Sohag	304	312,035
Qena	232	253,699
Aswan	124	89,505
Red Sea	28	8,611
New Valley	24	11,094
Matruh	39	17,161
Sinai	18	13,950
TOTAL	6,819	5,313,191

APPENDIX E

Governorate ASU Organization (June 1967)

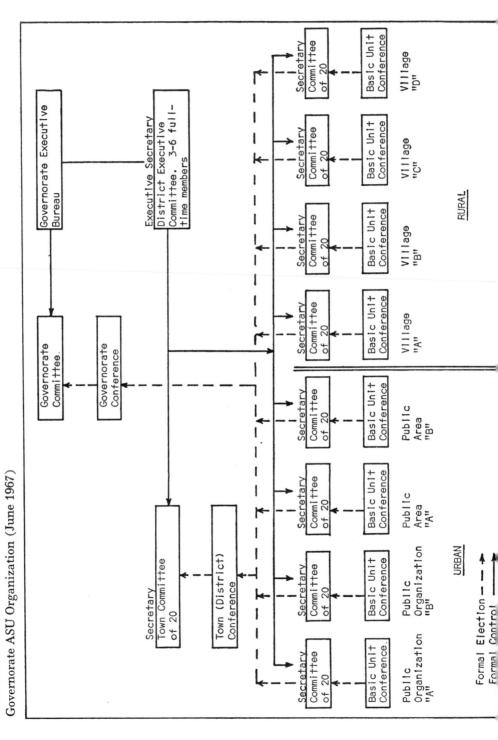

APPENDIX F

Number of Combined Units in the Governorates (1967)

Cairo	0
Alexandria	0
Port Said	1
Ismailia	0
Suez	0
Buheira	22
Damietta	6
Kafr al-Shaykh	12
Sharkia	25
Gharbia	25
Dakahlia	32
Menufia	17
Kalyubia	15
Giza	16
al-Fayyum	16
Beni Suef	16
Minya	27
Asyut	16
Sohag	29
Qena	21
Aswan	5
Red Sea	0
New Valley	0
Matruh	0
Sinai	0
TOTAL	301

APPENDIX G

Number of Villages under Each Village Council in the Governorate of al-Fayyum (1964)

Village Council	Number of Villages
Disya	7
Damu	4
'Azib	5
al-Ahun	3
Biyihmu	3
Sinhur	2
Fidyimin	3
Mutartaris	5
Tarsa	4
Qalhana	6
Qalmasah	3
Abu Jindir	9
al-Hazir	4
Minya al-Hit	5
Tatun	3
Abu Kasah	5
al-Hamula	4
al-Shuwashina	2
Tabhar	5
al-Ajmiyin	2
al-Nazla	2
Dar al-Salam	2
Sarsina	3
Qasr Rishuwan	2
Minshat al-Jamal	3

APPENDIX H

Number of Local Councils in the United Arab Republic

Governorate	1966 Population	1967 Budget thou. £E.	Governorate Council	Town Council	Village Council
Cairo	4,196,998	34,987	1	5ª	0
Alexandria	1,800,951	12,735	1	4ª	0
Port Said	282,876	3,787	1	1	0
Suez	264,025	2,803	1	1	0
Damietta	432,401	2,669	1	4	22
Dakahlia	2,279,139	9,079	1	10	98
Sharkia	2,125,376	8,448	1	10	82
Kalyubia	1,210,703	6,621	1	7	50
Kafr al-Shaykh	1,121,677	3,526	1	7	38
Gharbia	1,892,974	8,860	1	8	70
Menufia	1,467,600	8,097	1	8	78
Buheira	1,976,891	7,151	1	13	76
Ismailia	344,499	2,353	1	4	4
Giza	1,645,244	7,737	1	5	50
Beni Suef	934,008	4,753	1	7	41
al-Fayyum	930,961	4,302	1	5	42
Minya	1,702,969	7,297	1	9	100
Asyut	1,416,955	5,725	1	8	66
Sohag	1,684,576	6,061	1	10	70
Qena	1,469,769	5,323	1	8	64
Aswan	521,777	4,363	1	4	80
Red Sea	34,746	939	1	3	0
New Valley	60,306	1,198	1	2	0
Matruh	1,253,758	1,201	1	3	7
Sinai	—	—	1	1	0
TOTAL			25	147	977

ª Sections

APPENDIX I

Arab Socialist Union Organization (1970)

National Level

Chairman
Executive Committee
10 members

ASU Central Committee
150 members

National ASU Congress
(1) All members of the Governorate Congresses
(2) 50 members of the special election supervision committee

Governorate Level

25 Governorate Congresses
Delegates from each District

Governorate Committee of 20

Executive Officers
(1) Party Secretary
(2) Assistant Secretaries

District Level

210 District Congresses
Delegates from each Basic Unit

District Committee of 20

Executive Officers
(1) Party Secretary
(2) Two Assistant Secretaries

Village Level

7,584 Basic Units
All active members of the ASU

Basic Unit Committees
10 members per committee

Party Secretary

SELECTED BIBLIOGRAPHY

GOVERNMENT DOCUMENTS AND PUBLICATIONS

Egypt, Embassy, U.S. *Today's Egypt: The Agrarian Reform*. Washington, D.C.: Washington Embassy Publication, 1954.

Egypt, Government of. *Constitution of the Republic of Egypt*. Cairo, 1956.

Egypt, Ministry of Social Affairs. *Rural Social Welfare Centres in Egypt*. Cairo, 1951.

———. *Social Welfare in Egypt*. Cairo, 1950.

Egypt, Republic of. *The Permanent Council for Public Welfare Services*. Cairo: Société Orientale de Publicité, 1955.

Great Britain, Special Mission to Egypt. *Report of the Special Mission to Egypt*. Egypt No. 1, 1921; C. 1131. London, 1921.

———. *Correspondence 3534*, "Reports by Mr. Villiers Stuart: Reorganization in Egypt—Dufferin Report." No. 6 (1933).

———. *Report on the Conditions of the Agricultural Population*, by Sir E. Baring, No. 6 (Egypt). London, 1888.

United Arab Republic. *The Charter*. Cairo: Information Department, 1962.

———. *The Combined Units*. Cairo: Government Press, 1961.

———. *Law 124 of 1960 Concerning the Local Administrative System*. Cairo: Government Printing Office, 1960.

———. *Ministry of Social Affairs in Eleven Years 1952–1963*. Cairo: Public Relations Information Service, 1964.

———. *Research Report on Employment Problems in Rural Areas—UAR*. Cairo: Institute of National Planning, 1965.

———. Secretariat General for Local Administration. *New Patterns for Local Government in the United Arab Republic*. Paper to be submitted to the International Union of Local Administration meeting, Stockholm, Sweden, September 1967.

———. Socialist Youth Organization. Cairo: Ministry of National Guidance, 1966.

————. *Statistical Handbook 1952–66.* Cairo. Central Agency for Public Mobilization and Statistics, 1966.

————. *Statute of the Arab Socialist Union.* Cairo: Ministry of National Guidance, n.d.

————. *The Year Book 1964.* Cairo: Information Administration, 1964.

————. *The Year Book 1965.* Cairo: Information Administration, 1965.

————. *The Year Book 1966.* Cairo: Information Administration, 1966.

United Nations. United Nations Administration Seminar. *Les besoins et les possibilités de réaliser une décentralisation administrative en Egypte.* Istanbul, 1953.

————. Department of Economic and Social Affairs. *Community Development and National Development.* New York, n.d.

————. *Decentralization for National and Local Development.* New York, 1963.

————. Office of Public Administration. *Public Administration Aspects of Community Development Programs.* New York, 1959.

————. *Report of the Second Session of the Standing Committee on Social Welfare and Community Development.* E/C.N.14/187. New York, 1963.

PERIODICALS

A great deal of information for this study was gathered from newspapers and periodical sources. It would be tedious to list all of the articles perused. Reference to the more important may be found in the footnotes. The newspapers and periodicals found most useful were:

al-Ahrām (Cairo daily)

al-Ahrām al-Iqtiṣādī (Cairo bimonthly)

al-Akhbār (Cairo Daily)

Arab Observer (Cairo weekly)

Economist

L'Egypte Contemporaine

The Egyptian Economic and Political Review

al-Jumhūrīyah (Cairo daily)

Le Monde

New York Times

al-Ṭalīʿah (Arab Socialist Union weekly magazine)

Majallat al-ʿUlūm al-Siyāsīyah (Cairo monthly)

Miṣr al-Muʿāṣirah (Cairo quarterly)

BOOKS AND PAMPHLETS IN ARABIC

Aḥmad, Muḥammad Ḥasan. *al-'Ikhwān al-muslimūn fī al-mīzān* [The Muslim Brotherhood in the Balance]. n.p.: Matbaʿat al-Ikhā', 1946.

Amīn, Aḥmad. Qamūs al-'ādāt wa-al-taqālīd wa-al-ta'ābīr al-miṣrīyah [Dictionary of Egyptian Customs, Traditions, and Expressions]. Cairo: Maṭba'at Lajnat al-Ta'līf wa-al-Tarjamah wa-al-Nashr, 1953.

'Ammār, Ḥamid. *al-'Amal al-maydānī fī al-rīf* [Field Research in Rural Areas]. Sirs al-Layyān, 1955.

————. Fī binā' al-bashar [The Building of Human Beings]. Sirs al-Layyān, 1964.

'Amr, 'Umar, ed. *al-Mawsū'ah al-tashrī'īyah fī shu'ūn al-'idārah al-maḥalīyah* [Legislative Encyclopedia of Local Administration]. Cairo: Dār al-Fikr al-Ḥadīthah lil-Ṭibā'ah wa-al-Nashr, 1966.

al-'Aqqād, A. M. *Sa'd Zaghlūl: sīrah wa-tahīyah* [Saad Zaghlul: A Biography and a Tribute]. Cairo, 1963.

al-'Arabī, Muḥammad 'Abd Allāh. *Niẓām al-'idārah al-maḥallīyah* [The System of Local Administration]. Cairo: Dār al-Kalām, n.d.

'Aṭā, Muḥammad Muṣṭafā. *Miṣr bayna thawratayn* [Egypt between Two Revolutions]. Cairo: Dār al-Ma'ārif, 1956.

al-Bannā, Ḥasan. *Bayna al-'ams wa al-yawm* [Between Yesterday and Today]. Cairo: Maṭba'at al-Ḥurrīyah, 1961.

Barnāmij tadrīb sa'ādat ru'asā' majlis al-qaryah bi-muḥafaẓatay al-sharqīyah wa-al-munūfīyah [Training Program for the Village Council Chairmen in the Governorates of Sharqiyah and Munufiyah]. Sirs al-Layyān: 1966.

al-Ghallāb, Muḥammad. *Mushkilāt al-fallāḥ* [Problems of the Fellah]. Cairo: Dār al-Kitāb, 1946.

Ghayth, Muḥammad 'Atif. *al-Qaryah al-mutaghayīrah* [The Changing Village]. Cairo: Dār al-Ma'ārif, 1964.

————. *al-Taghyīr al-'ijtimā'ī fī al-mujtama' al-qarawī* [The Social Changes in Rural Communities]. Cairo: al-Dār al-Qawmīyah lil-Ṭibā'ah wa-al-Nashr, 1965.

Ghunaymī, M. R. *al-'Iṣlāḥ al-rīfī fī miṣr* [Rural Reform in Egypt]. Cairo, 1957.

————. *al-Takwīn al-'iqtiṣādī lil-qaryah* [Economic Structure of the Village] Cairo: Saḥīfat al-Khadamāt, 1956.

————. *Mazāhir al-bunyān al-'iqiṣadī al-zirā'ī fī al-rīf al-miṣrī* [Features of the Agricultural Economic Structure of Rural Egypt]. Cairo: Ṣaḥifat al-Khadamāt, 1956.

Ghurbāl, M. Shafīq. *Muḥammad 'Alī al-kabīr*. Cairo: Maktabat al-Nahḍah al-Miṣrīyah, n.d.

Ḥasan, Sālim. *al-'Ādāt al-miṣrīyah al-qadīmah al-bāqīyah ilā al'-ān fī miṣr al ḥadīthah* [Ancient Egyptian Customs Surviving until the Present in Modern Egypt]. Cairo: Bulletin de l'association des amis de l'art copte, 1936.

Haykal, Muḥammad Ḥusayn. *Zaynab, 'akhlaq wa manāzir rīfīyah* [Habits and Images of the Egyptian Countryside]. Cairo: Dār al-Hilāl, 1930.

al-Hilbāwī, Muṣṭafā 'Alī. *Fī al-rīf al-miṣri* [In the Egyptian Countryside]. Cairo, 1928.

al-Ḥusaynī, 'Ishāq Mūsa. *al-'Ikhwān al-muslimūn: kubrā al-ḥarakāt al-'islāmīyah al-ḥadīthah* [The Muslim Brotherhood: The Greatest Modern Islamic Movement]. Beirut: Dār Bayrut, 1952.

al-Ḥusnī, Kamāl Maḥmūd. "al-Tanmīyah al-'ijtimā'īyah lil-mujtama'āt al-maḥallīyah al-rīfīyah fī al-jumhūrīyah al-arabīyah al-muttaḥidah" [Community Development in the Rural Local Communities in the United Arab Republic]. *Majallat Tanmīyat al-Mujtama'* [Journal of Community Development] 12, nos. 1 & 2 (1965).

Khālid, Khālid Muḥammad. *Min hunā nabda'* [From Here We Start]. Cairo: Dār al-Nīl, 1950.

Malayka, Lewīs Kamāl. *al-'Alāqāt al-'insānīyah fī al-tadrīb 'alā tanmīyat al-mujtama'* [Human Relations in Training for Community Development]. Sirs al-Layyān, 1964.

———. *al-Jamā'āt wa-al-qiyādah fī qaryah 'arabīyah* [Groups and Leadership in an Arab Village]. Sirs al-Layyān, 1963.

al-Naggar, Aḥmad. *Bunūk al-'iddikhār al-maḥallīyah: al-kitāb al-sanawī* [The Local Savings Banks: Annual Report]. Cairo, 1965.

al-Rāfi'ī, 'Abd al-Raḥmān. *'Aṣr ismā'īl* [The Era of Ismail]. Cairo: Matba'at al-Nahḍah, 1932.

———. *Thawrat sanat 1919* [The Revolution of 1919]. Cairo: Matba-'at al-Nahḍah, 1946.

Ṣabrī, 'Alī. *Taṭbīq al-'ishtirākīyah fī miṣr* [Socialist Application in Egypt]. Cairo, n.d.

Sa'd, Sādiq. *Mushkilāt al-fallāḥ* [Problems of the Fellah]. Cairo, 1955.

Ṣaliḥ, 'Aḥmad Rushdī. *al-'Adab al-sha'bī* [Folklore]. Cairo: Dār al-Ma'ārif, 1954.

Sayf al-Dawlah, 'Iṣmat. *'Usus al-'ishtirākīyah al-'arabīyah* [Bases of Arab Socialism]. Cairo, n.d.

al-Sibā'i, Muṣṭafā. *'Ishtirākīyat al-'islām* [The Socialism of Islam]. Cairo, 1960.

al-Subkī, Muḥammad Fakhr al-Dīn. *Mudhakkirāt ṭabīb fī al-'aryāf* [Memoirs of a Rural Doctor]. Cairo, 1946.

Taḥūn, Sa'd Muḥammad. "Nash'at al-waḥdah al-mujami'ah lil-manzalat al-baqarī" [Development of the Combined Unit in Manzalat al-Baqari]. *Majallat tanmīyat al-mujtama'* [The Journal of Community Development] 12, no. 2 (1965).

al-Ṭamāwī, Sulayman. *Mabādiʾ al-qanūn al-ʾidārī* [Principles of the Administrative Law]. Cairo: Dār al-Fikr al-ʿArabī, 1963.

al-Taqārīr al-nihāʾīyah lil-lijān al-farʿīyah li-shuʾūn al-dirāsāt al-madanīyah lil-majālis al-qarawīyah [Final Reports of the Sub-committees for Field Research on Village Councils]. Cairo, 1962.

Yūnis, ʿAlī Fawzī. "al-Majālis al-qarawīyah fī al-jumhūrīyah al-ʿarabīyah al-muttaḥidah" [Village Councils in the United Arab Republic]. *Majallat tanmīyat al-mujtamaʿ* [Journal of Community Development] 12, no. 2 (1965).

BOOKS AND PAMPHLETS IN WESTERN LANGUAGES

Abdel Nasser, Gamal. *The Philosophy of the Revolution*. Cairo: Ministry of National Guidance, 1954.

———. *Egypt's Liberation: The Philosophy of the Revolution*. Washington, D.C.: Public Affairs Press, 1955.

———. *Speeches and Press Interviews, 1958–60*. Cairo: Information Department (U.A.R.), 1960.

Adorno, T. W.; Frenkel-Brunswik, E.; Levinson, D. J.; and Sanford, R. N. *The Authoritarian Personality*. New York: Harper, 1950.

Ahmed, Jamal Mohammed. *The Intellectual Origins of Egyptian Nationalism*. London: Oxford University Press, 1960.

Alderfer, Harold F. *Local Government in Developing Countries*. New York: McGraw Hill, 1964.

Alderfer, Harold F.; el-Khatib, M. Fathalla; and Fahmy, Moustafa Ahmed. *Local Government in the United Arab Republic 1964*. Cairo: Institute of Public Administration, 1964.

Alfort, Cecil. *One Hour of Justice*. London: Dorothy Crisp, 1946.

Allen, H. B., ed. *Rural Reconstruction in Action*. Ithaca, New York: Cornell University Press, 1953.

Almond, Gabriel A., and Powell, G. B. *Comparative Politics*. Boston: Little, Brown and Co., 1966.

Ammar, Abbas M. *Reorganization of the Egyptian Village*. Sirs al-Layyan, Egypt: Arab States Fundamental Education Centre, 1954.

———. *The People of Sharqiyah*. 2 vols. Cairo: Royal Geographical Society of Egypt, 1944.

Ammar, Hamed. *Growing Up in an Egyptian Village*. London: Routledge and Kegan Paul, 1954.

Anderson, J. N. D. *Islamic Law in the Modern World*. New York: New York University Press, 1959.

Apter, David E. *The Gold Coast in Transition*. Princeton: Princeton University Press, 1955.

———, ed. *Ideology and Discontent*. Glencoe, Ill. The Free Press, 1964

————. *Politics of Modernization*. Chicago: University of Chicago Press, 1965.

el-Araby, Mohamed Abdullah. *An Outline of Local Government in the United Arab Republic*. Cairo: Misr S.A.E., 1961.

Arnold, T. W. *The Caliphate*. London: Oxford University Press, 1924.

Ayrout, Henry Habib. *The Fellaheen*. Translated by Hilary Wayment. Cairo: Schindler, 1945.

————. *The Egyptian Peasant*. Translated by John Alden Williams. Boston: Beacon Press, 1963.

Baer, Gabriel. *A History of Landownership in Modern Egypt 1800–1950*. London: Oxford University Press, 1962.

————. *Scripta Hierosolymitama: Studies in Islamic History and Civilization*. Edited by Uriel Heyd. Jerusalem: Hebrew University Magnes Press, 1961.

Banfield, E. C. *The Moral Basis of a Backward Society*. Glencoe, Ill.: The Free Press, 1958.

el-Barawy, Rashed. *The Military Coup in Egypt*. Cairo: Renaissance Bookshop, 1952.

Baring, E. *Report of the Conditions of the Agricultural Population in Egypt*. Egypt, No. 6, 1888.

Batten, T. R. *Communities and their Development*. London: Oxford University Press, 1957.

Bayle, St. John. *Village Life in Egypt with Sketches of the Said*. 2 vols. London: Chapman, 1852.

Bell, Daniel. *The End of Ideology*. Glencoe, Ill.: The Free Press, 1960.

Benedict, Ruth. *Patterns of Culture*. New York: Houghton Mifflin Co., 1934.

Berger, Morroe. *The Arab World Today*. Garden City, N.Y.: Doubleday, 1964.

————. *Bureaucracy and Society in Modern Egypt: A Study of the Higher Civil Service*. Princeton: Princeton University Press, 1957.

————. *Military Elite and Social Change: Egypt since Napoleon*. Princeton: Princeton University Center for International Studies, 1960.

Berque, Jacques. *Histoire sociale d'un village égyptien au XXième siècle*. Paris: Mouton, 1957.

————. *The Arabs*. London: Faber and Faber, 1964.

Binder, Leonard. *The Ideological Revolution in the Middle East*. New York: John Wiley, 1964.

————. "The Integrative Revolution." In *Political Parties and Political Development*. Edited by Joseph La Palombara and Myron Weiner. Princeton: Princeton University Press, 1966.

Blackman, Winifred S. *The Fellahin of Upper Egypt.* London: George C. Harrap, 1927.

Blunt, Wilfred Scawen. *Secret History of the English Occupation of Egypt, Being a Personal Narrative of Events.* New York: Knopf, 1922.

Boktor, Amir. *School and Society in the Valley of the Nile.* Cairo: Elias' Modern Press, 1936.

Braibanti, R. and Spengler, J. J., eds. *Tradition, Values, and Socio-Economic Development.* London: Cambridge University Press, 1961.

Burckhardt, John Lewis. *Arabic Proverbs.* London: Quaritch, 1875.

Burke, Fred G. *Local Government and Politics in Uganda.* Syracuse: Syracuse University Press, 1964.

Cecil, Edward Herbert. *The Leisure of an Egyptian Official.* London: Hodder and Stoughton, 1921.

Chirol, Valentine. *The Egyptian Problem.* London: Macmillan, 1921.

Cleland, Wendell. *The Population Problem in Egypt.* Lancaster, Pa.: Science Press, 1936.

E. Combe. *L'Egypte ottomane.* Cairo, 1933.

Cromer, The Earl of (Evelyn Baring). *Modern Egypt.* 2 Vols. London: Macmillan, 1908.

Easton, David. *Systems Analysis of Political Life.* New York: John Wiley and Sons, 1965.

Erikson, Eric H. *Young Man Luther.* New York: W. W. Norton and Co., 1958.

Festinger, Leon. *A Theory of Cognitive Dissonance.* Evanston, Ill.: Row, Peterson, 1957.

Fisher, Sydney N. *Social Forces in the Middle East.* Ithaca, N.Y.: Cornell University Press, 1955.

Foster, George M. *Traditional Culture and the Impact of Technological Change.* New York: Harper, 1962.

Gadalla, Saad M. *Land Reform in Relation to Social Development in Egypt.* Columbia: University of Missouri, 1962.

Galt, Russell. *The Effects of Centralization of Education in Modern Egypt.* Cairo: Department of Education, American University, 1936.

Gardner, George H. "Social Correlates of the Transitional Phase of Change from the Traditional to the Modern Way of Life." Doctoral dissertation. Princeton University, 1961.

Garzouzi, Eva. *Old Ills and New Remedies in Egypt.* Cairo: Dar al-Maarif, 1958.

Gaudefroy-Demombynes, Maurice. *Les Institutions musulmanes.* Paris: Flammarion, 1946.

Geertz, Clifford. "Ideology As a Cultural System." In David E. Apter, ed., *Ideology and Discontent*. Glencoe, Ill.: The Free Press, 1964.

Ghallab, M. *La Survivance de l'Egypte Antique dans le Folklore Egyptien Moderne*. Paris: Paul Guethner, 1921.

Gibb, H. A. R. *Modern Trends in Islam*. Chicago: University of Chicago Press, 1947.

———. and Bowden, Harold. *Islamic Society and the West: A Study of the Impact of Western Civilization on Moslem Culture in the Near East*. London: Oxford University Press, 1950.

Grunebaum, Gustave E. von. *Medieval Islam*. Chicago: University of Chicago Press, 1946.

Gullick, Luther, and Pollock, James K. *Government Reorganization in the United Arab Republic*. Cairo: Ford Foundation, 1962.

al-Hakim, Tawfiq. *Maze of Justice*. Translated by A. S. Eban. London: Harvill Press, 1947.

Halpern, Manfred. *The Politics of Social Change in the Middle East and North Africa*. Princeton: Princeton University Press, 1963.

Hamady, Sania. *Temperament and Character of the Arabs*. New York: Twayne-Bookman, 1960.

Harbison, Frederick A., and Ibrahim, Ibrahim Abdelkader. *Human Resources for Egyptian Enterprise*. New York: McGraw-Hill, 1958.

Harris, Christina P. *Nationalism and Revolution in Egypt*. The Hague: Mouton, 1964.

Herold, J. Christopher. *Bonaparte in Egypt*. New York: Harper and Row, 1962.

Heyworth-Dunne, J. *Egypt: The Cooperative Movement*. Cairo: Renaissance Book Shop, 1952.

———. *An Introduction to the History of Education in Modern Egypt*. London: Luzac, 1939.

———. *Religious and Political Trends in Modern Egypt*. Washington, D.C., 1950.

Hicks, Ursula. *Development from Below*. London: Oxford University Press, 1961.

Hoffer, Eric. *The Ordeal of Change*. New York: Harper and Row, 1963.

Honigman, J. J. *Culture and Personality*. New York: Harper, 1954.

Hsu, F. L. K. *Aspects of Culture and Personality*. New York: Abelard-Schuman, 1954.

Humes, Samuel, and Martin, Eileen M. *The Structure of Local Government Throughout the World*. The Hague: Martinns and Nijhoff, 1961.

al-Husayni, Ahmed Ishak Musa. *The Moslem Brethren: The Greatest of Modern Islamic Movements.* Translated by John F. Brown and John Racy. Beirut: Khayat's College Book Cooperative, 1956.

Hussein, Ahmed. *Rural Social Welfare Centers in Egypt.* Cairo: Ministry of Social Affairs, 1951.

Hussein, Taha. *An Egyptian Childhood.* Translated by E. H. Paxton. London: Routledge, 1932.

————. *The Stream of Days: A Student at the Azhar.* Translated by Hilary Wayment. 2nd ed. London: Longmans, Green, 1948.

Hyman, H. H. *Political Socialization.* Glencoe, Ill.: The Free Press, 1959.

Issawi, Charles P. *Egypt at Mid-Century: An Economic Survey.* London: Oxford University Press, 1954.

————. *Egypt in Revolution.* London: Oxford University Press, 1963.

Kedourie, E. *Sa'ad Zaghlul and the British.* Vol. XI of *St. Anthony's Papers.* Edited by H. Hourani. London: Middle Eastern Affairs, 1961.

Khalid, Khalid Muhammad. *From Here We Start.* Translated by Isma'il R. el-Farqui. Washington, D.C.: American Council of Learned Societies, 1953.

Klingmuller, Ernest. *Geschichte der Wafd-Partie im Rahmen der gesamtpolitischen Lage Aegyptens.* Berlin: Druck Triltsh und Huther, 1937.

Kluckhohn, C., and Murray, H. A., eds. *Personality in Nature, Society, and Culture.* New York: Alfred A. Knopf, 1953.

Kotb, Sayed. *Social Justice in Islam.* Translated by John B. Hardie. Washington, D.C.: American Council for Learned Societies, 1953.

Lacouture, Jean and Simonne. *Egypt in Transition.* New York: Criterion Books, 1958.

Landau, Jacob M. *Parliaments and Parties in Egypt.* New York: Fredrick A. Praeger, 1954.

Lane, Edward W. *Manners and Customs of the Modern Egyptians.* New York: Everyman's Library, 1908.

La Palombara, Joseph. *Alternative Strategies for Developing Administrative Capabilities in Emerging Nations.* Bloomington, Ind.: Comparative Administrative Group, 1965.

Laqueur, Walter Z., ed. *The Middle East in Transition.* New York: Fredrick A. Praeger, 1958.

Lerner, Daniel. *The Passing of Traditional Society.* Glencoe, Ill.: The Free Press, 1958.

Levy, Marion. *The Structure of Society.* Princeton: Princeton University Press, 1956.

Levy, R. *An Introduction to the Sociology of Islam*. 2 Vols. Cambridge: Cambridge University Press, 1957.

Lewis, Bernard. *The Arabs in History*. London: Hutchinson, 1950.

Linton, Ralph. *The Cultural Background of Personality*. New York: Appleton-Century-Crofts, 1945.

Lloyd, George Ambrose. *Egypt since Cromer*. Vols. I and II. London: Macmillan, 1934.

Lozach, Jean. *L'Habitat Rural en Egypte*. Cairo: Imprimerie de l'Institut Français d'Archéologie Orientale du Caire, 1930.

Maddick, Henry. *Democracy, Decentralization and Development*. London: Asia Publishing House, 1963.

Mansfield, Peter. *Nasser's Egypt*. Harmondsworth, England: Penguin Books, 1965.

Marei, Sayed. *Agrarian Reform in Egypt*. Cairo: Imprimerie de l'Institut Français d'Archéologie Orientale, 1957.

Mead, G. H. *Mind, Self, and Society*. Chicago: University of Chicago Press, 1934.

Meinardus, Otto. *Christian Egypt: Ancient and Modern*. Cairo: Cahier d'Histoire Egyptienne, 1965.

Merton, Robert K. *Social Theory and Social Structure*. Glencoe, Ill.: The Free Press, 1957.

Naguib, Mohammed. *Egypt's Destiny*. London: Victor Gollanez, 1955.

Nassouhy, Mohamed Gamal el-Din. "Local Autonomy under National Planning: The Egyptian Experience." Doctoral dissertation. University of Southern California, 1965.

Newby, P. H. *The Picnic at Sakkara*. New York: Alfred A. Knopf, 1955.

O'Brien, Patrick. *The Revolution in Egypt's Economic System*. London: Oxford University Press, 1966.

Opler, Marvin K. *Culture, Psychiatry and Human Values*. Springfield, Ill.: Charles C Thomas, 1956.

Parsons, Talcott C. *The Structure of Social Action*. Glencoe, Ill.: The Free Press, 1966.

Ponsioen, J. A., ed. *Social Welfare Policy*. The Hague: Mouton, 1962.

Pye, Lucian W., and Verba, Sidney, eds. *Political Culture and Political Development*. Princeton: Princeton University Press, 1965.

Radwan, Abu al-Futouh Ahmad. *Old and New Forces in Egyptian Education*. New York: Bureau of Publication, Teachers College, Columbia University, 1951.

Redfield, Robert. *Peasant Society and Culture*. Chicago: University of Chicago Press, 1956.

Riad, Hassan. *L'Egypte Nasserienne*. Paris: Editions de Minuit, 1964.

Rifaat Bey, Mohammed Ali. *The Awakening of Modern Egypt*. New York: Longmans, Green, 1947.

Riggs, Fred W. *The Ecology of Public Administration*. London: Asia Publishing House, 1961.

Rivlin, Helen Anne B. *The Agricultural Policy of Muhammad Ali in Egypt*. Harvard Middle Eastern Studies, No. 4. Cambridge: Harvard University Press, 1961.

Robinson, Ronald; Gallagher, John; and Denny, Alice. *Africa and the Victorians*. London: Macmillan, 1961.

Rowlett, Mary. *Founders of Modern Egypt*. Bombay: Asia Publishing House, 1962.

Russell, Sir Thomas W. *Egyptian Service, 1902–1946*. London: John Murray, 1949.

Saab, Gabriel. *The Egyptian Agrarian Reform 1952–62*. London: Oxford University Press, 1967.

Sabry, Muhammad. *La Révolution égyptienne d'après des documents authentiques et des photographies prises au cours de la révolution*. Paris: J. Urin, 1919.

Safran, Nadav. *Egypt in Search of Political Community: An Analysis of the Intellectual and Political Evolution of Egypt, 1804–1952*. Cambridge: Harvard University Press, 1961.

Schacht, J. *Origins of Muhammedan Jurisprudence*. London: Oxford University Press, 1953.

Shalaby, Mohammed. *Rural Reconstruction in Egypt*. Cairo, 1950.

Shaw, S. J. *The Financial and Administrative Organization and Development of Ottoman Egypt*. Princeton: Princeton University Press, 1962.

el-Shinnawy, Mohamed Ali. "Community Development and Local Government in the Developing Nations: The United Arab Republic, India, and Pakistan." Doctoral dissertation. New York University, 1964.

Siffin, William J., ed. *Toward the Comparative Study of Public Administration*. Bloomington: Indiana University Press, 1957.

Smith, W. R. *Kinship and Marriage in Early Arabia*. Edited by Stanley A. Cook. London: A. & C. Black, 1903.

Sorel, George. *Reflections on Violence*. Glencoe, Ill.: The Free Press, 1950.

Stevens, Georgiana. *Egypt: Yesterday and Today*. New York: Holt, Rinehart, and Winston, 1963.

Stuart, Villiers. *Egypt after the War*. London: John Murray, 1883.

Tignor, Robert L. *Modernization and British Colonial Rule in Egypt 1882–1914*. Princeton: Princeton University Press, 1966.

E. Tyan, "Le Califat." In *Institutions de droit public musulman*. Paris, 1954.

Vatikiotis, P. J. *The Egyptian Army in Politics—Pattern for New Nations?* Bloomington: Indiana University Press, 1961.

Warriner, Doreen. *Land Reform and Development in the Middle East*. London: Oxford University Press, 1962.

Watt, William M. *Islam and the Integration of Society*. London: Routledge and Kegan Paul, 1961.

Weber, Max. *The Theory of Social and Economic Organization*. Translated by A. M. Henderson and Talcott Parsons. London: Oxford University Press, 1947.

Wheelock, Keith. *Nasser's New Egypt: A Critical Analysis*. New York: Praeger, 1960.

Witmer, H. L., and Kotinsky, R., eds. *Personality in the Making*. New York: Harper and Brothers, 1950.

Wittfogel, Karl A. *Oriental Despotism*. New Haven: Yale University Press, 1957.

Wylie, Lawrence. *Village in the Vaircluse*. Cambridge, Mass.: Harvard University Press, 1951.

Yates, William H. *The Modern History and Conditions of Egypt*. London: Elder and Company, 1843.

Zaki, A. M. *An Outline of the Local Government System in the United Arab Republic*. Cairo: Ministry of Local Administration, 1965.

Ziadeh, Farhat, J. *A Reader in Modern Literary Arabic*. Princeton: Princeton University Press, 1964.

ARTICLES IN WESTERN LANGUAGES

Adams, John B. "Communications and Change in an Egyptian Village." *Middle East Forum* 32, no. 3 (March 1957).

——. "Culture and Conflict in an Egyptian Village." *American Anthropologist* 59 (1957): 225–235.

Aiken, H. D. "The Revolt against Ideology." *Commentary* 37, no. 4 (April 1964): 29–39.

Ashford, D. E. "Nation-Building and Nationalism in the Middle East." *Middle East Journal* 18 (Autumn 1964): 421–430.

Asirvatham, E. "The Role of Local Self-Government in a Democracy." *Indian Journal of Political Science* 16, no. 3 (1955).

"ASU Programme for Youth—Pioneers of the Future." *Arab Observer*, February 14, 1966.

Baer, Gabriel. "The Dissolution of the Egyptian Village Community." *Die Welt des Islam* 6, nos. 1 & 2 (1961).

Beers, Howard. "Social Components of Community Development." *Rural Sociology* 23, no. 1 (March 1958).

Bell, Daniel, "The End of Ideology in the West." *Columbia University Forum* (Winter 1960): 4–7.

Doob, Leonard. "Attitudes and the Availability of Knowledge Concerning Traditional Beliefs." *Journal of Abnormal and Social Psychology* 59 (1959).

Dotson, Arch. "Democratic Decentralization in Local Self-Government," *Indian Journal of Public Administration* 4, no. 1 (1959).

Fertier, Francis. "Les forces sociales à l'oeuvre dans le nationalisme égyptien." *Orient*, no. 5 (1958).

Gardner, George H., and Hanna, Sami A. "Islamic Socialism." *The Muslim World* 56, no. 2 (1966): 71–86.

Hirabayashi, G. K., and el-Khatib, M. Fathalla. "Communication and Political Awareness in the Villages of Egypt." *Public Opinion Quarterly* 22 (1958): 357–363.

Horton, Alan W. "The Omda's Boy." *American Universities Field Staff: Report Service Northeast Africa Series* 11, no. 6 (1963).

Hussein, Ahmed. "Social Reform in Egypt with Special Reference to Rural Areas." *The Muslim World* 44, no. 1 (January 1954): 12–19.

Hussein, Aziza. "The Role of Women in Social Reform in Egypt." *Middle East Journal* 7 (Autumn 1953): 440–450.

Mattison, Beatrice. "Rural Social Centres in Egypt." *Middle East Journal* 5 (Autumn 1951): 461–479.

Mello, Lordello de. "Decentralization for Development." *Journal of Local Administration Overseas* 2, no. 1. (January 1963).

Metaweh, J. E. "An Egyptian Experiment in Functional Education." *Rural Sociology* 18, no. 4 (December 1953).

Noureddine, Ben Khader. "Le Parti unique—Est-il une solution?" *Jeune Afrique*, (December 1963).

Peretz, Don. "Democracy and the Revolution in Egypt," *Middle East Journal* 13, no. 1 (Winter 1959): 26–40.

Polson, Robert A. "Theory and Methods of Training for Community Development." *Rural Sociology* 23, no. 1 (March 1958).

Presthus, Robert V. "Weberian and Welfare Bureaucracies in Traditional Society." *Administrative Science Quarterly* 6, no. 1 (June, 1961): 1–24.

Rosenthal, Franz. "The Muslim Brethren in Egypt." *The Moslem World* 37 (October 1947): 278–291.

Sigell, Roberta, ed. "Political Socialization: Its Role in the Political Process," *The Annals of the American Academy of Political and Social Science* 361 (September 1965).

Sjoberg, Gideon. "Ideology and Social Organization in Rapidly Developing Societies." Paper presented to the Comparative Administrative Group Conference, University of Maryland, April 16, 1966.

Weerawardana, I. D. S. "Objectives of Local Government in Underdeveloped Countries." International Political Science Association Congress, Rome, September 1958.

Wickwar, W. Hardy, "Notes on Local Government Administrative Areas and Local Government Units in the Middle East," *Revue internationale des sciences* 24, no. 2 (1958): 148–151.

Zink, H. "Selected Materials for a Comparative Study of Local Government." *American Political Science Review* 50 (December 1956): 1107–1133.

INDEX

Abbasid Dynasty: 20
Abbas, Khedive: 31
administrators, rural: functions of, 11, 36, 59, 133, 168; attitudes of, 71, 142, 220–225. SEE ALSO bureaucracy, local
adult education: 146
agrarian reform. SEE land reform
Agricultural Bank of Egypt: 41
agricultural cooperatives: 68, 145–146, 162–163, 228–229
agricultural extension services: 182
Agricultural Laborers Union: 131–132
Aly Sabri: 111
Anglo-French Debt Commission: 33
Arab Socialism: 97, 110–114, 147, 157, 159–160
Arab Socialist Union: ideology and, 11, 173; development of, 101–102, 107, 133–134; organization and structure of, 117, 124–137; recruitment patterns in, 117–119, 127; membership in, 118–120, 122–123; administration problems in, 120–122, 150, 226; dismissal of members from, 133, 135; functions of, 137–149; political socialization through, 150–165; political influence of, 163; mentioned, 10, 68, 85, 118, 210, 242. SEE ALSO Liberation Rally; National Union
Arab States Training Center for Education for Community Development: 189
Arab tribal community: 16–18
arbitration: 148–149
Azhar, al-: 24, 54, 110

bāhith: 240
bakshish: 37, 78, 121, 162, 221. SEE ALSO bribery; corruption
banks, local savings: assumptions of, 231–232; selection of employees for,

232–234; training programs of, 234–242; rural development through, 244–247
baraka: 94
basic units (ASU): 118, 124, 161
basic unit conference: 124–125
basin irrigation: 40
Baring, Sir Evelyn (Lord Cromer): 41
Barudi, Sami el-: 34
bilharziasis: 222–223
birth control: 223–224. SEE ALSO family planning
Bisindilla: 130
black market: 146
blood revenge: 39
Bonaparte, Napoleon: 24, 32, 166, 168
bribery: 32, 88. SEE ALSO bakshish; corruption
British occupation: 36–42
bureaucracy, local: functions of, 141, 147; Arab Socialist Union and, 150; in Egyptian villages, 213–229
bureaucratic centralism: 213
bureaucrats, local: functions of, 71, 96; attitudes of, toward peasants, 167, 218–219, 221

cadastral survey: 29
central committee (ASU): 126, 128–129
chamber of deputies: 33
charisma: 10, 93–98. SEE ALSO Nasser, Gamal Abdel
Charter, National: provisions of, 101, 147, 156; Egypt and world history discussed in, 110–111; socialism described in, 111–112
children, training of: 61–64
combined units: 174–185, 210
communication: process of development and, 7; role of *'umdah* in, 119; Arab Socialist Union and, 140–142